Retirement Planning Expert

®

2020/21

Retirement Planning Expert

®

2020/21

Plan more, save more, earn more, live better and achieve a better retirement.
Fully up-dated for the UK 2020 budget and covering your home, tax, pensions, finance, property, work and volunteering, health, leisure and travel.

by
Allan Esler Smith, FCA

Publisher's note, disclaimer and terms of use agreement

Every possible effort has been made to ensure that the information contained in this book is accurate at the time of going to press, and the publisher and author cannot accept responsibility for any errors or omissions, however caused. No responsibility for loss or damage occasioned to any person acting, or refraining from action, as a result of the material in this publication can be accepted by the publisher or the author. The publisher and author make no representations or warranties with respect to the accuracy, applicability, fitness, or completeness of the contents of this book. Importantly, this book is only a guide and it is neither legal nor financial advice; it is no substitute for taking professional advice from a financial adviser or other professional adviser. Any potential tax advantages may be subject to change and will depend upon your individual circumstances and, again, individual professional advice should be obtained that is appropriate to your individual circumstances.

The publisher and the author do not warrant the performance, effectiveness or applicability of any websites or other resources listed in this book.

Published in Great Britain in 2020 by Quartertoten Productions Limited

www.allaneslersmith.com

ISBN Paperback   978 1 916377004
eBook ASIN   B08PPB5RRX

CONTENTS

ESSENTIAL STEP 3: EARN MORE

ESSENTIAL STEP 4: LIVE BETTER

ACKNOWLEDGEMENTS

I am indebted to my father, Stanley Smith, a retired senior civil servant and my wife Karen, whose assistance and guidance were invaluable. Frances Kaye introduced me to writing books on this subject and provided me with the greatest of help and support over many years and I remain very grateful. I also value incisive professional input and in this regard Martin Gorvett, a Chartered Financial Planner of Lavender Financial Planners Ltd, cuts an effective knife through the complexities and language of investments and pensions. On tax and weighing up the world's largest tax book, I am indebted to Graham Boar, a Tax Partner of UHY Hacker Young. Graham boils down complex issues into straightforward planning tips and guidance. And on legal matters, wills and powers of attorney I thank the father and son team of Mike and Tom Bottomley of Ewart Price Solicitors of Hertfordshire. Legal issues are so vitally important to smoothing the path of an estate and their 40 years' combined experience and resulting contribution and advice is appreciated. Thank you to Andy Cooper, Tony Ecuyer, David Falvey, Gillian Hannington, Paul Hewitt, Jonathan Lyon, Martin Joynes, Emma McKenzie and Graeme Swan for their help and assistance.

Allan Esler Smith FCA

Introduction

This book is about helping you adapt and thrive after the immense challenges we have faced in 2020 with an absolute focus on helping **you** to **achieve a better retirement by following my four essential steps**. The UK (and much of the world) will have lost many lives and this generation will encounter tax pain and national debt and probably unemployment of unimaginable proportions as the economy re-sets. All the more reason to re-set our own plans and hence this new book. I want to help you understand where you are now, where you want to get to and how **you** can achieve a better retirement.

The longer you have until retirement, the more you can do to improve your prospects, as so much flows from increasing your knowledge around pensions, investments and how they interlink with tax. This throws up an immediate challenge as the UK has one of the most complex tax regimes in the world and we must prepare for tax rises next year to help pay for the Covid-19 pandemic. There are then hundreds of opportunities to improve your retirement by saving more and earning that little bit better. But all that clever financial stuff ignores the more important goal of creating the life you seek from a great home, focusing on your health and personal relationships and enjoying hobbies, new interests and maybe volunteering (and giving something back to society).

A quick word on how you might make best use of my book and get the best out of the four essential steps. As you will see, perhaps I should call it a work book or manual for your retirement plan. Most of the chapters are relatively self – contained. It is not like reading a novel with a beginning, a middle and an end which you read in sequence. You can pick your way through the chapters depending on what is of most interest and relevance to you and then work out your plan and take some incisive actions based on my **top tips** (which you can't miss). Having said that, you probably should read through the opening two chapters first. They deal with the key issues of very basic financial planning and the central part of most people's lives – their home. The chapter on personal relationships could also be important as relationships may need adjustment as you glide towards retirement. I should explain up-front the term **'glide'**. I have presented retirement seminars for 17 years where I got the sense that many people were approaching a **'cliff-edge'** retirement. Suddenly they were on a course and maybe retirement came 6 months later - that's a cliff edge! Suddenly people were realising that there was so much more they could have been doing to plan and achieve a better retirement. On the other hand I've worked with many personal tax clients and tried to encourage the concept of a **glide-path** into retirement from about 10 years or more before retirement. That gives you a better chance to create the lifestyle you want. Just a thought! Let me outline my **four essential steps.**

THE 'PLAN MORE' ESSENTIAL STEP. I start by explaining the basics. There are **three phases of retirement** that you will travel through: the *'active retirement years'*, then *'the passive retirement years'* and finally *'retirement with care'*. The three phases could easily cover a thirty year period and your income and expenditure will change radically as you move through each phase. Few people really grasp the three phases and what this means for their finance and what they can do about it. Next I peel back the sometimes complex world of doing the retirement sums and show you how to do it. You then have the basis of a financial plan that is developed by the next three essential steps of retirement planning- hence my book!

THE 'SAVE MORE' ESSENTIAL STEP. Having defined a basic financial plan the focus shifts onto demystifying 'financial speak' and assessing the opportunities for you to save more by starting with one of your biggest assets **- Your Property and Home (Chapter 2).** The next big potential savings in most retirement plans will come from **Pensions (Chapter 3), Savings & Investments (Chapter 4) and Tax (chapter 5).** I try to cut through the waffle and get you focused on where you can really save money with loads of precise 'top tips'. For instance I expect tax 'pain' on its way next year and more predators stalking your wealth and point to some help. The UK has a magnificent financial services safety net in these difficult Covid-19 pandemic times and any associated recession. Straying outside the regime and its protections could cost some readers a fortune if a financial institution goes bust or you encounter a rogue adviser. By the way my tips come from experience as I worked in Insolvency and Corporate Recovery during the 1989 to 1993 recession and then as the Manager of the Investigations and Recoveries Unit at the UK's Investors Compensation Scheme (predecessor of the Financial Services Compensation Scheme). This has given me a useful perspective!

I didn't want to go over the top on cutting costs as we all need to try and live a bit better but I did recognise a need to tool readers up with more fire-power in **Cutting** costs, **Raising complaints** and fending off **Scammers (Chapter 6)**. The extent to which you find the 'save more' chapters on this book useful will depend on your personal circumstances. If you are newly retired with a good final salary scheme you may skim over the pensions chapter as you have a fixed and fairly strong pension base. On the other hand, if you are in your 40's and are a higher rate tax payer in a defined contributions pension scheme the pensions chapter may save you thousands of pounds (as I have seen many times in my work as a Chartered Accountant and Tax Advisor).

THE 'EARN MORE' ESSENTIAL STEP. The third essential step is considering how you can earn more. This is the other side of the economic equation on balancing the retirement plan. It may involve **Starting Your Own Business (Chapter 7)** or maybe the solution is to **find a '*better*' job (Chapter 8)?** These could be for big money or just help you earn some money for an extra holiday if you want to scale things down.

THE 'LIVE BETTER' ESSENTIAL STEP. The fourth essential step is the most important section of all. It's about living better as we glide into and through retirement. It's about retuning your **Personal Relationships and Health (Chapter 9)** and perhaps the best of the lot, **Leisure and Holidays (Chapter 10)**. Life, however, comes with some inevitable bumps and bruises and challenging or sad times. Taking care of our young people or elderly relatives can also present financial and emotional challenges. For many readers these may happen at the same time and hence the tips for the 'Sandwich Generation' (Chapter 11). That chapter also covers wills, power of attorney and executors to help you start these difficult conversations. I close the 'live better' step with two final pages that are all about **Your Plan (Chapter 12)**. It is where **you** make notes to plan **your** actions and follow up research to help achieve a better retirement. I have also left some extra space at the top of each page throughout the book (a bit like a work book) for you to make any extra notes. A final thought if I may - the key to a better retirement is to start your plan and actions as early as possible so that you do not have a cliff-edge retirement. I'd suggest you aim for a glide path into the life you want to create. You could, therefore, share this book with younger members of your family as **it's never too early to start your plan**.

Life has changed for all of us in 2020 and, overall, my **four essential steps** of plan more, save more, earn more, live better **will help you achieve a better retirement as we progress through 2021 - guaranteed!**
Allan Esler Smith FCA

Chapter One

Plan more for the three phases of retirement.

"Excellence is never an accident. It is always the result of high intention, sincere effort, and intelligent execution; it represents the wise choice of many alternatives - choice, not chance, determines your destiny."

ARISTOTLE

Could this be the year where you make some changes to your retirement planning? The circumstances in the Autumn of 2020 are unique and unmatched in the majority of the population's living memory. In short the Covid-19 pandemic has caused many of us to have a re-set moment. So how can you adapt and thrive? It's actually quite simple and boils down to my four essential steps where you **plan more, save more, earn more, live better** and, ultimately, achieve a better retirement. It all starts with improving your planning – the first of the four essential steps and this chapter.

This chapter at a glance

- *Understand the three phases of retirement (active, passive and with care) and, ultimately, the life you wish to lead in <u>each</u> of these retirement phases.*
- *Use a simple approach to doing the sums and start your own retirement plan.* The word 'budget' or 'plan' can send most sane folk running to the

hills. But let's face facts from the start of this book. The life you wish to lead in each phase of retirement will come at a cost and the simple fact is that people struggle to estimate the reality of the cost of the lifestyle they aspire to and also struggle to determine what funds they may have in retirement. This chapter therefore sets out an approach to help put you in a better position and provides signposts to further help.

Pre-retirement planning- it's never too soon to start

It's never too soon to start your pre-retirement planning. Ideally you are reading this in your 30s or 40s as the earlier you start the more time you have to build plans and adapt them. In your 50's and 60's there are still lots of things you can do to achieve a better retirement so read on. What life do you want to create as you move into retirement – how does it look in terms of location, lifestyle, holidays and use of time? Everyone will be different and each lifestyle will have a different standard of living. As you get older the money you will need to achieve it will change as, indeed, will your activity levels. This is the starting point of your retirement plan.

The three phases of retirement

Active retirement

This is so important. Once you understand this point about the first of the three phases of retirement you're on your way. Your active retirement years start when you leave your regular full time work or you sell your business and will usually occur anywhere from your fifties to late sixties. The ten to twenty years after this are your 'active retirement years'. You may choose to 'just' downsize the regular job to a less stressful position with perhaps less hours so that you maintain a very active life and enjoy a decent income to supplement your pension and savings. This is becoming increasingly available from more progressive employers who understand the benefits of retaining and rewarding experience with the introduction of flexible working policies.

You are still 'buzzing' and enjoying a great social life with more holidays and more hobbies and may even relocate within the UK or abroad. It will still be an expensive time and you will probably eat into those savings you had built up so that you can enjoy these years to the full. It should be an expensive, but rewarding, period of your retirement and probably the best of the three phases of retirement.

Passive retirement

Your passive retirement years are generally in your late seventies and eighties. Work income may have largely dried up and you are now mostly reliant on pension income and any savings that are left after you were having a whale of a time during the active retirement phase. Any part time job or business you run may provide some extra money for more holidays or buying a new car. Finances will be tighter and you will also probably have to accept there will inevitably be changes in what you can and cannot do as medical issues arise. Associated with this will be questions about your location and proximity to social and medical facilities and, overall, you will be reassessing if your home remains cost efficient to your lifestyle, manageable and in the right location. This is possibly the cheapest of the three retirement phases.

Retirement with care

As you reach your late eighties and your nineties your income may rely solely on state and occupational pensions and your spending will need to be cut to meet your income. Medical and other care needs may dictate what you do and where you live. Your home may need to be used to underwrite care home fees which can average about £35,000 per year without medical care and £45,000 per year upwards with medical care. It would be much less if care is arranged in a home environment. Handle these figures with care as there can be huge variations in the averages depending on location, lifestyle choices and amenities provided. This is possibly the most expensive phase of retirement if the cost comes from eroding your capital (the equity in your house) each year This may conflict with your ultimate inheritance and gifting plans and so you may now see how the whole 'picture' comes together and how you need to focus on Chapter 1, Your Home and Property and on Chapter 5, Tax to help your planning around the equity in your house.

> **Top tip**
>
> Grasp and understand the three phases of retirement and how your income, savings and expenditure patterns will change over the three phases. The earlier you 'do the sums' and then increase your knowledge around retirement planning the better chance you have of reaching and maybe even exceeding your ambitions.

Know your £ numbers - money in/money out

So you will have to accept that once you retire there will inevitably be changes in your financial affairs over three distinct phases. Your income will change but so, too, will your pattern of expenditure. Many people worry about this, but the good news is that provided you are prepared to do a little planning things will work out better. The earlier you do this the better as you will have more time to plan how you can influence the key numbers either by saving more, increasing your tax planning, earning more or cutting costs.

The starting point, not least for your peace of mind, is to spend time putting together an annual budget and assessing your current pension and savings plans and, importantly, the lifestyle you want to create in retirement. If you are someone who has always had a personal budget when you were working then things should be pretty straightforward and you simply need to take a hard look at your changed income and expenditure once you retire and over the three phases of retirement. However, some people operate on a sort of auto budget during their working life. They get used to an income level and then in the light of experience know more or less what they can afford to do on that budget without thinking about it a great deal. But even they must understand that things will change on retirement and very few forty and fifty year olds grasp the reality of their pension and savings plans and what that will mean in reality for their retirement years. Before they know it they are at a cliff edge retirement and wishing they had planned a glide path retirement.

If you are not used to personal budgeting it may seem a bit daunting. But that is really not the case: unless your financial affairs are extremely complex, budgeting is no more than simple addition and subtraction. You simply add together all your likely actual income and subtract from that all your estimated expenditure, and if the two balance then you can rest easy. For three decades I've watched accountants claiming this as their own territory but it's not and it's actually really easy! It may take a little time when you first do it but you will find it time well spent. It becomes much easier once you have the basic figures in place for the first time.

Income

Let's start with your income calculations, which should be relatively straightforward. You start by inserting on the template at the end of this chapter your current income - nothing could be easier.

Then set out your estimated income based on the year you will retire on another template. This needs some more work but it should be straightforward to get an estimate of any pension entitlements. Those entitlements might come from your previous employment or from any private pension provision you might have made. Such pensions are, however, taxable. In your calculations you would need to make an allowance for any tax due on them, less tax allowances such as the tax free 'Personal Allowance' (much more in Chapter 5, Tax). State Pensions are not taxable at source. However, the tax authorities will usually adjust your Personal Allowance to take account of what you receive in State Pension and use that to set an appropriate tax code for your employment or private pensions which usually means those pensions are paid net of basic rate tax. I know, I know... it's starting to get complex but hang in as that's as complex as it gets.

An additional point about a State Pension is that some people retire before pensionable age. In those circumstances they may have to use any savings and investments to balance the books until such time as they become eligible for their State Pension. One positive thing about this is that when the State Pension does eventually arrive they may well feel better off.

You then need to estimate any income you expect from investments or savings – again taking account of any tax that may be due, albeit there are beneficial new tax breaks that allow you £1,000 of interest tax free if you are a basic rate taxpayer and £500 for higher rate tax payers (£0 for additional rate taxpayers). Finally, you may have prospects of some further paid work (employed or from your own new small business) after you start your retirement or perhaps you may plan to serve as a non-executive director on some advisory body or quango or just take a little job doing something you've always fancied. Any income from such sources should be included – again allowing for Income Tax and National Insurance (the latter continues until you reach state retirement age).

Already you may be feeling out of your depth but as you work through the chapters that follow your knowledge will improve on the above and, as a result your plan will improve.

Expenditure

You start by inserting on the template at the end of this chapter your current expenditure based on the categories below. Then do the all-important sanity check by checking the bottom line expenditure to what you spend each month as shown on your bank accounts and credit cards over a year. If it does not match you've missed something which needs to be added in. In reality, and in my experience, most people significantly underestimate their expenditure. Don't fall into this trap and do the sanity check. Then set out your best estimate of expenditure based on the life you want to create when you aim to retire on another template. Estimating expenditure in the future, while perhaps slightly more complex and less precise than income, is also relatively straightforward. The first thing is to identify the current costs as above and as a base line and then flex these based on how your expenditure is likely to change as you pass through the three phases of retirement. This is another complex bit but bear with me... ignore inflation and in accounting terms base it on the present days value and I'll explain why later in this chapter. If expenditure on certain areas is shared with others you need to check how circumstances change. Broadly speaking, expenditure is likely to fall within the following areas:

- food and drink
- household and personal costs
- travel (including cars)
- leisure (especially holidays)
- sundry expenditure
- big one-offs.

Food and drink

What is purchased and what it costs can vary greatly from family to family. Your eating and drinking habits may increase in the active retirement years, reducing in the passive years and then again reducing further in the retirement with care years.

Check through everything you spend on food and drink over, say, a two-month period (and probably go back to pre Covid-19 times) and use that figure in your estimates as a starting point. Remember to include eating out. If you have not done this before the total will surprise you but don't be put off.

Household and property

The obvious items are utilities, rent, council tax/rates and water rates and insurance. Factor in any outstanding mortgage although many plan to end mortgage payments well before or around the time they are due to retire so that should represent a major saving in retirement. There are other items such as telephone, broadband, mobiles and TV package payments. You also need an amount to cover upkeep ranging from window cleaning to decorating to minor repairs. As you reach passive retirement you may need some part-time help with the heavier gardening tasks and larger gardens. It is always the major repair and maintenance household costs that tend to trip up any budget from updating bathrooms to needing roof repairs. Rather than making no provision set something aside when doing the sums. The biggest future change is retirement with care and care home costs as already highlighted.

Travel

Cars are expensive and if you have two cars it's time to ask if you really need 2 cars especially if you right-size and relocate your property (more in Your Home and Property, Chapter 1). If you were provided with a company car while working this could mean quite significant additional expenditure starting at the purchase price and adding road tax, insurance, servicing, replacement parts, MOT and any subscriptions to motoring organisations. Also, don't forget that cars don't keep going forever, so you may need to think about setting something aside for a replacement every 5 years. The good news is that many new cars come with exceptionally good three-, five- or even seven-year warranty provision so do shop around and look for value here – even if you do have to give up that cherished 'brand' that you have always bought. If you prefer a monthly budget a 'Personal Contract Purchase' ("PCP") loan may work better over 24, 36 or 48 months. You can pay a one off fee (called the final balloon payment) to take ownership of the car or hand it back and your obligations end. There are too many pros and cons on PCPs to go into here but you can start to explore the option on moneysaving expert (search for 'personal contract purchase'.)

Leisure

The whole idea of retirement is that you should have more time to enjoy yourself. While some of the most enjoyable things in life are free others do require some expenditure. Club fees and any other social clubs you are involved with or join to broaden your horizons will come with some cost but this is possibly what you have been waiting for so pay and enjoy. Much more is set out in Chapter 10, Leisure and Holidays. But probably the main item of expenditure could be long haul holidays and then other shorter routine holidays/ trips – you will almost certainly have more time for these and this cost may rise significantly in the active retirement years. This is a difficult area to estimate but you should not ignore it and should make your best guess as this may underpin another quality side of your better retirement. If you are overly ambitious you can cut back, and conversely if you are overly careful you may find you can afford to do more than you anticipated. Don't forget holiday insurance and the fact that premiums tend to increase as you get older.

Sundry expenditure

You will need to set aside something to cover sundry expenditure. These may be relatively small amounts that, taken individually, you may scarcely notice but which can mount up. For example, if you buy a newspaper every day of the week this could well amount to something in the region of £500 over the whole year. Similar comments apply to the odd morning coffee. There is also the occasional gift or not so occasional if it involves grandchildren and, indeed, presents and gifts are usually the biggest component of this category - underestimate this at your peril. The list could go on and on as, by their nature, sundries are virtually impossible to define. You need to look at your own lifestyle and set aside a reasonable amount each month to cover this type of expenditure. This could be one area where there is an element of trial and error, and it may just take a little time to get the full measure of what you might need. But it would be unwise to ignore it, as it will mount up over the year.

The big one-offs

The life stages of your family members needs some thought. The millennials and

Generation Z (more at Chapter 11, Sandwich Generation) face the prospect of high debt and not being able to own their own house and you may want to help? Do you wish to help with wedding costs? The average cost of a wedding in 2019 was £31,000 which may seem astonishing and more recently we may have seen many folk have beautiful and memorable weddings for a fraction of that cost. Perhaps the Covid-19 pandemic 're-set' will help us all rethink weddings costs?. University costs (fees, accommodation and maintenance costs) run, potentially, to £50,000 over 3 years. Maybe there is also a house deposit (£20,000)? Have you earmarked some of your savings and investments for such events and if so how much and when and ensure you include these in your plan. It is especially tough for those under 25 year olds as they are dealing with significant University loans (following the changes introduced in 2012).

Older generations are, therefore, looking at ways they may be able to help which will become all the more focused as we re-set after the Covid-19 pandemic. At the same time these older generations will look into gifting away inheritances at a much earlier stage than may have happened in previous generations with improved knowledge and planning around inheritance tax (more at Chapter 5, Tax).

Again, you may be feeling out of your depth but as you work through the chapters that follow your knowledge will improve and, as a result your plans will improve.

Balancing your books

Having set everything out, the next step is to see if it all balances in the future against the lifestyle you wish to create. If at the first count income balances with expenditure and your savings and investments look like you can cover any big one off payments then you are either very lucky or you are a financial genius. If income and savings exceed expenditure you have no problems, and after checking that there are no errors in your figures you can go and book an extra holiday! The likelihood is, however, that you will find that expenditure exceeds income and savings.

In these circumstances you might find you still have time to save more by perhaps increasing your pension income in the future. One way is by deferring income now that you pay higher rate tax upon to a later point in time when you may be paying a lower rate of tax. Or maybe you go and earn more. All will become clear as you work through the next two essential steps on retirement planning about 'save more' and 'earn more'. Again the earlier you start these actions the better.

As a final check just make sure that you have included everything in the income column – for example have you missed a pension entitlement or an investment? You might also look at the possibility of further paid work (part-time) in your active retirement years. Or, if radical rebalancing is required, you may need to look at releasing capital in your home by downsizing, relocating, selling off part of your garden for a house to be built on (if you are lucky enough to have a big garden with access) or via some form of equity release. Much more on this is set out in the chapters that follow with the result that your plan will improve (more in Your Home and Property Chapter 1).

It will probably be necessary to re-review your expenditure as time passes and your plan develops. There are certain areas where you can't do much – you will still need to eat, most household and property-related expenditure cannot be avoided and if you keep the car the running costs will be largely unchanged. The likelihood is that you will need to look at your leisure/holiday expectations and cut back a bit – at least until you see how things pan out after a few years. You may also need to look at your sundry expenditure and ensure you are not overly indulgent.

How to go about it

You can't keep all of this in your head; as a minimum you need a yearly budget to look at your life now as you have the evidence in the form of bank statements and credit card bills and then go about setting it all out. The table at the end of this chapter gives a proven outline of how you might do this. Just look at the general headings and ignore the detail of splitting it into months at this stage. The headings are not set in stone as people have differing patterns of income and expenditure and you need to tailor it to your own personal needs and circumstances. The intention of the table is to give you a broad framework within which you might operate and start to understand your current budget and how you can manage that and then develop the current budget through the three phases of retirement.

While you may be able to get by with a yearly budget, it is probably worthwhile to take just a little more time and set everything out on a monthly basis. Many payments, and probably some income, do not occur on a regular monthly basis – many bills come in quarterly, insurance policies are often paid annually and holidays and other breaks tend to be irregular. It is therefore much easier to keep track of things if you operate on a monthly basis. This also has the advantage that you can see if things are not quite working out as you go along, rather than being surprised at the end of the year. In this respect it is very unlikely that in practice everything will work out as you plan. There can be unforeseen expenditure, some things may cost more than you have estimated, and you may even find your income increases. All of this is easier to deal with if you can adjust things on a monthly basis to compensate for what will probably be inevitable changes.

Then move on and specifically track how your savings and investments become diluted (if expenditure exceeds income) and what happens as you progress through the active years and into passive years (perhaps less expenditure) to then the retirement with care years (when your home may be used to finance care home fees).

One final suggestion is to put it all on a spreadsheet. If you have been used to dealing with spreadsheets in your working life this will not be difficult. The sort of very simple spreadsheet suggested at the end of this chapter is very easy to set up and run. It would certainly be worthwhile as it enables you to update things virtually automatically, and an additional advantage is that when it comes to the next year all you need do is slot in updated figures and the spreadsheet does the sums automatically.

A final word on doing the sums

Don't be put off by all of this – you do not need to follow the suggestions slavishly. The intention has been to start you thinking about the way your financial affairs might change when you retire and then pass through the three phases of retirement. Those more used to financial modelling will spot that I have not mentioned the effects of inflation and how this can erode your finances (and budget). They're probably right but for now I just want to get us thinking more clearly about the big numbers around projected income and expenditure and I've assumed that inflation will effect both income and expenditure in broadly the same way. This makes things simpler and is not unreasonable for the purposes of this exercise.

Remember that everyone has different circumstances and will have a different retirement lifestyle ambition so you just need to pause and think about your own situation. If you follow the suggestions in this chapter, adjusted as necessary to your own personal needs, then you should have better control over your affairs. But don't forget that personal budgeting is not a precise science; you have to be flexible and prepared to make adjustments as you go along. If things just seem too complex then the answer is very simple and you just need to engage the services of a good financial advisor or accountant who will be used to shaping these sorts of projections and can also adapt quite easily for 'what if' scenarios.

The most important message of this chapter is the earlier in life you do this sort of exercise the better chance you have of achieving the retirement you seek.

Top tip

The key to improving your initial plan now lies in the four sections of this book: plan more, save more, earn more and live better and you will ultimately achieve a better retirement. If you turn now to the final pages at Chapter 12 you will see possibly the most important pages of all. It was written for you and remember the quote at the start of this chapter and the punchline is repeated below. Is it time to make your first entry? It's your choice.

"Choice not chance determines your destiny."

ARISTOTLE

Useful reading

For further help and information the following should prove useful:

The free and impartial advice at the government funded website www.moneyadviceservice.org.uk and these two sections:

Budgeting and saving section: The 'managing money' sub-section and the 'budget planner'.

Pensions and Retirement section: The 'Managing money and planning ahead' section and the 'managing money' sub-section.

RETIREMENT PLANNING EXPERT 2020/21

BUDGET AND PLANNER	Month 1 and repeat monthly	Annual total
INCOME		
Private/work pension received (after tax)		
State Pension (less any tax due)		
Any other pension (after tax)		
Interest on savings (after tax)		
Dividends from investments (after tax)		
Paid work (after tax)		
Any other income		
Total income (A)		
EXPENDITURE		
Food and drink		
Food and drink (eating in)		
Meals out (and drinks)		
Total food and drink		
Household and personal		
Mortgage or rent		
Council tax/ rates		
Water rates		
Insurance		
Electricity, gas and oil		
Clothing		
Telephone, mobile and broadband		
TV packages		
Decorating, repairs and maintenance		
Garden upkeep and maintaining		
Hair, beauty and health		
Cash spending		
Other/ contingency		
Total household and personal		
Transport/car		
Petrol/fuel		
Tax		
Insurance and breakdown cover		
Service, parts and repairs		
Any other regular transport costs (train, taxi etc.)		

Total transport/car		
Leisure		
Clubs, gym, hobbies, theatre etc.		
Short trips and holidays		
Major long haul holidays		
Pets		
Total leisure		
Sundries, gifts and presents		
Total expenditure (B)		
Surplus/deficit to carry forward each month (A–B)		
Attach notes on any forthcoming big one-offs (and how these will be funded)		

Notes and calculations

Reminder: Take any action points or follow up points to Chapter 12, Your Plan For A Better Retirement.

Chapter Two
Your home and property

"Home is the place that goes where you go, yet it welcomes you upon your return. Like a dog overjoyed at the door. We've missed you is what you hear, no matter how long you have been gone."

MICHAEL J ROSEN

Some of the biggest solutions on achieving a better retirement can flow from property and this is where we start on the 'save more' chapters in this book. If you need a refresher on the approach set out within this book and structure go back and revisit the introduction chapter. Remember the essential four steps as you work through this book; plan more, save more, earn more, live better and achieve a better retirement. Your home is likely to be a significant part of your wealth if you own or costs if you rent and the centre of your social and family life. The glide path into retirement offers a perfect opportunity to reappraise your home and your values and priorities around 'the home'. It may help you save a fortune and help you achieve a better retirement if it is up for review in the retirement lifestyle you wish to create. Indeed this may have been brought more into focus by experiences or thoughts during the Covid-19 pandemic and the re-set moment many of us are experiencing. In any event your home and property may be a big part of your intended retirement expenditure and this review might give pointers to some savings and opportunities. If so you will see why this chapter is a good start for the 'save more' essential step of retirement planning.

The home is a central part of lives for both economic and sentimental reasons.

The sentimental reasons are emphasised by a number of old familiar sayings 'Home is where the heart is', and 'There's no place like home' and by Michael J Rosen as quoted at the head of this chapter - I love that quote. It is our space, our comfort, our shelter, our retreat and a place to welcome family and friends. That is not likely to alter once you retire and it is likely to remain at the centre of your social and domestic life. On the economic side of the equation many home owners will have cleared their mortgage by the time they retire and this can be a real financial bonus. The Office for National Statistics show that 74% of people aged over 65 owned their homes outright in England in 2018, up from 56% in 1993. Economic factors flow from the size and age of the property – the bigger and older the property the more it costs to maintain and maintenance costs will only increase over time as the property ages and you perhaps become less agile and self-sufficient. The biggest economic factor is location and the Office of National Statistics House Price Index summary available at ww.gov.uk shows London and the South East have an average house price almost double the North West.

Country and government office region	Average price	Annual change
England	£261,795	4.9%
Northern Ireland (Quarter 3 - 2020)	£143,205	2.4%
Scotland	£161,510	4.3%
Wales	£170,604	3.8%
East Midlands	£204,581	5.0%
East of England	£305,764	4.8%
London	£496,485	4.1%
North East	£136,262	3.3%
North West	£176,976	6.0%
South East	£336,763	4.0%
South West	£275,376	6.4%
West Midlands Region	£208,497	4.0%
Yorkshire and The Humber	£174,450	5.4%

Source: Office of National Statistics: UK House Price Index summary, September 2020

This chapter will mention tax issues but remember this is only a guide and it is neither legal nor financial advice; it is no substitute for taking professional advice from a financial adviser or other professional adviser. Any potential tax advantages may be subject to change from future budgets and will depend upon your individual circumstances, and individual professional advice should be obtained.

This chapter at a glance

As a quick guide, this chapter covers in detail a number of aspects of home and property that you should consider:

- *Future proofing the place you call home is important.* This means taking an in-depth look at where you currently live and deciding if it will work for you in your retirement - it is called 'right-sizing' your home.

- *Right-sizing your property costs.* Equity release, downsizing in the area, staying put and moving to a completely new area all present pros and cons. *Suggestions and help are provided.*

- *Moving abroad or taking a second home abroad* can look brilliant through rose-tinted glasses. Find out more and some options in this chapter.

- *Using your home to earn money.*

Reassess your property needs and priorities

Your home will hold many sentimental attachments and it will be a tough assignment right at the start of this book and journey but it is now time to reassess what you actually require in a home and where you want that to be. Importantly this review has to consider your likely changing circumstances over your future years. With life expectancy in the UK on average at 85 years for men and 87 years for women you can start to think how you would like to live through the three phases of retirement as set out at Chapter 1. Remember it's never too soon to start planning.

Why do people 'right-size' their home for retirement?

The common reasons for moving home in the approach to retirement or during retirement are:

- To help create the life they now want to live.
- To reduce costs and increase the wealth they have to spend on enjoying their life.
- To be closer to family.

- Due to actual or anticipated changes in health (bungalows/no stairs etc.).
- Due to changes in marital status.
- In the current Covid-19 pandemic environment to take advantage of generous temporary stamp duty 'holidays' that presented a 'cost' obstacle before the temporary change to the tax regime - at Autumn 2020 I don't know how long it will last beyond the current end date of 31 March 2021.

What to consider when planning a home for the future?

There will be many sentimental and economic factors that will influence your decision. Everyone will come at this differently. The following questions may help you take this big question a little further on some sentimental factors:

- Where is the life you want to create?

- What cultural and hospitality facilities do you need nearby?

- What healthcare facilities do you need nearby?

- What size of town or city would you need 'nearby' (what is 'nearby' and what quality of transport links including airports)?

- What climate would you like and accept or not accept?

- What outdoor activities and clubs/associations/ interests nearby would count as a bonus?

- What home and garden safety needs do you have or may need to have?

- Are there considerations for pets?

- Will you have good support networks in the area – family and friends? If not how do you feel about developing these? Again, if there are no family or friends in the new area do your plans include having a spare room and 'space' for them to stay with you?

- What if your health and other circumstances change?

- If one person in a relationship is unhappy in a location then ultimately both of you will probably be unhappy.

The economic factors are easier. Right-sizing presents a straightforward opportunity to change the financial position and your retirement plan in two significant ways:

Proceeds from the sale of your existing home less the purchase price of a new home (including all costs, including stamp duty which is being reduced until 31 March 2021) will give either a surplus or a loss. If this is your only property the surplus is called a 'gain' and is tax free (more in Chapter 4, Tax) and there for your retirement plans. Briefly for now, this flows from the UK tax regime where, currently, any surplus (or 'gain' to use tax terminology) is free from tax. It's why people invest in extending and building up their home. With current tax rules there may also be no inheritance tax until over a million pounds and currently (and until 31 March 2021, unless the rules are changed) there are stamp duty holidays. If there is a loss (for instance you are moving to a more costly house) the loss needs to be funded from the finances in your retirement plans.

The second aspect is the ongoing cost of upkeep (utility bills, council tax/rates and insurance), repairs and maintenance. Usually big homes cost more to maintain and old homes require more upkeep unless they have been modernised with new insulation, heating, water systems and electrical systems. Smaller homes usually cost less to maintain. On the other hand new homes tend to require less upkeep and are more energy efficient although garden space can be smaller. New home developments that are 'packed in' means you can be significantly overlooked by neighbouring properties. It is a case of comparing the numbers and seeing how the ongoing costs of property upkeep and maintenance change according to the size of property, age of property and location and how this can change your financial plan. If it's a saving then you usually keep saving on upkeep, repairs and maintenance year after year and the amount can be significant and help you achieve a better retirement.

Releasing funds: the options of equity release, downsizing or relocating

If there is a significant gap between the retirement lifestyle you desire and the actual reality of your pension income and your investment income there are a few options that can make another significant impact on your finances in retirement. The first is earning more by taking a job, starting a business or perhaps letting out a room and this is covered elsewhere in this book. Another option is accessing the equity stored in your property by either (a) borrowing money against your property through an equity release scheme to help provide additional income, or (b) freeing up wealth by right-sizing which means downsizing or relocating. Essentially you are converting wealth that is stored up in a property into income to spend but each route comes at a price and with pros and cons.

Staying put and using equity release

The process of equity release works by you taking out a mortgage on your property whilst continuing to live there and then receiving a lump sum or drawing down funds against that mortgage. Interest then rolls up on the mortgage debt, which will be repaid when you do come to sell the house and downsize or move into alternative accommodation. The interest on the mortgage may be slightly more than on other commercial mortgages.

The industry was subject to significant mis-selling in the late 1980s and early 1990s when some financial advisers persuaded elderly homeowners to re-mortgage their houses and then gamble on the stock market to try and achieve returns to beat the mortgage interest. It went spectacularly wrong for many with the intervention of some poor selling techniques and rogue advisers, the recession, stock market turmoil and high interest rates. I was personally involved in reviewing the damage across the UK as Manager of the Investigations and Recoveries Team at the Investors Compensation Scheme (the predecessor of the current UK safety net the Financial Services Compensation Scheme). Millions of pounds of compensation was paid out to disadvantage investors and, unfortunately, many claims by investors had to be turned down as investors had strayed outside the UK safety net by not dealing with an authorised financial advisor. I provide more hints and tips around this theme at Savings and Investments, Chapter 4

For now, if arranged properly, equity release mortgages may give you an option to consider against 'right-sizing' but these things still carry an instinctive risk as the interest just rolls up in the background. So it is vital to get trusted relatives on board to help you fully appraise any equity release scheme and look at it from all angles. A good independent financial adviser who is not connected with the marketing and promotion of an equity release scheme should be able to help you understand the financial implications and help you consider other property related options. More on finding a good financial advisor is set out in Savings and Investments, Chapter 4. For the equity release perspective the Equity Release Council is the industry body and it aims to facilitate the safe growth of the equity release market (www.equityreleasecouncil.com).

Some positives about equity release:

- You can stay in your home.

- In terms of long-term care planning equity release can be useful if you're looking to fund care and stay in your own home.

- All Equity Release Council members offer a "no negative equity guarantee" which means that, no matter what happens to the housing market, customers will never owe more than the value of their home.

Some negatives to consider about equity release:

- The compounding effect of interest at 4% or 5% should not be under-estimated as interest builds on interest. Ensure you understand how this adds up over 5 years, 10 years and 20 years (on top of the actual mortgage that was obtained). David Byers wrote an article in The Sunday Times, 9 February 2020 *'Equity release turns on the money tap - at a high price'* and he stated *"With equity release, the debt typically doubles every 14 years. So if you borrow £50,000, 14 years later you will owe £100,000, and after 28 years it will be £200,000."*

- Your family will receive a smaller inheritance as some of the value in your home, maybe all of it if you live long enough, will go to the mortgage provider.

- The fees to arrange the equity release. Before signing anything get everything set out in writing so that understand absolutely everything about all fees involved including: adviser's fee paid by you, valuation fee, mortgage fee, solicitor's fees and most importantly any Early Repayment Charge (ERC). Also get confirmation (in writing and beforehand, of course) of any commission payable by the lender to your adviser for you taking out an equity release product. ERC's must be understood as they can vary from 5% to 20% commented David Byers in the Sunday Times article referenced immediately above. Adam Williams in The Sunday Telegraph, 6 September 2020 in an article 'Cashing in on soaring house prices? Beware fees' warned that *"Older homeowners could be wasting thousands by using expensive equity release advisers."* The article questioned why investors were paying fees of 1.99% or 2.25% to equity release advisers as part of the fees to arrange the equity release. It also highlighted that some equity release advisers were also receiving commissions from equity release lenders. The article highlighted how some equity release firms charged a flat fee of £395 and a further £595 as an arrangement fee. The answer - no if's, no but's ... just get clarity on everything, as above, in writing before signing anything.

- The money released may affect your state benefits.

- Borrowing may be limited to about 35% of the value of your home.

- If you wish to downsize in the future the equity remaining after repaying the mortgage and interest may limit your choice and options. Could this point to downsizing or 'right sizing' at an earlier stage to avoid double disruption and costs? More on these alternatives below.

- You retain responsibility for maintaining the property and paying the bills.

Top tip

Equity release fees and costs must be clearly set out and understood. If you do decide to consider equity release get at least two quotes from advisers and get clarity in writing on all fees, charges and commissions payable before you sign or agree to anything.
There should be no rushed meetings and being asked to 'just sign here' to proceed- if that's the approach run a mile. Take a time-out, reflect and discuss with relatives. Any quality adviser with be delighted to see you taking this considered approach.

If you do go ahead with equity release, think carefully about whether you need all the funds in one go or if you can draw it down in tranches. The latter is called a 'drawdown lifetime mortgage' and is usually cheaper on interest costs as you don't draw the money until you need it and, therefore, save on the interest costs on the amount deferred. This could be useful if your needs were, say, £10,000 now in year one for a holiday of a lifetime, £25,000 between years three and five to help with a child/grandchild's three years of university accommodation and subsistence costs and £25,000 at some future point to help with a house deposit or wedding or such like for a child/grandchild.

Downsizing or Relocating

You should also consider if there is a 'better way' – for instance is downsizing a better option for some of the benefits of, potentially, a brand new home, new view, the right size, lower property running and maintenance costs and lower council tax/rates? Add on a more manageable garden and proximity to the shops, facilities and services which you might need for the next phase in retirement. Against this, issues such as a smaller space and new neighbourhood can be considered together with the costs of buying and selling (which may include expensive stamp duty albeit there are currently Covid-19 pandemic related stamp duty holidays). The money released may affect your state benefits.

Another factor to consider is whether it is better to downsize/right size at the present time rather than in the future and before you get too set in your ways. Perhaps the younger the better as it may help with developing new social circles? Again it's potentially a big number so it is worth repeating that there are generous stamp duty holidays available on transactions completed before 31 March 2021 and your solicitor will set out more information as part of the house purchase transaction.

In addition you could achieve a double win by not only 'right-sizing' but also look at relocating to a new area where property prices are cheaper. Or with a relocation to a cheaper area you could still have a similar size house if 'size' is important to you but free up significant equity. The regional variations in house prices as shown in the table at the head of this chapter are significant especially if you are moving out of a sought after area or high price region.

If you are considering moving to be closer to your family don't overlook the fact that everyone is now more mobile than has been the case in the past. While they may appear settled just now, new opportunities or challenges may mean that they themselves may need to move again – leaving you stranded in your new home, away from both old friends and family.

If you are thinking about moving to a new area that seems more attractive then check it out very carefully. Don't place too much reliance on lists of so-called (over-priced?) best places to live. They may well have their attractions but you need to be sure they meet your particular requirements. Ideally, before moving it would be sensible to spend some quality time in the new area (i.e. weeks and weeks and over different seasons), checking out what it is really like, whether it will meet your changing needs and whether you would be comfortable there socially. And don't forget that the social aspect is likely to be even more important to you in retirement.

Assess all those recreational and medical positives and negatives. Don't forget the hidden intelligence that is lying around on the internet, such as TripAdvisor reviews of restaurants and Facebook sites for local community groups, which can all be quite telling/reassuring. If you move from a high cost area to a lower cost area it is difficult to unwind the decision years later due to house price inflation (and how it accumulates and the gap widens) and paying stamp duty and other costs again. Could renting out your property and renting in the new location provide a solution to this possible issue whilst you give it a trial period (but you may miss the stamp duty holiday this year until 31 March 2021, currently)? Finally many commentators say that 'property prices always go up' but from the 1970s onwards the UK has seen several property crashes. You must therefore consider the potential impact of the Covid-19 pandemic and whether there may be another crash once furlough support changes or ends. Combines this with the ending of mortgage payment holidays, any increase in stamp duty (after the end of the stamp duty holiday) and the potential for the number of house evictions increasing and all of this may influence your timing if you are downsizing.

Top tip

The equity release market is very high profile and gets much attention. Consider it but you should also consider 'right-sizing' and whether downsizing/ relocating makes better financial and emotional sense. You may even get a super new all-mod-cons living space with a nice new view and retain a big surplus to have fun with or pass on.

Staying put and maybe increasing the home size

Many people who retire choose to stay put in the same area where they have lived for years rather than being tempted to move to some apparently ideal new situation. These reasons include being close to where they used to work, or near their families for whom they provide 'grandsitting' support (enabling their adult children to work), and staying within reach of friends and where their social networks are. Many people also find it reassuring to remain with their local medical practice and other medical facilities, which could prove a blessing in later life when more support may be needed.

Even if staying put there may be adjustments to consider to take account of your new circumstances; if more space is required to accommodate boomerang kids (children who return to the family home after university/college - more in Sandwich Generation, Chapter 11) try reviewing these four options, ranging from economical to expensive.

- *Economical.* Invest in a garden room – these have boomed in quality and reduced in price in recent years and range from a glorified wooden shed to fully insulated and double-glazed structures. Some require no planning permission and some can be built in less than a week. They can provide accommodation solutions which range from simple storage to a hobby room to living accommodation. The size of the building will influence whether or not you need any planning permission or approvals and your local authority will be able to provide further information.

- *Fairly economical.* A garage conversion is another popular way to increase space in your home; it is reasonably simple and can be surprisingly cost-effective. If you propose to add a room above your garage, any scheme would be subject to appropriate planning permission being granted. This is needed because of the extra height and alteration to the roof line. Rooms above a detached garage make an ideal guest suite, office, study, granny annex or somewhere to carry out a noisy hobby. If you convert a garage you may worry about where you put your car but don't forget that modern cars seem quite capable of surviving without the protection of a garage. Otherwise, a cost-effective car port could be added in as part of the scheme.

- *Quite expensive.* One possibility might be to extend your existing property. If you're considering doing building works, check out both planning and building regulation controls. Some smaller extensions to the rear or side of a property can often be built without having to make a planning application, provided that the design complies with the rules for permitted development (see www.planningportal.gov.uk). But make sure you carefully check the particular rules for the area in which you live as building without the necessary approval can have serious consequences. Expect tighter rules for conservation areas and listed properties. Obtain quotes from more than one contractor and ask for references or visit their last job. The lowest quote may not necessarily be the best one with regard to the vital quality factor. Friends or your professional adviser can assist with recommendations before you go ahead with any works. Keep things in proportion – extra bedrooms aren't an advantage unless there are sufficient bathrooms or shower rooms and many now prefer the convenience of en-suite facilities. Remember to keep the planning paperwork and electrical certificates as these will be needed when you come to sell the house.

- *Expensive but provides radical new space and environment.* Buying the property next door: if your budget allows, becoming your own neighbour allows more space than an extension without leaving the neighbourhood. This option is neither cheap nor simple and professional advice from an architect is essential. Even if you live in a flat you might be able to buy the adjoining unit or the one above or below, then knock through or install a staircase to achieve double living space. Any construction work being undertaken must, of course, adhere strictly to planning and building regulations. Engaging a good architect will be worth the money as cutting corners will just come back to haunt you when the property is eventually sold. If you can continue to live at the property while work is progressing this can cut down costs as temporary rentals of less than six months can be hard to find; you will also be able to monitor security and work efficiency.

> **Top tip**
>
> **Garden rooms have improved in quality and reduced in cost and may not need any planning permission – is this the solution to a need for space and a new outlook?**

Moving abroad – full-time or part-time

If you're planning to retire abroad, the complexities and risk of a property purchase increase due to the dual factors of dealing in a foreign language and with foreign law where rights and remedies differ to the UK. Just now there are added complications and uncertainties as the relationship between the UK and the rest of Europe will change dramatically as a result of Brexit and some generous tax breaks will be lost. You will pay more tax in some European countries so take advice from a tax adviser that knows the relevant tax regime. Brexit may also impact lending, residency rights and health care. It is very difficult to assess the implications of this for those living abroad and if you are contemplating a move you will need to keep a very careful watch on developments as we Brexit and move into 2021. What you really need to look out for is definitive information from government sources as it emerges at www.gov.uk.

The other less obvious factor is the way things just work differently in overseas countries and this can be frustrating - just ask anyone that lives abroad. But if you're relaxed and flexible then that will help make any transition that little bit better.

Top tip

A great place for a holiday is not necessarily a good place to live permanently or part-time.

Some ways of protecting yourself when buying property abroad include:

- Spend an extended period in the area at high and low season before you commit yourself to a purchase.

- Get a good solicitor. This is easier said than done but take recommendations from trusted friends and their network and try to identify a solicitor with offices in both the UK and the country you are buying in as this can smooth transactions (especially complex ones where there may be an extra risk factor). Get all documents translated if you are signing them and they are in a foreign language.

- Make sure the solicitor you use is independent and not involved in the sale in any way.

- In particular keep a very careful watch on any changes affecting those living abroad emerging from the negotiations relating to the UK exit from the European Union.

There are many websites offering advice and information on retiring abroad. Have a browse through the following:

- www.gov.uk – Britons preparing to move or retire abroad;
- www.buyassociation.co.uk – section on advice on retiring abroad and homes

   abroad;

- www.shelteroffshore.com – information on living abroad;

- www.expatfocus.com – provides essential information and advice for a successful move abroad.

If you have the necessary funds another option would be to continue to live at home and buy another property abroad, especially if you are downsizing. If you can afford it, this might give you the best of both worlds. You would still have all the comfort and security of your home base but be able to escape to the sun from time to time as the mood takes you. To ease the financial burden you might consider letting the property out, particularly at peak times. You would, however, need to carefully check the local rules and regulations relating to letting property – these can vary from country to country and indeed from area to area.

If you do go for that 'home in the sun' as a second property the following budget planner will help you put some flesh on the likely returns to help inform your decision:

- First off, assess the structure and accommodation set-up and assess the cost of one-off adaptation work – security system, en-suites, new kitchen, fencing, roof integrity and the like.

- Income – expected weekly rental x number of weeks. Use Owners Abroad or equivalent sites to assess potential weekly rentals (the amounts can vary in high season), less:

- accountancy and tax (you may be able to do it yourself for UK taxation but are there returns required in the foreign country);

- advertising;

- bank charges;

- cleaning and laundry between occupiers and annual deep clean;

- electricity (higher if you have a heated pool and air conditioning);

- annual safety testing;

- gas/oil if appropriate;

- insurance – buildings and public liability (and loss of rental, i.e. utilities failure etc);

- maintenance – house;

- maintenance – pool;
- letting agent fees;
- property service charge (flats and holiday-type villages with communal land/facilities);
- property tax of foreign country;
- local tax/rates of the area the property is in;
- gardening;
- security – annual maintenance and call-out fees;
- telephone/broadband;
- satellite or cable television;
- water rates/charges;
- administration costs (post, stationery).

> **Top tip**
>
> **That second home in the sun could cost a lot more than you think and restricts holiday getaway flexibility. But if you do the numbers first it could be a fantastic opportunity and make for a perfect retirement.**

Counting the cost of a house purchase

In order to fund a house purchase remember to do the numbers and budget for costs of between 4 and 14 per cent of the value of a new home (the higher the purchase price the higher the percentage due to Stamp Duty). So add up Stamp Duty, legal fees, search fees, removal charges, survey fees, estate agents' commission and a provision for decoration and furnishings and you can refine the cost of moving. Remember agents' fees vary and range from hundreds of pounds via online offerings to thousands of pounds for the traditional high-street agents. And don't pay too much for your new house. An asking price is just that – an asking price. So do your homework on websites such as Rightmove and Zoopla which list the actual selling price of all houses in the street or area for the last decade; consider additions and extensions undertaken by the seller and gain more intelligence on price. Overlaying this are the general market conditions – is it a buyers' or sellers' market? Look at the sales price divided by square feet of the accommodation – this gives a useful indicator. But overriding this and governed by the golden rule of 'location, location, location' is the fact that the truly wonderful properties are often hard to find and even harder to secure so be prepared to research, graft and undergo a bumpy journey if you set your sights really high.

When buying a new home, especially an older property, a building survey is essential before committing yourself. This costs upwards of £500 depending on the type and size of property but it may provide you with a comeback should things go wrong. Also, an early review of environmental surveys will help you avoid being sold 'a stinker' – a home built on historic landfill (check the Environment Agency website and search 'historic landfill') or a property in an area of high flood risk (search the Environment Agency website for 'flood map for planning'). Helpful to home buyers, for a small charge, the Land Registry allows members of the public to seek information directly about the 23 million or so properties held on its register via the Land Registry website: www.gov.uk/government/organisations/land-registry.

Your protection

The Property Ombudsman scheme provides an independent review service for buyers or sellers of UK residential property in the event of a complaint. It also covers lettings agents and residential leasehold management. As with most ombudsman schemes, action can be taken only against firms that are actually members of the scheme. See the Property Ombudsman website: www.tpos.co.uk.

Removals

Costs vary significantly depending on the type and size of furniture, the distance over which it is being moved and other factors, including insurance and seasonal troughs and peaks. Shop around and try a quote from just outside your local area as neighbouring removal firms are always keen to get a slice of the action. The British Association of Removers (BAR) lists approved member firms who work to a code of practice, see the website: www.bar.co.uk.

Home security

Your local neighbourhood watch should be able to advise you on home security arrangements. Age UK provide a helpful booklet, *Staying Safe*, which can be downloaded from www.ageuk.org.uk. Why not have a street meeting and invite your local crime prevention officer along to give a talk – it helps to be able to connect that face to a name if you really do need help.

Living in leasehold

An ever-increasing number of people move into a flat in retirement. If you go down this route three of the big issues to grasp are the length of the lease, your obligations to others and the size of the service fee. The general rule is that the longer the lease the more the property is worth. So know the length of the lease and who owns the freehold of the building (maybe an investment company, a private investor, or ideally the leaseholders themselves in the form of a management company). With the advent of 'right to manage', leaseholders do not need to own the freehold but will be able to manage the building as if they were the freeholder. Leaseholders should be aware of their responsibilities, such as keeping the inside of the property in good order, paying their share of the cost of maintaining and running the building, behaving in a neighbourly manner and not contravening things as set out in the lease, such as subletting their flat without the freeholder's prior consent, or keeping a pet if the lease clearly states this is not permitted.

The leaseholder has the right to expect the freeholder to maintain the building and common parts. The leaseholder will be required to pay a 'service charge' to the freeholder (or their managing agent) to maintain, repair and insure the building as well as to provide other services, such as lifts, central heating or cleaners. These charges can vary massively but must be 'reasonable'. Leaseholders have a right to challenge the service charge if they feel it is 'unreasonable' via the Leasehold Valuation Tribunal (LVT) but it's better to clearly understand the service charge before you even view a potential leasehold property. For further information see Leasehold Advisory Service (LAS), www.lease-advice.org, and Association of Retirement Housing Managers (ARHM), www.arhm.org.

Retirement housing and sheltered accommodation

Hopefully you will still be in good physical health at the time of your retirement. However, as time moves on it is inevitable that you will start to slow down and may find it increasingly difficult to maintain your existing property. At that stage, you may need to start thinking about the need to move to retirement housing or sheltered accommodation. You probably do not need to take any direct action as you retire; rather it is something that you could usefully keep at the back of your mind. And, of course, you also need to consider any potential changes in your partner's well-being.

The terms 'retirement housing' and 'sheltered accommodation' cover a wide variety of housing but are designed primarily to bridge the gap between the family home and residential care. There are many well-designed, high-quality private developments of 'retirement homes' on the market, for sale or rent, at prices to suit most pockets. As a general rule, you have to be over 55 when you buy property of this kind. Positives include 24-hour emergency alarms or on-site wardens and built-in design features such as walk-in showers and raised plugs. There can be a positive social community. Some 'villages' have been developed to offer on-site amenities and some developers have identified a need for luxury-type units including a swimming pool. Negatives may include a no-pets policy, high service charges (these must be factored into any decision and, again, probably before you even view a potential property), smaller space than you are used to and a closer proximity to neighbours. Resale values can also be poor and press reporting indicates some owners encounter significant reduced property resale values when the property is later sold. A check on resale values should be undertaken on any proposed purchase and, if there is no historic data, check similar sites. Banks normally don't lend on these properties. More information around assessing the welfare aspects of such properties is set out in the Sandwich Generation, Chapter 11.

Earning money from property

Your home doesn't have to be a drain on your finances. If you need some spare cash or a regular source of income, there are several ways beyond holiday lets as covered earlier which could make you money from your home.

- *Rent a room scheme*: This is the government's incentive that allows owner–occupiers and tenants to receive tax-free rental income if furnished accommodation is provided in the main – or only – home. The maximum amount you can earn is £7,500 per year. If you live in a suitable area, you could find a commuting lodger who only wants the room on week nights – see websites such as Monday to Friday (www.mondaytofriday.com) or www.airbnb.co.uk. Remember you will lose some privacy and you will need to manage any risk to you and your property.

- *£1,000 tax free property allowance*: You can also earn £1,000 from letting out your home and not pay any tax via the HMRC property allowance. If you own a property jointly with others, you're each allowed the £1,000 allowance. See Gov.UK and search 'tax free allowances on property and trading income'.

- *Rent out your drive*: Some areas of the United Kingdom are chronically short of available parking for people going to work or travelling from a nearby airport. Try www.justpark.com for more information.

- *Your home in lights*: It is possible to rent out your home as a film or TV set, particularly if it is quirky or charming. You can list your home via an online agency such as Film Locations (www.filmlocations.co.uk), or Amazing Space (www.amazingspace.co.uk), although agencies will take a fee if your home is used.

- *Host students*: Offer your home as a base for a foreign language or exchange student. This pays typically £100 per week. Contact your local language schools, colleges and universities to see if they offer a pairing service for would-be lodgers and hosts.

- And finally, make money from clearing your clutter and surplus possessions that could be converted into cash. Obvious outlets are eBay and the local car boot sale and you could also try facebook marketplace.

Buy to Let

Buy to let properties have become an increasingly challenging investment. The recent 'hits' taken by this sector include increased stamp duty on second homes and restrictions on the amount of mortgage interest that you can deduct if you are a higher rate taxpayer. The other wider economic challenge is over the affordability of housing and whether this may prompt more/other action to supress house price increases. Up to 2020 the prospects of a capital gain has been one of the factors that property investors hoped for and, indeed, probably attained. Will this continue in the light of the Covid-19 pandemic where I expect there to be tax 'pain' later in 2021 to help repay the national debt. For instance, I believe Capital Gain Tax will probably change significantly in 2021 and may move to income tax rates. This would mean the tax on the profit (gain) from second home sales will move from being taxed at the Capital Gains Tax rates for a second property at 18%/28% to income tax rate rates of (presently) 20%, 40% or 45%? Time will tell. After that it comes down to the numbers and factoring in the cost of finding tenants and managing the property if you decide to outsource these tasks to an agent. Then factor in your time in 'managing' the activity. Finally factor in the risk of you ending up with a 'tenant from hell' and being left with unpaid rent, damaged property and lots of stress. At the end of the day one of the key issues is the bottom line 'yield' (income less costs as a percentage of the amount you invested in the property). How does this compare to investment returns which you can earn for little or no effort?

Top tip

This is a big area so just purchase the book 'Successful Property Letting' by David Lawrenson (January 2020 edition, published by Robinson).

Furnished holiday lettings

Furnished holiday lettings at home or abroad - these still benefit from ample tax breaks and the mortgage interest caps do not presently apply. To get the tax breaks there are strict rules over the number of days that the property must be available for short term lettings; the number of days actually let and restrictions to stop lettings of more than a month to one person counting towards short term lettings. The invisible benefits are the availability of a holiday home for you to use when it is not let out and this can provide a lovely retirement lifestyle if you find the right property. Remember the golden rule of property 'location, location, location'. For further information read HMRC Guidance note HS253 Furnished holiday lettings.

> **Top tip**
>
> **Fewer houses are being bought for buy to let due to a more challenging tax environment. The tax burden on furnished holiday lettings are much less onerous (at Autumn 2020) and these may give a better investment yield.**

Commercial property and a Self Invested Personal Pension (SIPP)

Commercial property is another option and there is the bonus of a big tax break as (currently) it can be held as part of a Self Invested Personal Pension with the property, in turn, providing an investment and then income in retirement planning. This is significant as residential property cannot be held in a SIPP. A good Independent Financial Advisor who specialises in pensions will be able to guide you on this (more at Pensions, Chapter 3) but also note the word of caution in Chapter 3 about protection in SIPPs when things go wrong or if there is a financial crash.

Property investment funds

Finally there are also property investment funds. When the economy is doing well there are more business tenants seeking space for their premises. If there is high demand then landlords can charge higher rents and investment funds that specialise in property tend to do well. If there is a recession the opposite happens. It is another route into property where the charges are lower and the risk is spread.

Useful reading

The Equity Release Council is the industry body of the equity release market www.equityreleasecouncil.com

Successful Property Letting by David Lawrenson

www.expatfocus.com – provides information and advice on moving abroad

> **Reminder: Take any action points or follow up points to Chapter 12, Your Plan For A Better Retirement.**

Chapter Three
Pensions

"The question isn't what age I want to retire. It's at what income."

GEORGE FOREMAN

This chapter on pensions could be tough reading as pensions are a complex subject and full of jargon. In summary if you have a final salary defined benefit pension (where the pension just keeps on paying as long as you live) and are retired or nearly retired you are in a good position and perhaps can skip over this chapter. For everyone else particularly those with plenty of time until retirement with defined contribution pension schemes (where there is a pot of money for a pension and when it's gone 'it's gone') there is much to review and some very big tips in this chapter. Some of the tips involve tax advantages that may disappear soon under the tax 'pain' we are expecting to pay for the national debt that was built up due to the Covid-19 pandemic. Therefore, this chapter features early in the 'save more' section of my book and the knowledge you gain will hopefully help you achieve a better retirement.

Pensions provide the main income in retirement so George Foreman's quote at the head of this chapter seems to be spot on in to-day's flexible pension environment. Chapter 1, 'plan more' underlined the importance of determining the level of income we want to have in retirement. In 2020/21 we have more control than we had a decade ago over both the age we retire and how we turn-on/turn-off pension income. This is because the world of pensions has changed radically in the UK in recent years due to two main drivers. The first is the flexibility in careers with extended and flexible working being possible beyond the state retirement age if that's what you want. This includes the potential to take a top up or part time job that can allow you to reach the income you need depending on the phase of retirement and your needs at that time. The second is the most radical change in living memory in the UK pensions world that came with pension changes introduced in 2015. This created a more flexible pension environment that, potentially, allow you to turn off/turn on the pension income and bring in more tax planning to work with your pension planning. Then, finally and importantly, we have the re-set moment created by the Covid-19 pandemic that has caused many to reappraise the life they want to create and also the security of their pensions (from market risk and any recession risk).

The downside, however, is that pension planning is the biggest financial decision you will make (probably even bigger than a mortgage) but gets little attention, is poorly understood and is surrounded in baffling 'finance speak'. For that reason, financing your retirement through pensions is put on the back burner and too many people get a nasty shock when reality strikes at the cliff edge of retirement. A common theme is that pensioners are 'disappointed' that they hadn't grasped the issues and opportunities earlier. By retirement day or when sitting in a retirement planning course paid for by your employer it is often too late to do anything meaningful and make a significant impact to increase your income in retirement. At that cliff edge 'too late' stage there are, still, some other options to work around the harsh reality of a modest pension and higher living aspirations. The first option is to work longer perhaps under a flexible work scheme that some more enlightened employers implement to help retain experience in their business. Or you could go and find a new job or start your own small business to ramp up your income and another option could include raiding your savings and investments. A second option is perhaps rightsizing your house or relocating to a cheaper area or using an equity release scheme to release capital in your home to give you more money to spend. The third option is to reset your lifestyle and costs and learn to live off less money. All these options and more are outlined in this book to help give you some ideas to put in your plan at the end of this book. Best of all, however, if you have plenty of time (and under the 'it's never too early to start planning ethos of this book) is the opportunity to start making some changes now so you have a more tax efficient income and can glide into retirement.

Importantly, this chapter is only a guide and it is neither legal nor financial advice; it is no substitute for taking professional advice from a financial adviser or other professional adviser. Any potential tax advantages may be subject to change and will depend upon your individual circumstances, and individual professional advice should be obtained.

This chapter at a glance

- *Mind the gap.* The reality of pensions you may receive (and when) and recognising the gap in your retirement income aspirations. Pointers to possible changes in the tax regime that may influence your pensions and tax planning.

- *Information to help you understand your State Pension entitlement and any company and private pension entitlement.*

- *Guidance about defined pensions options and pension drawdown facilities that provide flexibility on planning your retirement income.* Drawdown, tax free amounts and other tax opportunities and pitfalls are explained.

- *Pointers to free guidance offered by the government's impartial service about your defined contribution pension options.* Book in your appointment via www.pensionwise.gov.uk.

- *Reminders about the importance of getting proper financial advice.* Investment risk has increased in the current Covid-19 pandemic and, if the sums involved are significant, the benefits of quality advice and options should outweigh fees that you may have to pay. Always ensure your adviser is on the Financial Conduct Authority register at www.fca.org.uk.

- *Beware of the 'pensions predators'.* They range from crooks in suits trying to get you to move your pension before age 55 into some scheme which, in reality, could hit you with massive tax charges to over-charging advisers. In the current Covid-19 pandemic you also need to be sure of your Financial Services Compensation Scheme coverage and there could be a wake-up call in here for those relying on a SIPP.

- *Combine your pensions planning with your savings plan to finance your retirement.* But also keep half an eye on the tax implications (which can change) of both, as therein lie both opportunities and pitfalls.

The 2020/21 'big picture'

The buck stops with you

Pensions freedom and many of us living longer means there is a greater responsibility on you to understand and plan around your pension. Whilst the buck stops with you and this chapter will give you a great start, consider engaging a financial adviser registered with the FCA where you need further help or the numbers are large.

How long have I got?

I struggled writing this paragraph so here goes. Everyone is different but no one is immortal and so I've turned to the simplicity of the Office of National Statistics ("ONS") who estimate that a male aged 65 in 2020 has a life expectancy of 85 (and a 2.9% chance of reaching 100). A female of the same age has a life expectancy of 87 (and a 4.9% chance of reaching 100). But note that there are big variations in how long you may live depending on location, wealth, health and your lifestyle choices - sometimes by 5 years or more. I'm glad I've got that bit out of the way!

How much could I need? Average expenditure

Chapter 1, 'plan more' will have shown you how to develop your own financial plan and assess your own expected lifestyle and expenditure over the three phases of retirement. But as a sanity check Which research identified retired households spent a shade under £2,110 a month (or £25,000 a year) on average in 2020 and about 4% to 5% less than the previous year due to Covid-19 pandemic. Which research indicated retired households would spend around £40,000 a year if spending included long haul holidays and a new car every 5 years.

Pension access ages and 25% tax free

The minimum age you can take money from a pension is currently 55 (it rises to 57 in 2028) but employer pension schemes are able to set their own rules on accessing pensions so the access age could be higher. Generally speaking most defined contribution schemes (explained below) let you access the money at 55 (or 57 from 2028) and employer schemes have a higher age.

You may be able to withdraw up to 25% of your pension tax free. This is fairly simple for defined contribution schemes but final salary schemes (again explained below) are a little more complicated and a calculation involving a 'commutation' works out a reduced final salary in lieu of taking 25% of your pension tax free.

Tax pain is on its way and related pension issues

Tax and pensions go hand in hand due to significant differences in the tax rates you pay under income tax. For many years I have seen much press speculation before each budget about the government taking action to reduce tax reliefs on pension payments but the threat has only been partially addressed by amending some allowances. More in Chapter 5, Tax and in the section that follows on immediately below.

Playing the tax bands ... while you can

One way of increasing your income in retirement is by playing the tax bands in the years when you are earning. This has particularly good impact if you are earning above the higher rate tax band (£50,000 in 2020/21) and even bigger impact if your earnings are in the 'tax kill' zone of £100,000 to £125,000. The tax 'kill zone' is described further in Chapter 5, Tax. Pension planning can shift income from being taxed at 40% to being taxed at 20% (and then it gets even better as a quarter of your pension pot may be able to be extracted free). It can even, potentially, shift tax from being taxed at 60% in the 'kill zone' to 15% (deriving from extracting pension at 20% but with a quarter of the money shifted being tax free). Phew - it is complicated but worth digging into and any next budget may include changes to the rules as part of the future tax 'pain' that I'm expecting later in 2021. For the moment (Autumn 2020) there is still an opportunity to shift more earnings into a pension after taking independent professional advice.

Top tip

Get to a better understanding of your income now and what it will be in retirement and look at ways of shifting income from being taxed at a higher rate now to a lower rate later when you draw your pension (subject to reliefs and allowances outlined below and, of course, your current spending commitments). This offers big opportunities at present but those could tighten or close as part of any future tax 'pain' regime to pay for the Covid-19 pandemic. In terms of scale I'd say this should be an urgent priority for many readers of this book.

The pensions expectation and 'mind the gap'

The Office of National Statistics measures the average weekly UK pay (including bonuses and before tax) and in May 2020 this was £505 a week so about £26,200 per annum. As a very rough rule of thumb a reasonable retirement goal is to expect an income in retirement of between 40 and 75 per cent of your employed earnings. Four examples detailed below will help you see how much you need to be saving in pensions to bridge the gap between State Pension and your retirement income ambitions. Many people are surprised at how much you need to build up in your pension pots to achieve the sort of lifestyle you wish to create. Note the size of the pots in the 4 example below and how much income they may provide and for how long. Note what happens to the different pensions and what happens when the pots run out. All four examples assume that no significant savings or investments have been built up (or they are ear marked for one-offs) and that retirement income is being financed only by pension income.

Case study 1. Theresa is aged 66 and is on average earnings of about £26,200 and her pension aspiration is to have an income in retirement commencing in 2021 at about £19,650 before tax (75% of earnings). Theresa has no final salary pension so she will depend on how she has built up her other pension pots and the numbers will work like this. [The term 'final salary' pension is explained later in this chapter but for now it means a great form of pension income as it pays a percentage of your final salary and just keeps on paying year after year no matter how long you live.]

Theresa can probably expect to get a State Pension of about £9,100. This means she would need a pension pot of £281,000 to generate a 25% lump sum of about £70,000 and then further pension income of about £10,540 rising by the Retail Prices Index ("RPI") each year. This gives Theresa a total income in retirement before tax of about £19,650 (then increasing by RPI) for an estimated 20 years. The tax free lump sum is assumed to be allocated to 'one-off' expenditure - perhaps a new car, kitchen and a holiday fund for the next 10 years whilst she enjoys her active retirement phase. She can then expect to gear down her spending as she moves into passive retirement when her pension pot runs out at about the age of 85 and then lives on just her State Pension with equity in any home or state benefits paying any subsequent care home fees. If she wants more income in the 86 plus years then she just needs to redo the numbers and reduce the £11,500 drawn from her pension pot over 20 years to make the numbers work.

Case study 2. Let's next look at **Boris** a high earner aged 66 with his own business bringing in around £100,000 per annum (from salary and dividend income). He also has an old employer final salary scheme from the 1980's which will pay about £12,000 per annum from the age of 66. His retirement goal from 2021 is an income in retirement commencing at about £43,500 before tax. His numbers will work like this.

Boris can probably expect to get a State Pension of about £9,100 and will also receive £12,000 per annum from his final salary pension scheme (after taking a 25% tax free lump sum). He will have needed to build up a further pension pot of around £600,000 to generate a further 25% tax free lump sum of about £150,000 (which he may have ear-marked for a holiday home abroad) and the pension pot will then pay further pension income of around £22,500 per annum rising by RPI for an estimated 20 years to reach the £43,500 income before tax goal. To achieve this he would have been paying in about 25% of his £40,000 income in 1990 and consistently paying in about 25% each year up to the £100,000 income level in 2021 when he retired (this assumes his income increased at a steady rate between 1990 and 2021). By about 86 his pension pot will be exhausted under these assumptions and it will be 2041 and Boris can expect to then live on just his State Pension and final salary pension. Originally in 2021 these were about £9,100 and £12,000 but by 2041 both will have risen by approximately RPI to protect their equivalent purchasing power. This should still allow Boris some nice extras in his passive/ care home years.

Case study 3. Next is **Keir**, aged 66 in 2021 who has substantial public service and a 'good' final salary pension of about £25,000 per annum before tax and after commutation which could have provided him a tax free lump sum of approximately £75,000 (the before-commutation amount may have equated to about two-thirds of his final salary as he had always served in the public service) and a State Pension of about £9,100. Again the lump sum is assumed to be allocated to 'one-off' expenditure - this time being set aside to help with the children's future university fees and anticipated future weddings. Keir's income in retirement of about £34,100 before tax will just run and run for as long as he lives (increasing by about the retail price index to protect him against inflation).

Case study 4. A final illustration could be useful. **Angela** is aged 66 in 2021 and hoping for an income in retirement at about the average annual expenditure level of £26,200 and has no final salary pension. Her income will be a State Pension of about £9,100 and a pension income of about £17,100 per annum rising by RPI for an estimated 20 years. For tax efficiency and flexibility she takes 25% as the usual tax free lump sum and places this in ISAs over several years (contributing in £20,000 a year from age 66 for a number of years) and then draws on the ISA funds as a form of extra income each year for long haul holidays, luxuries and new cars every 5 years. Angela would need to build up a pension pot of about £456,000 to achieve this so that she can put £114,000 away as the tax free savings in investments and draw off this as explained leaving a £342,000 pension pot. Then, when aged 86, she would live on just her State Pension in her passive / care home years as per the first example, Theresa.

So could you retire 5 years earlier?

The above examples are at a high level and serve to illustrate some of the numbers and how this could, in turn, relate to you. The main focus is to help you identify potential gaps in pension expectations and how some pensions 'run out' and thus the importance of knowing what you are likely to receive and for how long. The key next step for you is to do some preparation work and get to grips with your own pension position and then consider options if you find a gap. The younger you are reading this chapter the better as you could knock 5 years off your retirement plans. This could be good news for a younger woman who envies her mother who received the state pension at age 60 in 2009. She now faces a state retirement age of 68, will live longer and may have taken career breaks to start a family. The trick for younger readers is easier than you think:

- Draw up you plan.
- Join your workforce pension scheme or set up your own pension.
- Contribute more than the minimum net of tax contribution of 4%.

Martin Gorvett, a Chartered Financial Planner, of Lavender Financial Planners Ltd, has helped hundreds of individuals understand and bridge the gap. Martin advises:

"For many the kick-starter for funding a pension comes from our first job. In our early years we may accumulate several small pension pots as our career progresses. It's important to keep track of what you have and ensure that inertia doesn't creep in. Whilst in the early years you may only be able to afford to contribute a little towards your pension, every pound is important. The more you can fund in the early years the longer it has to grow (the effect known as "pound cost averaging"). Those starting later in their life face a daunting reality. The rule of thumb is that you should take your age, half it and that is the percentage of earnings that you should then start to contribute. For example, someone who starts at 50 should contribute 25% of their earnings to a pension to have any chance of having a decent retirement. Whereas someone who starts at 20, should contribute 10%."

The buck stops with you part 1: Understand your State Pension entitlement

The State Pension is a regular, weekly payment from the government and is funded by National Insurance contributions and based on the amount you have contributed. Because people are living longer the state could not afford to fund the State Pension for the previous retirement ages of 65 (male) and 60 (female). Therefore, since 2010 we have seen the retirement age for women increasing and other previously laid-out plans on pension age increases being accelerated. Put simply, the funding solution was met by equalizing the retirement ages of men and women and then making both wait longer to receive it. The State Pension is being paid at age 66 for both sexes by 2020, then it moves to 67 by 2027, increasing again to age 68 by 2037–39. The www.gov.uk website and a search for 'State Pension calculator' will give the age at which you will receive yours.

The State Pension and related additional elements to it have changed over the years and this has led to further confusion. The latest change took place in April 2016 when a new flat-rate pension structure was brought in for those retiring after 6 April 2016. Those who retired before then remain on their old scheme.

To qualify for the 'old' State Pension scheme and receive a full basic State Pension you required 30 years' full National Insurance (NI) contributions. For 2020/21 the full single-person basic state retirement pension is £134.25 per week which will rise by 2.5% in 2021/22. If you're married or have a civil partnership and both you and your partner have built up a State Pension, you'll get double this amount.

Some people also receive an additional State Pension (also called the State Second Pension or, before 2002, it was called SERPS), which is the government's earnings-related additional pension. How much additional State Pension you get is complicated and depends on your National Insurance contributions and whether or not you 'contracted out'. You will have been contracted out if you opted for National Insurance contributions to be diverted to a work or personal pension. There is then a range of further options including: deferring your pension (by deferring it you can have a bigger pension when it starts); adult dependency increases (for a husband, wife or someone who is looking after your children); Pension Credit (an income-related benefit); payments to an overseas address; provisions for married women and widows; divorce, death and disputes; and the Christmas bonus. More detailed information can be found at www.gov.uk and at www.pensionsadvisoryservice.org.uk, whose help is always free.

Then we have the new 'simpler' regime for those retiring after 6 April 2016 which pays £175.20 per week for 2020/21 (about £9,110 per annum) if you have the 'full' 35 years of service. For 2021/22 the amounts will increase by 2.5% under the Governments current triple lock promise which states it will increase state pensions by the greater of average earnings, prices as measured by the Consumer price Index or 2.5%. This is a good result for pensions in 2021/22 but could the triple lock be abandoned as the Government grapples with balancing its books post Covid-19?

You will get a reduced amount providing you have at least 10 qualifying years on your National Insurance record. You will receive a proportionate amount if you have between 10 and 34 qualifying years and you may receive more if you have accrued SERPs or State Second Pension. But don't worry too much as the simple and easy step is to get a State Pension forecast as shown immediately below.

Early retirement and your State Pension

Because some people retire early they can mistakenly assume it is possible to get an early State Pension. While the information may be correct for some employers' schemes it does not apply to the basic State Pension.

Next steps – getting that State Pension forecast

You can request a pension statement estimating your State Pension based on your current National Insurance record. You can apply online at www.gov.uk/check-state-pension, by telephone on 0345 3000 168, by text phone on 0345 3000 169 or by post to:

The Pension Service 9
Mail Handling Site A
Wolverhampton
WV98 1LU

Top tip

Nearly half the population is not prepared for retirement. Spend 10 minutes getting your State Pension forecast.

If you don't have full NI records you may be able to buy missing years from the HMRC. This is usually a sensible option to explore especially if you are in good health and expect a long life.

Top tip

Get an estimate for buying missing years from The Pension Service and do the numbers and make a choice. You may find that it is comparably the cheapest way to secure extra guaranteed income.

Sources of further free help or advice on the State Pension

- The Pensions Advisory Service: www.pensionsadvisoryservice.org.uk.
- www.pensionwise.gov.uk;
- The Service Personnel and Veterans Agency: www.gov.uk/government/organisations/veterans-uk.
- Citizens Advice: www.citizensadvice.org.uk.

The buck stops with you part 2: Understand and control your other private pension income

Private (or personal) defined contribution pensions and 'drawdown'

Private (or personal) defined contribution pension schemes are a pension 'pot' from which future pension income payable to you will depend on the investment growth of your contributions. These contrast massively with defined benefit schemes which are often known as 'final salary' pension schemes and were the norm until the late-1980s (more below). Defined contribution pensions are now the norm.

The 2014 Budget brought in 'pensions liberation' in April 2015. In the 'old world' most people bought an annuity with their defined contribution pension pot on retirement. The annuity then provided a fixed income for life. The 'old world' system attracted criticism as it was perceived as representing poor value and some annuities were miss-sold to those in ill health or were unsuitable as they may have resulted in no or limited financial protection for dependents on the death of the annuity holder.

The 'new world' of pensions liberalisation resulted in a dramatic change and since April 2015 everyone now has a right to access their defined contribution pension pots from age 55 and no one is forced to buy an annuity. Instead we have the new concept of 'drawdown' and this is just financial speak for taking money out of your pension as an income. You'll have 25% tax free and then pay income tax depending on your tax band. The risk, however, is that you may outlive your pension pot and exhaust your funds as there is not the same certainty that annuities provided (albeit you could purchase one if this proved more suitable). The other risk is the fact that financial markets fluctuate. So what happens if the markets collapse just as you are about to start drawing on your funds? Some readers may remember the Japanese asset price bubble of the early 1990's (Nikkei 225 at 13,000 in December 1985, rising to 39,000 4 years later in December 1989 before crashing to 14,400 in August 1992) and a decade of despair that followed for investors. Or some others will remember the US bear market of 2007 to 2008 (between October 2007 and June 2009 the Dow Jones Industrial Average, Nasdaq Composite and S&P 500 all fell 20% from their peaks in 2007). More recently we had the collapse in many worldwide financial markets as a result of the Covid-19 pandemic and a subsequent partial or full recovery but where will the markets now head as we move into a recession? Fluctuations vary according to the risk that you have selected for your funds. The bigger the risk the bigger the potential fluctuation.

Top tip

If you have significant funds in defined contribution pensions you must, therefore, understand and accept your risk levels and consider adapting your approach if you consider there is a risk of a deep recession. In the current Covid-19 pandemic remember the buck stops with you but quality advice and assistance from an adviser can help so arrange a review if you have not had one in the last year (and if you haven't that may tell you something).

Related to this is another risk and that is one of complacency. Most people just accept the charges proposed by an advisor/ pension provider and do not shop around. However plans are hard to compare in terms of risk, reward and fees and other charges. Martin Gorvett, a Chartered Financial Planner, of Lavender Financial Planners Limited, explains the fee structure on advice and what to look out for in fees, charges and costs when considering defined contributions and 'drawdown':

"More often than not people are tempted to avoid professional fees in favour of directly accessing retirement products. If you have the knowledge, all well and good. Just look out for the 'unknown, unknowns'. Professional fees do vary and have historically been hidden. However, the modern financial planning advice market is designed to provide a service based on value, not a toll gate to products. Regulated Financial Planners will charge a fee relevant to the work expected of them. This will either be fee or percentage based. Average costs in the industry have dropped from 5% to around 3% over recent years. Some advisers will take this further to somewhere between 1-2%. Don't be afraid to challenge the fee being charged. A good Financial Planner will be able to justify their fees. Thankfully

the modern pension market is designed to be portable. Very few modern financial contracts harbour surrender penalties. If there are they will be disclosed at the outset. Again, don't be afraid to ask for clarification. Typically you would expect to pay fees as a percentage of your fund, although some pension contracts operate in £'s. There are three layers of cost to an advised product:

Advice – typically between 0.5% and 1%
Product – typically between 0.25% and 0.35%
Investment – typically between 0.2% (for a passive solution) and 1.8% (for an actively managed solution)

As with other industries, going direct to a provider could end up costing you more, as the retail price of direct offerings may be higher."

The fee band range above could be a range of fees from 0.95% to 3.15%. On a £300,000 pension pot that equates to a staggering spread of 2.2% or £6,600 a year. Over 20 years that amounts to £132,000 and a fee review that takes an hour could add (effectively) tens of thousands of pounds to your pensions' pot so a fee review would be time very well spent. Watch out also for any 'tie-ins' – these are exit fees that are payable if you wish to move advisers/providers. Consider also the non-fee side of things as the quality of dialogue you have with your financial adviser and, importantly, how well they link in with your other advisers (for instance any accountant/tax adviser) are just as important. Then there are the returns offered and then actually attained by the adviser. These two 'quality factors' could add tens of thousands of pounds to your pension pot. The quality factor is difficult to weigh up but if you never hear from your financial advisor in a way that is tailored to you and if don't have a quality annual review with your financial advisor then that probably tells its own story and it's time for that review and perhaps a change?

Top tip

The key issue on adviser and pension firm fees is the quality of interaction with you, pension performance and fees. Get absolute clarity on all fees and precision on any exit fees and review the fees you are paying. Review your financial advice set up to see if you can get a better service/ fee structure.

In drawdown you can take as little or as much as you need and therefore income levels can be varied to take advantage of other income you may be earning (perhaps from a new part-time job, or having started a small business) or whilst waiting for the State Pension to kick in. This might make your tax affairs more efficient and could save you money and you should ensure your financial adviser is working with any tax adviser you have retained to try and leverage these benefits for your ultimate benefit. The point is that you can then manage your income more easily to take advantage of the zero rate and basic rate tax bands more efficiently and this may save you tax and provide more of an income (as flagged up earlier in a top tip). Importantly, the new regime ensures you can now pass on your pension on death to a loved one more tax efficiently up to the age of 75 because up to that age defined contribution pension pots do not form part of someone's estate for Inheritance Tax purposes. Under previous rules there used to be a 55 per cent Pensions Death Tax. Now, if you die before 75 there is no tax to pay on funds passing from defined contribution schemes. A death after the 75th birthday will be subject to your pension beneficiaries' marginal rate of Income Tax. Most pension experts agree that pensions liberation is a good thing but also add a note of caution. Martin Gorvett advises:

"Modern pension flexibilities have helped enormously in making my clients' retirement strategies more efficient. For those with other savings, pensions have become an efficient way of handing your wealth on to those whom you leave behind. But with these freedoms comes temptation and a lot of new responsibility. At the other end of the spectrum, there's a danger that some pension savers will draw their pension savings and fritter it all away without any constraints to hold them back. Most pension providers are acting as a second line of defence for savers looking to draw pension benefits under flexi-access. They will ensure that professional advice has been considered and that savers aren't being scammed."

Top tip

Plan carefully when first drawing down pension benefits under 'flexi-access' as emergency HMRC tax codings can cause havoc. HMRC may assume that your income continue each month for the tax year at the level you first draw down on the pension pot. If you draw a significant amount of income early in the tax year as a 'one off' you may invoke 40 or 45 per cent tax on your pension income as HMRC may assume this will continue and assign a tax code accordingly. You can sort out any overpaid tax with HMRC and get it back later but, alternatively, drawing a notional amount (£100) first, or by drawing later in the tax year may avoid this.

Annuities - shop around!

Since April 2015 and pensions flexibility you are no longer compelled to buy an annuity if you have a defined contribution pension to fund your pension. The concept of annuities needs some explanation as the option of purchasing an annuity still remains. When you buy an annuity you hand over a lump sum (your pension fund after taking out 25 per cent of it as a tax-free lump sum) to an insurance company in return for a regular, guaranteed income for the rest of your life called an 'annuity' and the income is subject to income tax. Under the current rules the earliest age you can do this is 55 (increases to 57 in 2028). Once you have bought your annuity, the income you receive is effectively free of investment risk. The risk has been transferred to your provider. There is little danger of running out of money, as your provider has to pay you for as long as you live.

When you approach retirement your pension company will contact you about purchasing an annuity and provide you with a quotation, which will tell you the amount of money you have in your 'pension pot', the amount of tax-free lump sum you are entitled to take and the level of income you will receive each month (should you convert your pension fund to an annuity with them) and will explain the options available to you including flexible drawdown. Ali Hussain reported the 'Return of the pension annuity sales scandal', Sunday Times 22 November 2020 explaining:

"Pensions freedoms were supposed to end the misery of savers being sold low-paying annuities by insurers... About six in every ten savers take the annuity or drawdown plan offered by their pension company rather than rivals who offer better rates. In some cases, failing to find the best annuity could cost pension savers with a £100,000 pot as much £23,000 over a 30-year retirement."

Top Tip

Shop around for better annuity and drawdown pension deals with an Independent Financial Adviser registered with the Financial Conduct Authority or after taking free help from the government funded Pension Wise (www.pensionwise.gov.uk).

Beware of pension predators as set out further later in this chapter.

Types of annuities

There are several different kinds of annuity. The most basic is a *level annuity*. This pays you a fixed income for the rest of your life. If you die, the income usually stops. And — crucially — it will not change if prices rise. So in an inflationary world, your annuity will lose real value every year. For example, if inflation averages 4 per cent per year, the purchasing power of your annuity income will halve in 18 years.

To avoid this you could buy an *increasing annuity*. Here, the amount of income you receive will rise in line with inflation each year, or by a set percentage. And if you are worried about your insurance company keeping a large chunk of your pension fund should you die after only a few years of retirement, you could buy a *guaranteed annuity*. So if you bought a five-year guarantee, and you died after two years, your nominated beneficiary (your spouse perhaps) would receive annuity income for another three years.

Another option is a *joint-life annuity* where your partner can receive some or all of your pension income if you die before them. If you want to take a bit more of a risk, you could choose an *investment-linked annuity*. Here you start with an initial level of income while your fund is invested in an insurance company's with-profits fund. If the fund makes a profit, your income goes up. If it loses money, however, your income goes down.

Your health can also have a significant impact. If you are a smoker or have an illness, you may be eligible for an *enhanced annuity* or *impaired-life annuity*. These pay a higher annual income than a standard annuity. In short, the annuity provider is betting that you won't live as long, so it can afford to pay you more.

Other annuity options

If you don't want to buy an annuity because of low rates, there are a number of strategies you can use. One is known as *phased retirement*. This is where you set up a series of annuities and drawdowns with 25 per cent tax-free lump sums. You will get a lower starting income but if you think annuity rates are going to rise it might be worth considering.

Another possible option is *fixed-term annuities*. Here you set up an annuity for a fixed period (say 5 or 10 years). You get paid an income for the fixed term but at the end of the period you have a guaranteed pot of money to reinvest again. As with phased retirement, your income will be lower than from a standard annuity.

Finally, remember that due to pensions flexibility you can now avoid buying an annuity and, instead, manage your own defined contribution pension under flexible drawdown as outlined above.

Self-invested personal pensions (SIPPs)

If you want to use a pension to save for your retirement, you don't have to give your money to a fund manager in a personal pension provider. Instead you can manage your own retirement fund with a self-invested personal pension (SIPP). You can buy a range of asset classes, from stocks to bonds to gold bullion (though you can't buy fine wines or residential property). Monthly contributions can be as low as £50 or as much as 100 per cent of your annual salary (subject to the tax restrictions set out further below). These were designed for people who wanted to play a more active part in their investment strategy. The investments that can be held in the SIPP are quite wide and can even include commercial property, and for this reason some owners of small businesses may look at holding their commercial property within their SIPP to good end effect. A specialist pension adviser should be able to assist further. Martin Gorvett, Chartered Financial Planner advises:

> "Specialist pension products, SIPPs, are becoming a lot more mainstream but be warned a product bearing this title doesn't always promise full functionality. If you are venturing away from the more traditional investment routes, especially buying commercial property, it is important to ensure that a 'pure' SIPP is used where you are a co-trustee of the SIPP and hence a co-landlord of the property. Just be careful that if you don't need a 'pure' SIPP, you aren't inadvertently paying for one.
> "SIPPs" have become somewhat of a buzz word for pension wrappers. Ensure that the functionality of the product meets your needs (and nothing else). A SIPP can be anything from a drawdown providing an open architecture personal pension to a full blooded personalised pension trust that has the capacity for esoteric investments. Just check the label first."

If you are someone who finds the idea of investing your own money daunting, a SIPP may not be for you and I also set out a major wake-up call on SIPPs in the section below in this chapter 'Protection when things go wrong or if there is a financial crash'.

How much should you pay in?

The more precise number should flow from your own plan but as an indicator (and maybe a shock?) Martin Gorvett provided a basic rule of thumb earlier in this chapter saying you 'should take the age you start your pension and halve it. Put this percentage of your pre-tax profits (or before tax salary) aside each year until you retire.' So for a 45 year old with no real pension provision it would be 22.5 per cent of your profits/salary for the next 23 years (until aged 68) and they may attain a reasonable retirement pension income. This reinforces one of the key messages in this book that it is never too early to start your retirement planning so you have a better chance of achieving the retirement you want to create.

Restricting tax relief on pensions

You can save as much as you like towards your pension but (and it is a big but) there is a limit on the amount of tax relief you can get. For that reason, linking savings together with pensions can be wise for your retirement planning and especially for high earners. The rules on how much you can contribute and still receive relief have been tightened over recent years and it is currently £40,000 per year. There are provisions to use three previous years' unused allowance and if this becomes a potential issue the sums involved would usually justify specific professional advice. Another restriction, called the 'tapered reduction', hits big earners as it reduces the amount of tax relief that can be obtained on pension contributions for taxpayers with 'adjusted income' in excess of £240,000 in 2020/21 (previous year was £150,000 so care is needed when utilising the three years back provision outlined just above). Where an individual is subject to the taper, their annual allowance will be reduced by £1 for every £2 by which their income exceeds £240,000 subject to a maximum reduction of £30,000. The annual allowance of £10,000 will, therefore, apply to taxpayers with adjusted income of £210,000 or more.

The other big restriction on the tax relief available on pension contributions is the 'lifetime allowance', which limits the maximum amount that can be paid into pension savings tax efficiently to £1,073,000 in 2020/21. The 'cap' has been slashed significantly since 2011/12 when it had stood at £1,800,000 and there are HMRC protection schemes which preserve, for instance, £1,250,000 of lifetime allowances existing at 5 April 2016 – more at www.gov.uk and search for 'pension schemes protect your lifetime allowance.'

Timing of withdrawals – don't shoot yourself in the foot

Receiving tax relief on £40,000 of contributions and the back-dating provisions of unused relief is a valuable planning tool for tax efficiency, especially, for the small business owner who may face volatile income streams and variable spending patterns or those facing redundancy (for any payments beyond the initial £30,000 relief from income tax). Once you start withdrawing taxable income from your defined contribution pension pot a barrier comes down. After that date tax relief on contributions into a pension will be limited to £4,000 per year – this is known as the 'Money Purchase Annual Allowance'. This along with some other measures are to prevent the 're-laundering' of pension income back into pensions to try and get double tax relief on the tax-free element of a withdrawal. There are some exemptions to this rule for small pension pots where withdrawals can be taken without being subject to the reduced allowance. If in any doubt check it out with a financial adviser who is a pensions specialist and carefully consider your future income and anticipated pension contributions before starting to draw down on your pension as this action could restrict the future tax efficiency of contributions.

Top tip

Tax rules and tax reliefs can and do change and their exact value depends on each individual's circumstances; however, pension savings are <u>currently</u> one of the most tax-effective investments. As the numbers increase so does the tax efficiency opportunities and risk (subject to allowance caps as outlined) and planning at this level should be undertaken with a financial adviser registered with the Financial Conduct Authority ("FCA"). Further restrictions on the extent of tax relief that can be obtained on pensions seem inevitable as part of the tax 'pain' that can be expected later in 2021 so an urgent review should be undertaken so that any planning can be implemented as soon as possible. The door could shut on any emergency budget, or by the end of the tax year on 5 April 2021. On 6 April 2021 a new tax year opens up and further planning could be considered for implementation that day if appropriate.

Employer pension schemes

Types of employer pension schemes

The pension that your employer offers may be 'contributory' (you and your employer pay into it) or 'non-contributory', which means that only your employer does. There are four main types of employer pension:

- a final salary pension scheme (a defined benefit scheme and often considered to be the 'king' of pensions for those lucky enough to have one and who had promotions late in their careers);
- another defined benefit pension scheme called a 'career average' pension scheme;
- a defined contribution money purchase pension scheme; and
- a defined contribution group or personal pension scheme.

Final salary pension scheme

Final salary pension schemes are known as a type of defined benefit scheme. You build up a pension at a certain rate – one-sixtieth is quite common – so for each year you've been a scheme member, you receive one-sixtieth of your final salary as a pension. The pension benefit keeps paying for as long as you live and, therefore, the cost and risk of funding the pension sits with the employer. This is, potentially, a very big win for employees given extending life expectancy rates. Many private sector employers have exited this sort of arrangement as the cost of funding them has become just too onerous. The biggest winners of all are those employees who secure big salary increases towards the end of their employment.

If you work for one of the few remaining employers with a final salary scheme you would need a compelling reason not to join it. Again you would probably need a compelling reason to shift the benefits to another scheme after you leave the employer. Whilst this holds true some large employers have been offering increasingly large sums to buy leavers out of their scheme. Some considerations may make this a worthwhile option to review with an independent financial adviser registered with the FCA. Perhaps the prompt could be that the amount offered seems 'too good to be true'. On review factors such as health concerns of the future pensioner and/or the spouse pension being low may make the option more viable. One other factor could be the inheritance tax breaks which apply to defined pension contribution pots as these do not apply to final salary scheme payments on the death of the pensioner. Once in a defined contribution pot and under 75 the inheritance tax breaks may apply which could be tax free money for the recipient. It is vital to remember that any such review would need to be undertaken by an Independent Financial Adviser, regulated by the Financial Conduct Authority. Martin Gorvett, Chartered Financial Planner, provides some guidance on this:

> *"Final salary pension schemes are usually the 'golden goose' of the pensions world as these schemes just keep paying, which will be a nice win if you live to over 100. Only in the rarest of exceptions would there ever be a need to shift out of a final salary pension scheme – if you are unmarried or fear decreased mortality due to health concerns you may wish to seek advice on this topic. If you are tempted to move your final salary benefit to a defined contribution scheme just make sure that the temptation isn't driven by the ability to invest into an unregulated investment vehicle that promises the earth as happened with some British Steel workers. Also, there is only modest risk, as if a salary-related occupational scheme or the sponsoring employer gets into financial trouble, the Pension Protection Fund can provide some protection - normally of up to 90 per cent of your expected pension, subject to a cap (more at www.pensionprotectionfund.org.uk)."*

Career average pension scheme

This is another type of defined benefit scheme and differs from the final salary pension scheme outlined above as the benefit (your pension) is worked out using an average of your earnings in the time that you're a member of the scheme, rather than the final salary.

Money purchase pension scheme

These are defined contribution schemes, as described earlier and therefore provide additional benefits through flexible access options and inheritance tax breaks (up to age 75). The money paid in by you and your employer is invested and builds up a fund that buys you an income when you retire; significantly, the funding risk sits with the employee (in contrast to the defined benefit alternatives above where the funding risk sits with the employer). The fund is invested, usually in stocks and shares and other investments, with the aim of growing it over the years before you retire.

You can usually choose from a range of funds to invest in. The Pensions Advisory Service has an online investment choices planner to help you decide how to invest your contributions (see www.pensionsadvisoryservice.org.uk and go to 'choosing investment funds').

Group/personal pension scheme

These are also money-purchase schemes and a defined contribution scheme so, again, the funding risk sits with the employee but there are additional benefits through flexible access options and inheritance tax breaks (up to age 75). Typically, your employer offers access to a personal pension plan, which you own, and can take with you if you get a new job. Your employer will choose the scheme provider, deduct the contributions you make from your salary and pay these to the provider, along with their employer contributions.

Automatic enrolment

This was introduced in 2012 because people in the UK were living longer but were not saving enough to finance their increasing retirement. Auto-enrolment (as it is called) was designed to help shift the responsibility away from the state and towards the individual and their employer. It commenced in October 2012 and now covers all employees.

To be eligible an individual must live in the UK, be between 22 and State Pensionable age and earn more than £10,000 a year. Some employers may offer schemes which better the auto-enrolment rates but for all other employers each individual will pay 5 per cent of their pre-tax income between £6,240 and £50,000. Their employers will pay a minimum of 3 per cent. Many employers use the National Employment Savings Trust ("NEST") as their pension scheme for auto-enrolment purposes. This is a national defined contribution workplace pension scheme established by the government to support auto-enrolment. It is transportable between employers and has relatively low charges. More at www.nestpensions.org.uk. Other auto-enrolment schemes are available.

Whilst auto-enrolment is starting to help address the pensions gap it still seems to be a modest provision in the context of the pension aspirations of many. Will we see bigger percentage increases in years to come?

Questions on your employer pension scheme

If you have a query about your company pension they (or their delegated representative) should be able to assist with the usual questions that arise such as:

Could you have a refund of contributions if you were to leave shortly after joining? What happens if you become ill or die before pension age? What are the arrangements if you want to retire early? What will your pension be on your present salary? What spouse's pension will be paid on the death of the pensioner? Can a pension be paid to other dependents? What happens if you continue working with the organisation after retirement age?

Top tip

With all forms of employer pension scheme check the answer to this question. "What is the maximum amount or percentage the employer will match or contribute?" Then review if you are missing out on free money to help boost your retirement. I only say this a few times in this book but this is an urgent and vital step- as free money does not happen often in life!

Other pension opportunities and issues

Lifetime Individual Savings Account - a different pension?

The lifetime ISA (LISA) has been available since April 2017 for adults provided they were aged under 40 when they opened the account. There is an annual contribution limit of £4,000 and savers will receive a 25 per cent government bonus. The intention is to encourage individuals to save towards their first home or for retirement once aged 60. They could be an early step in a new approach to pension funding where taxed money goes in and is tax-free on the way out (with the 25 per cent government bonus being a welcome addition). This switches the traditional pensions world on its head. The difficulty for many imminent retirees is that it is currently only available to the under-40s and lack of availability as not many of the traditional ISA providers have introduced the product. In addition better tax relief can currently be obtained by higher and additional rate tax payers using traditional pensions.

Individual Savings Account - for a top up 'income' or 'rainy day' planning

ISAs provide significant tax breaks as you do not pay any tax on the interest or the income (dividends) you make and there is no Capital Gains Tax if shares in your ISA soar. They are not, however, tax free on death and could be subject to the 40% Inheritance Tax charge if the Estate is above tax exempt levels.

You can currently (2020/21) put up to £20,000 into an ISA so that is £40,000 between yourself and your partner. There is no age restriction as found with the Lifetime ISA as outlined immediately above. Whilst pensions win for overall tax efficiency ISAs are a great second option for any savings or investments that are not tax sheltered already and for any free money that you receive (lottery, gaming or inheritance) or excess income received that you wish to 'put away' if you have used up your pension lifetime allowance or beyond the pension annual allowance.

Minimum retirement age

The minimum age at which you are allowed to take early retirement and draw your pension is 55 and rises to 57 in 2028 maintaining a 10-year gap from the State Pension age. It may be possible to draw retirement benefits earlier if you are in poor health and unable to work.

Other help in retirement - benefits

Pension Credit is an income-related benefit. It's an extra payment that guarantees most people over 65 a minimum income, and many people fail to claim it. For single pensioners with a weekly income (including pension) below £173.75 (£265.20 for couples). Pension Credit will top you up to £173.75/ £265.20. You might get more if you're a carer or disabled. You must live in England, Wales or Scotland (there are separate rules for Northern Ireland) and you won't get pension credit if you move abroad permanently. For more information visit www.gov.uk and go to 'Pension Credit'.

Death and divorce

On death pensions are normally passed on free of inheritance tax and if you are over state pension age your state pension may increase. Contact the pension service to check your state pension entitlement. Private pensions will usually follow the 'expression of wish' form detailing the intended recipient. Occupational defined benefit schemes will usually pay any tax free lump sum remaining and then any income forms part of the survivor's taxable income. Defined contribution pensions and a death before 75 means the pension pot is paid to the survivor tax free and where death is over 75 schemes will usually pay any tax free lump sum remaining and then any income forms part of the survivor's taxable income.

Top tip

Review your expression of wish forms held with your pension schemes. Do they still meet your wishes? They can be amended easily via your current provider. Consider it as a Will for your pension.

Divorce can see pensions split in a number of ways and what can be divided also depends on where you live in the UK. The options may include offsetting (where one person keeps their pension and another keeps another asset for instance the home); sharing (where the pension is shared between two parties and this can be now or deferred) or by informal agreement which is then documented and formalised. There is substantial free trusted advice and assistance available from the four organisations referenced at the end of this chapter at 'free trusted advice' and therefore further analysis is not detailed here. These organisations together with any legal advice that may obtained may also assist couples separating.

Protection when things go wrong or if there is a financial crash

You would normally approach the Pensions Ombudsman if the pension scheme manager (or trustees) and the Pensions Advisory Service are unable to help. The ombudsman can investigate complaints of maladministration by the trustees, managers or administrators of a pension scheme or by an employer. The ombudsman will assist with disputes of fact or law with the trustees, managers or an employer. The ombudsman does not, however, investigate complaints about mis-selling of pension schemes, a complaint that is already subject to court proceedings, or those that are about a state social security benefit. The Pensions Ombudsman has also taken on the role of Pension Protection Fund Ombudsman, which helps final salary pension scheme members who are at risk of losing their pension benefits owing to their employer's insolvency. Members below the scheme's normal retirement age will receive 90 per cent of the Pension Protection Fund level of compensation plus annual increases, subject to a cap and the standard fund rules. More at www.pensions-ombudsman.org.uk.

Some aspects of complaints about pensions can be investigated by the Financial Ombudsman Service (FOS), such as complaints about the suitability of advice to start a personal pension arrangement (perhaps they would have been better off being advised to join, remain or top up their employer's company pension scheme). More at www.financial-ombudsman.org.uk. The interaction between the FOS and the Pensions Ombudsman can seem confusing but don't worry too much as they have good arrangements to point you in the right direction if you end up with the wrong ombudsman.

The financial turmoil that arose from the Covid-19 pandemic and the potential for the UK entering the greatest recession most of us will have seen could be the shock needed to reassess our pensions 'exposure' under the current UK safety net arrangements. Unlike occupational pension schemes where the Pension Protection Fund can provide some protection there are different protections on personal pensions and SIPPs. For a salary-related occupational scheme if the sponsoring employer gets into financial trouble, the Pension Protection Fund can normally (under current arrangements) provide a pension of up to 90 per cent of your expected pension (and there is more above on employer pension schemes).

In marked contrast the protection on annuities, personal pensions and SIPPs is currently through the UK financial services safety net the Financial Services Compensation Scheme ("FSCS" and see fscs.org.uk for further information). Cover varies and if you are unsure you should ask your financial adviser to review your position and advise if any changes are required to optimise your compensation protection.

1   Pensions that are provided by UK-regulated insurers that are 'contracts of long-term insurance'. This could be a fund in a personal pension or an annuity. Where FSCS can pay compensation, they will cover the pension at 100% with no upper cap. FSCS cannot confirm whether individual plans with specific providers would be classed as 'contracts of long-term insurance' or not – you would need to speak to your provider directly or check with your financial adviser.

2   A share in your SIPP goes bust akin to Northern Rock in 2008. There is no FSCS cover as FSCS does not protect investment losses arising from poor financial losses.

3   A fund goes bust or a series of funds go bust that are not 'contracts of long term insurance'. There is no FSCS cover as FSCS does not protect investment losses arising from poor investment performance.

4   The bank or banks which hold the SIPP or personal pensions cash goes bust. Usually the FSCS would expect the cash deposit to be held by the SIPP/personal pension (not the member) and would look through the SIPP/personal pension to regard the member as the eligible claimant for up to £85,000. This may leave some exposure where the member holds cash in excess of the £85,000 per bank.

5   Where the SIPP/personal pension provider is negligent in advising on or arranging investments or scheme assets and the customer has suffered loss the customer may have a claim under the FSCS's rules up to £85,000.

6   Where the SIPP/personal pension provider goes bust. This could be a complex area but where a regulated firm owes a civil liability to a customer in connection with a regulated activity (e.g. for negligent advice/due diligence), and the customer has suffered loss, the customer may have a claim under FSCS compensation rules up to £85,000. If a SIPP provider has failed but there is no shortfall in SIPP assets (which should have been ring-fenced from the provider's own assets) and the SIPP provider does not otherwise owe a civil liability to customers (e.g. for negligent advice/due diligence), customers would not have an FSCS claim.

Top tip

If you have a SIPP in any format or a personal pension that is not a 'contract of long term insurance' review (with your independent financial adviser) and assess your holdings against FSCS compensation limits that may apply if there is a financial crash and consider adjusting your holdings accordingly based on the advice you receive from your IFA.

Beware of predators stalking your pension

Beware of anyone claiming that they can help to cash in a pension early and before you are 55. Whilst initially attractive, the sting in the tail is that you could face a tax bill of more than half your pension savings. The Pensions Advisory Service call it 'pensions liberation fraud' and warn that it is on the increase in the UK. The main warning signs are unsolicited text messages and phone calls, a transfer overseas and seeking to access a pension fund before the age of 55; the crooks also try to create some false urgency.

To counter this you must always check that any financial adviser is registered with the Financial Conduct Authority; always obtain a written statement about any tax charges; never allow yourself to be rushed into agreeing to a pension transfer; and create a 'time out' to check things out. The benefit of dealing with a financial adviser who is registered with the Financial Conduct Authority is the safety net if things go wrong – in the form of the Financial Ombudsman Service – and, if the firm fails and is insolvent the protection offered by the Financial Services Compensation Scheme.

Six must-do steps in 2021

Martin Gorvett, Chartered Financial Planner, of Lavender Financial Planners Ltd, helps you get to grips with financing your retirement with his six 'must do' steps to help you firm up on your preparations. Perhaps some of these should feature in your own plan?

1. *Keeping track of your retirement goals*. Retirement is not uniform. Everyone has different expectations. Start by understanding your likely expenditure by splitting your spending into three categories:

   —*must-have*: day-to-day living costs such as food and heating etc. (see the budget planner set out in Chapter 1);

   —*like-to-have*: a holiday twice a year;

   —*nice-to-have*: a new car, a new kitchen or a legacy for the children.

   Consider how these categories will change during the phases of retirement. Then you can start to consider the income you need to meet your personal retirement goals.

2. *Don't rely on the state*. The State Pension is certainly no substitute for private pension provision and other savings but it does provide a secure guaranteed baseline income on which to build. Ensure you understand what

you will be entitled to and when from the State Pension.

3. *Retirement isn't just a pension.* You may need professional help to think differently about your goals for later life and how you want to finance them. The traditional view is that your pension provides income, and other investments are viewed as 'rainy day' funds.

4. *Understand just how long retirement could last and the effect of inflation.* A 65-year-old can now typically expect to live for another 22 years, and in all likelihood may well live a lot longer. Any income that will finance your retirement that is not inflation proofed will reduce in value over time. Getting the investment strategy right may sustain the funds for longer and may provide the desired investment returns while also limiting volatility.

5. *Pensions are still the most tax-privileged savings.* Pensions still offer the best tax breaks for mainstream savings. Where else can you get tax relief on contributions, tax-free investment returns and take 25 per cent out tax-free? Treat the pension annual allowance of £40,000 like your ISA allowance of £20,000 and save, save, save.

6. *Your pension is now perhaps the most efficient device for sheltering part of your wealth (the pension fund) from Inheritance Tax (IHT) if you are under 75.* Look upon this as part of your savings armoury and, potentially, save 40 per cent for those you leave behind by carefully planning how you create your savings and pensions and which you draw from first.

Martin also explains that modern pensions allow much more flexibility than ever before. 'Flexi-Access' – modern pension freedoms – which can allow you to 'mould' your pension income (and tax-free cash) into any shape you wish.

> *"With expenditure typically higher in the early years, planning can ensure value if extracted from your pension savings when you need it most. Retirement income doesn't have to come from the pension alone. Having a variety of different savings and investments can achieve the optimum tax-efficient income. Do take professional advice – the benefits arising usually justify any cost."*

Other help and advice

Lost previous pensions

In addition to understanding your current pension scheme, you may also need to chase up any previous schemes that you can't seem to track down due to takeovers and mergers. The Association of British Insurers report that people typically move house 8 times in a lifetime but that few remember to tell their pension schemes about their change of address and over time £19.4 billion of pension pots has gone unclaimed for around 1.6 million people. That's nearly £13,000 per pension pot. For free help tracking down a pension go to www.gov.uk and then to 'Pension Tracing Service'.

Trustees or managers of your pension scheme

These are the first people to contact if you do not properly understand your benefit entitlements or if you are unhappy about some point to do with your pension.

Useful reading

There are three government funded organisations that can provide free, trusted help.
Book a free appointment with Pension Wise from the age of 50 to understand more about your pensions and access free and quality help at pensionwise.gov.uk.
The Pensions Advisory Service provides general information and guidance on pension matters and assists individuals with disputes about pensions. It can also help you find missing pensions schemes. More at pensionsadvisoryservice.org.uk.
The moneyadviceservice.org.uk can also help you get a high-level understanding of your choices for using your pension pot.
In addition citizensadvice.org.uk has good free information on pensions.

Reminder: Take any action points or follow up points to Chapter 12, Your Plan For A Better Retirement

---

Chapter Four
Savings and investments

"An investment in knowledge pays the best interest"

BENJAMIN FRANKLIN

This chapter follows close on the heels of the chapter on pensions as the two subjects are interlinked. They often work well together in the active phase of retirement when expenditure tends to be much higher. The phases of retirement are important and were outlined in Chapter 1. The active retirement phase is when you may be spending more of your retirement fund reserves which are held in your savings and investments and, perhaps, drawing on more of your pension where this is allowed if you have pensions flexibility (as per Chapter 3, Pensions). In the active retirement phase you still have the appetite and energy to devour all those things set out in the 'live better' chapters of this book and many of the activities come at a financial cost. Just like pensions the world of savings and investments is poorly understood and filled with 'financial jargon'. This chapter will help you invest in more knowledge on savings and investments as Benjamin Franklin's famous tip urges at the start of this chapter. The 'save more' and second essential step of my retirement planning approach is therefore taking another big step forward in this chapter. Basically with an improved knowledge on savings and investments you will 'save more' and you will achieve a better retirement.

This chapter at a glance

- *How to find a good financial adviser and the importance of getting proper financial advice.* The benefits obtained from good financial advice should more than outweigh the fees that you may have to pay. Always ensure your adviser is on the Financial Conduct Authority register at www.fca.org.uk.

- *Understanding risk and reward especially in the current Covid-19 pandemic and understand your Financial Services Compensation Scheme protection limits.*

- *How to save more by combining your pensions planning with your savings plan to finance your retirement.*

- *Be alert to the tax implications (which can change) of both, as therein lie both opportunities and pitfalls. Tax efficient savings and investment products include* ISAs, LISAs, some National Savings products and some higher risk alternatives.

Importantly, this chapter is only a guide and it is neither legal nor financial advice; it is no substitute for taking professional advice from a financial adviser or other professional adviser. Any potential tax advantages may be subject to change (from future budgets) and will depend upon your individual circumstances, and individual professional advice should be obtained.

How do I find a good financial adviser and why should I have one?

Two easy questions to ask but not so easy to answer. You are free to manage your own savings and investments and this may interest you especially if you have a good knowledge of the financial markets. Financial advisers offer an alternative for a fee and their knowledge and skills may remove the work from you and, potentially, improve returns over the long term. Another alternative is a financial services company which sells funds, shares, related products and provides you with information through its website to assist you in making decisions. They make money from dealing and transaction fees which will usually be less than a financial adviser's overall fees. My tips on finding a good financial adviser would be:

- One of the biggest wealth warnings in this book is to always ensure your adviser is on the Financial Conduct Authority register at www.fca.org.uk - if not you are left outside the impressive UK regulatory safety net if things go wrong. If a financial adviser gets things wrong you will usually have a remedy against them and their professional indemnity insurance or can escalate matters to the Financial Ombudsman Service. If the financial adviser goes bust, there may be compensation payable by the Financial Services Compensation Scheme ('FSCS' more below - see section on 'protection').

- Always trust your instincts – if in doubt walk away and find another adviser.
- Look for recommendations from trusted family, friends or other professional advisers and then talk to at least two financial advisers before deciding.
- Look very closely at the attention your advisor gives to fully understanding where you are in life, when you may need to access your savings and investments and your appetite to take risk with your savings and investments. The adviser's assessment of your appetite for risk should help the adviser recommend more suitable products. The higher your appetite for risk the higher the variation in returns. For instance a high risk investor may expect returns that could rise by 10% to 20% per annum or during a surge of optimism. Equally they would not be surprised by a fall of 10% to 20% or maybe more during an investment shock as happened around most of the world in March and April 2021 as a result of the Covid-19 pandemic. A no risk investor will expect no downside risk and may accept returns of 1% to 2% per annum with all savings and investments managed within FSCS limits. An investor's appetite for risk can change over time and it is not uncommon to see risk reduce as the retirement years approach as individuals may not wish to see their funds eroded by the highs and lows of the stock market.
- Consider all relevant costs so that you can understand the actual net return over a year to you. The financial adviser's costs are either paid by fees from the return they make for you (perhaps an hourly rate) or they may charge a percentage of the funds they manage. In addition there may be charges levied by the fund management company itself. These should all be set out for you in writing before proceeding.
- A good financial adviser will gain a complete understanding of both you and your partner's wealth and in the event that one of you is incapacitated or dies the financial adviser's knowledge and advice will be invaluable to the person remaining (especially if they were not the one used to the finances). So both of you need to be happy with the financial adviser if you have a

partner.

- A good financial adviser will usually work with your other professional advisers including solicitor and any accountant/tax adviser to assist your overall tax efficiency. If not you should consider changing things.

Paying for financial advice - understand the fees. Then review and renegotiate the fees.

Charges vary widely and should be set out clearly on any proposal letter provided to you before you decide to engage a financial adviser. Check that everything fee and charge wise is understood before you sign up including adviser fees, product provider fees, any hourly rates, annual management fees and any fee charged if you move advisers (exit fees). The following may assist you in understanding the types of financial adviser, the types of cost and the range of fees. You can then make a more informed decision and renegotiate fees as appropriate.

Restricted or Independent Financial Adviser

The distinction is important because it lets you know whether you are dealing with an adviser who can offer you solutions from a restricted pool of providers /solutions (restricted) or an adviser who can offer products/solutions from across the market (independent).

Likely fee components

There may be an initial advice fee to assess your circumstances and assess what you can invest in. This may be 0.5% to 5% of the sum invested or hourly rates of £200 to £275 or even higher. Further fees can involve the following:

Ongoing advice fee 0.2% to 1.25% per annum on the amount invested for the financial adviser.

Fund charges 0.2% to 1.9% per annum for the funds you are invested in.

Platform charge 0.1% to 0.45% for the financial organisation that the financial adviser selects to manage your investments.

There may also be exit fees if you change advisers or platforms.

The above rates are taken from a survey conducted by the Sunday Times and published on 17 November 2019 *"Beating the fees muddle"* by Ali Hussain. Generally speaking the larger the portfolio the lower the % fee. Sometimes VAT is added to the fee.

The newspaper headline about 'fees muddle' sums up the dilemma for investors as fees and charges can be significant when added together and are sometimes difficult to clarify. They may be acceptable in an environment where you are consistently receiving high returns. But what happens if markets move against us and returns reduce or capital sums start to erode?

Top tip

Obtain clarity on the type of adviser you are dealing with and double check they are registered with the FCA. Obtain written details of the entire proposed fee structure. Compare and contrast and don't be afraid to negotiate if selecting an adviser for the first time or renegotiate with an existing adviser. Any saving secured will mount up to a very tidy sum if you take a twenty year horizon.

Savings and investing

Money in savings and deposit accounts at banks has been earning minimal interest in the last year (maybe 1% if you are lucky) and the value of funds held in banks was being eroded by inflation which had been hovering around 2% to 3% for several years. As at August 2020 inflation had lowered to just 0.5% due to Covid-19 pandemic financial impacts. A year ago the gap between interest and inflation was causing real pain to many who had led thrifty lives and saved for old age in traditional bank accounts. But that pain on traditional savings is now easing, to be replaced by a different sort of pain and one more focused on investors. This is flowing from the potential risk of a financial turmoil arising from the Covid-19 pandemic and the size of the national debt in the UK. The words 'financial collapse' will send shivers down the spine of any investor.

However, where there is risk there is also opportunity and investing into the shares of a company, or funds, bonds and other investments has never been easier. This chapter will help shine a light on the risks and rewards of investing and the vital role of knowledge, quality financial advice and an improved knowledge of the UK safety net if things go wrong. I think that 2021 will see more investors getting better at managing their investment and savings risk (more on this below).

Remember also the Individual Savings Account (ISA) annual limit is £20,000. This allows savers to protect part of their wealth from Income Tax and Capital Gains Tax. Between a couple and over several years that can equate to a powerful tax-free fund that can help in retirement. Also, the first £1,000 (£500 for higher-rate taxpayers) of interest and the first £2,000 in dividends (2020/21) will not be subject to Income Tax on your self-assessment return – another useful tax-planning tool. For those who are interested in saving and investing for retirement, and for the long term, the principles remain the same. Martin Gorvett, Chartered Financial Planner of Lavender Financial Planners Ltd explains the golden rules:

"Keep the costs down; shelter as much money from the tax office as you can; buy assets when they are cheap and sell when they are expensive (albeit that few people have the financial knowledge or crystal ball to really make a success of this but the motto, generally, is worth remembering). To be a successful investor you have to be disciplined. You need to decide on a strategy, allocate your money to your investment accordingly, then stick with that through the ups and downs that the markets will inevitably bring. Remember once a market has fallen, the stock it contains are 'on sale'. Equally when markets are at an all-time high, it could be overpriced (although markets should always continue to increase in value over the long term)."

There's a big difference between 'saving' and 'investing'. Investing is for the long term. It is money you can put away for your retirement, and in the long run it should grow more rapidly than in a savings account. If you are saving for a shorter-term goal, perhaps in less than five years, then you're looking to get the most interest paid on your money. Martin Gorvett provides more valuable insights and tips:

1. *Buy what is right for you and don't believe everything you read or hear*. Just because an investment works well for someone else doesn't necessarily mean it will be right for you. Social media promotions can be misleading. Ensure that the investment provider is regulated by the FCA; you don't have to wander off the beaten track just to avoid the herd.

2. *Remember that the Financial Services Compensation Scheme* does not protect investment losses arising from poor investment performance or if the company you have bought shares in goes bust.

3. *Diversify and don't put all your eggs in one basket.* Consider spreading your risk by diversifying across a mixture of asset classes, industry sectors and geographical areas. When the value of one asset is falling, another might be rising so could help to compensate.

4. *Invest for the long term.* Adopt a strategy and stick with it. Investing isn't a matter of 'timing the market', it is about 'time in the market'. Similarly, try not to get emotionally attached to your investments. Review and rebalance your portfolio regularly to ensure you haven't strayed from the original strategy.

5. *Take professional advice.* Investing is not free. Every avenue to market has a cost. Professional advisers will have a tried-and-tested process, often accessing institutional prices, rather than retail classes available to direct investors.

6. Lastly, *don't risk investing money that you can't afford to lose*. Investments carry a huge caveat – you may get out less than you put in. So don't overstretch, stick within your means and know when to walk away.

Since everyone has different financial aims, there is no 'one-size-fits-all' approach to investing. In very simple terms, there are four different types of saving or investment that you could consider:

1. *Cash savings.* Made into a bank account or cash ISA. These are generally short-term and offer easy access to your money and lower risk, so the potential returns are much less than other types of investment.

2. *Bonds and gilts.* Effectively, an IOU from the government or big companies. When you buy one you are lending money that earns an agreed fixed rate of interest. Government bonds (called gilts) are backed by the state and hopefully are as good as guaranteed. Corporate bonds carry greater risk in the event that the issuing company goes bust or cannot afford to repay you but because of this element of risk they offer the possibility of improved returns.

3. *Shares.* Sometimes referred to as 'equities', this basically means putting money on the stock market. You can do this by buying shares in individual

companies or by investing through a professionally managed investment fund, such as a unit trust.

4.   *Investing in property.* Directly as a buy-to-let investor or as a furnished holiday let investor or indirectly through certain investment funds. Property prices go down as well as up, and it can take time to sell property and get your cash back. This is dealt with at Your Home and Property, Chapter 1.

Top tip

"Investing should be more like watching paint dry or watching grass grow. If you want excitement, take $800 and go to Las Vegas"

Paul Samuelson, Nobel prize winner in economics.

He is saying that if you think investing is gambling then you are doing it wrong.

Sources of investable funds

These are the common sources where you will usually find funds to invest:

- *Long term savings built up out of excess income over expenditure.*

- *Commuted lump sum / 25% tax free from your pension*: One-quarter of your pension can usually be taken as a tax-free lump sum. The remainder will then be paid out subject to the ordinary rates of Income Tax.

- *Insurance policies (such as endowment policies)*: Designed to mature on or near your date of retirement. These are normally tax-free.

- *Profits on your home*: If you sell it and right-size to less expensive accommodation (more at Chapter 1). Provided this is your main home, there is no Capital Gains Tax to pay.

- *Redundancy money, golden handshake or other farewell gift from your employer*: Currently you are usually allowed £30,000 redundancy money free of tax.

- *Sale of SAYE and other share option schemes from an employer*: The tax rules vary according to the type of scheme and the rules are liable to change with each Budget statement.

- *Inheritance or a big lottery/premium bond win*: Self-explanatory!

Some key saving and investment products

Investments differ in their aims, their tax treatment and your tax objectives and the amount of risk involved. Your investments should be tailored to provide either income to supplement your pension or capital appreciation to build up over time for the longer term or a mix of both depending on your needs and the products you are likely to encounter are outlined below.

National Savings and Investments (NS&I)

The main reason for saving with National Savings and Investments is that they are secure as they are backed by HM Treasury and if that institution goes bust we may as well all pack up. Investments were flooding into NS&I in the Summer and Autumn of 2020 as investors sought to protect themselves from risk and take advantage of decent interest rates. More recently the interest rates offered have been slashed down. More information is at nsandi.com about their products:

- *Investment accounts*. Save from £20 up to £1 million per person with no notice, no penalty. Gross income is taxable. Option to save regularly.

- *Income Bonds.* Useful if you need a monthly income and easy access to your money. The minimum investment is £500 and the maximum is £1 million per issue, per person. Gross income is taxable.

- *Direct saver*. Save from £1.00 to £2 million with no notice, no penalty. Gross income is taxable.

- *Direct ISA and Junior ISA.* Interest is tax-free.
- *Premium Bonds*. The maximum amount that can be saved into Premium Bonds is £50,000. Prizes range from £25 per month to £1 million. Prizes are paid out tax-free every month. The rate used to calculate the prize fund is currently (Autumn 2020) 1%. The 'fun' of investing up to £50,000 per person in premium bonds provides a tax-free 'average' return that beats many routine savings accounts (but you may do better in ISAs and if you shop around); you can get a return of the capital within days (so it is easy to access, if need be). Prizes range from £25 up to a million pounds. The odds

of winning a prize each month were £34,500 to 1 (for every £1 bond).

Top tip

For those with very large savings who don't wish to carve up their funds into £85,000 blocks for Financial Services Compensation Scheme protection ('FSCS' – more below) NS&I is attractive as it is backed by HM Treasury.

Variable interest accounts

The accounts include instant access accounts, high interest accounts and fixed-term savings accounts. For 2020/21 the first £1,000 of interest earned is tax-free, reducing to £500 for higher-rate taxpayers and £0 for additional-rate taxpayers. If you only have State Pension income and bank interest in 2020/21 you don't pay income tax in 2020/21 until you have more than about £9,400 in savings interest. This is estimated by adding the personal allowance at £12,500, the £5,000 starting savings allowance and the personal savings allowance at £1,000 to give a total of £17,850. Then deduct the State Pension of about £9,100 (it could be more so adapt to your own figure) which gives £9,400. If you largely rely on your savings income and believe you are or have been paying excess tax you can reclaim this from HMRC using form R40 or reclaim it through self-assessment.

Top tip

During a recession, such as the one caused by the current Covid-19 pandemic, if your funds are not with NS&I (see above) and should the bank or building society get into serious financial difficulty up to £85,000 (double that if in joint names) of your money will be protected under the Financial Services Compensation Scheme. The cover can increase for up to 6 months to £1 million for certain life events (for instance moving home). More on the FSCS at the end of this chapter and at fscs.org.uk where you can also check out banks and their different brands (some of which combine under one limit so be careful in your selection).

Gilt-edged securities

Gilts, or gilt-edged securities, are bonds issued by the UK government that offer the investor a fixed interest rate for a predetermined set time, rather than a rate that goes up or down with inflation. You can either retain them until their maturity date, in which case the government will return the capital in full, or sell them on the London Stock Exchange at market value. Index-linked gilts are government-issued bonds – glorified IOUs – that you can buy to obtain a guaranteed rate of return over inflation. Gilt interest is paid gross (before tax). No Capital Gains Tax is charged on any profit you may have made, but equally no relief is allowed for any loss. Importantly during the Covid-19 pandemic the government guarantees the payment of interest and the repayment of the capital sum.

Permanent interest-bearing shares (PIBS)

These are a form of investment offered by some building societies to financial institutions and private investors as a means of raising share capital. They have several features in common with gilts including a fixed rate of interest that is set at the date of issue. The interest is usually paid twice yearly; there is no Stamp Duty to pay or Capital Gains Tax on profits. Despite the fact that PIBS are issued by building societies, they are very different from normal building society investments.

Unit trusts and Open Ended Investment Companies ('OEICs')

Unit trusts and OEICs are forms of shared investments, or funds, which allow you to pool your money with thousands of other people and invest in world stock markets. They are simple to understand, you get professional management, there are no day-to-day decisions to make and they invest in a broader spread of shares so that your risk is reduced. The minimum investment in some of the more popular funds can be as little as £25 per month or a £500 lump sum. Investors' contributions to the fund are divided into 'units' (and the term is changed to 'shares' in OEICs) in proportion to the amount invested. As with ordinary shares, you can sell all or some of your investment. The key differences between the two are:

1. *Pricing*: When investing in unit trusts, you buy units at the 'offer price' and sell at the lower 'bid price'. The difference in the two prices is known as the

spread. An OEIC fund, contrastingly, has a single price, directly linked to the value of the fund's underlying investments. All shares are bought and sold at this single price.

2. *Flexibility*: An OEIC fund offers different types of share or sub-fund to suit different types of investor. The expertise of different fund management teams can be combined to benefit both large and small investors. There is less paperwork as each OEIC will produce one report and accounts for all sub-funds.

3. *Complexity*: Unit trusts are more complex, which is one of the reasons for their rapid conversion to OEICs. Unit trusts allow an investor to participate in the assets of the trust without actually owning any. Investors in an OEIC buy shares in that investment company.

4. *Management*: With unit trusts, the fund's assets are protected by an independent trustee and managed by a fund manager. OEICs are protected by an independent depository and managed by an authorised corporate director.

5. *Charges*: Unit trusts and OEICs usually have an upfront buying charge, typically 3–5 per cent, and an annual management fee of between 0.5 and 1.5 per cent. It is possible to reduce these charges by investing through a discount broker or fund supermarket, but this means acting without financial advice. Charges on OEICs are relatively transparent, shown as a separate item on your transaction statement.

Investment trusts

One of the benefits that investment trusts offer is to income investors. While open-ended funds must pay out all the income they receive, investment trusts can hold some back in reserve. This can allow them to offer a smoother and more certain return. There are four major advantages that an investment trust has over a unit trust or OEIC:

- *Cost*: The initial charges on unit trusts are usually lower.
- *Gearing/ borrowing*: Investment trusts can borrow for investment purposes. Unit trusts, however, are usually restricted by regulation. When markets are rising, and the trust is run well, gearing should deliver better returns.
- *Size*: Investment trusts tend to be smaller than unit trusts and more focused

on their investment objectives.

Tracker funds and exchange-traded funds

Tracker funds and exchange-traded funds ('EFTs') are investments that seek to mirror the performance of a market index. As they track the market or index they can go down as well as up. EFTs are listed on a stock exchange and provide minute by minute pricing during trading hours.

Ordinary shares listed on the London Stock Exchange

Public companies issue shares as a way of raising money. When you buy shares and become a shareholder in a company, you own a small part of the business and are entitled to participate in its profits through a dividend, which is paid annually or a few times a year. It is possible that in a bad year no dividends at all will be paid. The money you invest is unsecured. This is vital and means that, quite apart from any dividends, your capital could be reduced in value – or if the company goes bust you could lose the lot. The value of a public company's shares is decided by the stock market. The price of a share fluctuates daily. Stockbrokers will buy or sell the shares on your behalf and you will be charged both commission (which can be as low as £6 a trade) and Stamp Duty (the latter is currently 0.5 per cent).

In 2020/21 an individual can receive £2,000 of dividend income tax free. A special income tax rate of 7.5 per cent is payable through your self-assessment if further dividend income takes you beyond £14,500 of income (personal allowance of £12,500 and dividend allowance of £2,000). This increases to 32.5 per cent if it falls in the higher rate tax band and then increases further to 38.1 per cent if it falls in the additional rate tax band (tax bands are set out in Chapter 5, Tax.

Top tip

An important wealth warning on shares – the financial pages of the Sunday newspapers carry regular stories about investors who have been scammed into buying worthless shares traded on some obscure stock exchange. Just as many column inches are devoted every year on investors who have bought some sort of bond offering glamorous interest rates (but which is not covered by the Financial Services Compensation Scheme (FSCS). Don't be caught out by the scammers – read the advice in the Cut Costs, Complaints and Scams, Chapter 6 and check if FSCS cover applies and get the answer in writing.

Tax advantaged investing

Individual Savings Account (ISA)

An Individual Savings Accounts ("ISA") is a 'tax wrapper' that holds cash or investments and the effect of the 'wrapper' is to provide significant tax breaks. It shields the cash and investments so you do not pay any income tax on the interest or capital gains tax on the profits you make. They are not, however, tax free on death and could be subject to the 40% Inheritance Tax charge if the Estate is above tax exempt levels. Shop around for the best rates and take full advantage of your annual allowance. You can currently (2020/21) put up to £20,000 into an ISA. Some ISAs are 'flexible' which allow you to replace money that you take out of your ISA, without eroding your £20,000 allowance – only if you do so within the same tax year. On death your spouse will inherit an Additional Permitted Subscription (APS) allowance equal to the value of your ISA. This may help your tax-free funds remain so for your spouse. The APS does not apply to ISAs passed to children/others on death.

Top tip

It is usually easier to protect your pension from Inheritance Tax on any wealth being passed down to children. Therefore, if you expect Inheritance Tax on your estate, it may be better to live off your ISAs than pensions so that more is left in a pension to pass on tax efficiently. Some pensions may not have been set up in a manner that allows this so professional advice is usually recommended to help understand and leverage this tax planning opportunity.

Top tip

If inheritance tax ('IHT') planning is driving your ISA investment decisions you may be able to avoid your ISA savings being subject to IHT on your death by investing in Alternative Investment Market ("AIM") shares within your ISA that specifically meet a niche tax exemption called Business Property Relief ("BPR").

This is about as complex as this chapter gets but it illustrates a point as shares that qualify for BPR fall outside of the scope of inheritance tax as long as the shares have been held for at least two years, and are still held at the time of death. This is a bit niche and is a higher-risk investment but it offers a window to leave ISA funds to beneficiaries free from IHT (albeit remember that funds passing on death to a spouse are exempt from IHT - more in the Tax chapter). This may of course change under the 'tax pain' that may come later in 2021.

Lifetime Individual Savings Account (LISA)

A Lifetime ISA ("LISA") is another 'tax wrapper' which became available from April 2017 and offers those under 40 a pensions or house purchase savings device where interest is tax free and there is no capital gains tax on the growth of investments. Provided you start a LISA before 40 years old you can then keep saving into it until you hit 50. The big reason to take out a LISA is the government will give you up to £1,000 of free cash every year but there are significant restrictions on what you can spend the LISA funds on. Here is how it works. You can save up to £4,000 a year either by a lump sum or saving regular amounts and the government will then add 25% as free cash into the fund. The restrictions are fairly simple as the LISA can only be used for either a pension after age 60 or savings towards a first home. Significantly the property can cost up to £450,000 across the UK so there is no outside London cap of £250,000 as found in the Help-To-Buy ISA.

If one of the two events does not happen and you draw out the funds you will lose the free cash and may receive less than you initially invested although there are allowances to retain the bonus if you die or are terminally ill. You are free to transfer it to another provider and you are allowed to split the overall ISA limit of £20,000 for 2020/21 between an ISA and a LISA (LISA up to £4,000). You can have a LISA and a Help to Buy ISA but you can't get the first-time buyer's bonus on both but you could, for instance, use the Help to Buy ISA on a home and then retain the LISA for retirement.

As outlined in the pensions chapter a downside on pensions planning through a LISA is that better tax relief can currently be obtained by higher and additional rate tax payers using traditional pensions. At present only a small number of companies sell this product.

LISAs can also be used to assist in purchasing your first home and can be withdrawn tax free if all the following apply (or retirement at age 60):

- the property costs £450,000 or less
- you buy the property at least 12 months after you open the Lifetime ISA
- you use a conveyancer or solicitor to act for you in the purchase - the ISA provider will pay the funds directly to them
- you're buying with a mortgage.

If you withdraw cash or assets for any other reason you will pay a withdrawal charge which recovers the government bonus you received on your original savings. The charge is currently 20% and it goes up to 25% on 6 April 2021.

Top tip

LISA's seem attractive at first glance for the under 40s looking to plan their retirement but better tax relief can currently be obtained by higher and additional rate tax payers using traditional pensions. The LISA is better than a Help-To-Buy ISA for properties between £250,000 and £450,000 outside London.

Enterprise Investment Scheme, Seed Enterprise Investment Scheme, Venture Capital Trusts and Social Investment

This may be a bit niche but is important to flag up as these schemes are often used by entrepreneurs and high or additional rate tax payers to save tax in return or taking a risk. Unquoted companies (i.e. those whose shares are not traded on a recognised stock exchange) can face problems when trying to raise finance. The Enterprise Investment Scheme (EIS) offers tax relief at 30 per cent for amounts up to £1,000,000 (increased to £2,000,000 if anything above £1,000,000 is invested in knowledge-intensive companies. The Seed Enterprise Investment Scheme (SEIS) offers tax relief at 50% on up to £100,000 if the shares are held for three years. The risk level of such investments is high and specialist advice and recommendations should be secured before venturing down this path, albeit the tax breaks prove enticing to some with the appropriate risk attitude and, perhaps, with specialist knowledge of the business concerned (perhaps through family or other connections).

Another variant is venture capital trusts (VCT), where tax relief can be secured at 30 per cent on new shares up to £200,000 in any tax year providing the shares are held for five years.

A final variant is Social Investment tax relief which helps social enterprises raise finance by offering tax relief to investors. These can be set up by community interest companies and charities and offer investors 30 per cent tax relief and capital gains tax breaks. These tax breaks may be subject to change as part of the 'tax pain' expected later in 2021.

Martin Gorvett, Chartered Financial Planner explains more:

> *"With restrictions on the amount of tax relief available to investors through pensions (£ 40,000 per annum) and ISAs (£ 20,000), the use of EIS/VCTs/SEISs has become more mainstream for higher rate and additional rate tax payers. These products should be approached with your eyes very much wide open. You are getting tax relief for a reason. They are high risk investments by their very nature and should be approached on their risk merits, rather than the tax relief available.*
>
> *SEISs carry the highest of risk. That's why you get 50% relief. Next EIS's with 30% after three years. Finally VCTs offer 30% relief but over 5 years. Taking more time to achieve profit status. Once the tax relief period has expired, ditch them or reinvest for more relief. Don't let inertia sink in. Some products reduce risk by the investment choices they make, such as Solar Power, renewable energy and 'peer to peer' lending. They are worth researching.*
>
> *How do you tell which will succeed and which will fail? In short you can't. Expect a third of your investment to fail, one third to do nothing and one third to do well. It's the latter third that makes up the return you achieve. Alternatively seek the use of EIS/VCT/SEIS platforms where significant due diligence has already been completed. Don't be tempted by online crowd funding type operations, these 'opportunities' tend to be the ones the professionals have already discounted. Tread carefully, take advice and invest within your means."*

Business asset disposal relief

Further tax breaks are also available under Business Asset Disposal Relief (which used to be called Entrepreneurs Relief) which enables a low 10 per cent Capital Gains Tax rate on selling shares in, for instance, a family company. The relief has now been reduced to £1 million which potentially saves £100,000 on a disposal that could have been charged at 20% Capital Gains tax. There have been suggestions that this relief may be further reduced in future budgets as part of a review of Capital Gains Tax and this now seems more likely given the 'tax pain' expected later in 2021.   Martin Gorvett also has some thoughts on entrepreneur's relief:

"As a business owner Entrepreneurs Relief is your new best friend. It allows you to sell a trading business and avoid high taxes on the value you extract. Just don't leave the decision too late. Shares in an unlisted business are also Inheritance efficient if held for more than two years. Make sure you remember to at least consider re-entering the arena in later life."

Investing for your child/grandchild

Children without any other form of income don't pay income tax in 2020/21 until they earn more than £18,500 in savings interest. This is the personal allowance at £12,500, the £5,000 starting savings allowance and the personal savings allowance at £1,000 all added together. To deter parents from giving away cash to children to reduce the parent's income tax on savings there is a basic tax rule where money given by a parent or step parent that generates more than £100 per year in interest is taxed at the parent's tax rate. The interest on money deposited by grandparents isn't caught by this rule and parents saving into a Junior ISA avoid this potential tax trap as it is tax free.

Children's Savings Accounts: All you need to set this up is the child's birth certificate. Interest rates are currently as high as 3.5 per cent (per moneysaving expert, November 2020) if you shop around as the banks and building societies are keen to sign up new potential customers as early as possible.

Junior ISA (JISA): You can currently save up to £9,000 a year into a JISA (2020/21). The child can take control of the account at 16 but can't access the fund until 18 when it is usually converted to an adult ISA. There is both a cash variant and a stocks and shares variant of the Junior ISA and both can share the one annual limit. The interest is tax free so the £100 parent's tax rate rule does not apply.

Child Trust Funds (CTF): All babies born between September 2002 and 2 January 2011 got £500 or more free from the government to save in a CTF. Children born after December 2010 are not eligible for a child trust fund. However, accounts set up for eligible children will continue to benefit from tax-free investment growth and you can still add £9,000 a year tax-free. Withdrawals will not be possible until the child reaches 18. These are now a defunct product and with less competition the interest rates tend not to be as good as a JISA (which you can switch to).

Child's pension: For really long-term saving, pay into a pension. Your child/grandchild takes control at 18, but can only access the money aged 55. Tax relief currently applies so the government will top up a payment of £2,880 to the limit of £3,600. Martin Gorvett says:

> "What better way to teach your child about the value of long-term savings. If you start a pension for them early enough, the effect of compound growth will give them a huge step up the retirement savings ladder when they themselves begin to focus on their own financial future."

Help to Buy ISA: These accounts were available from banks and building societies but were closed to new accounts on 30 November 2019. If one was opened before then you can keep saving into your account until 30 November 2029 when accounts will be closed to additional contributions. They offer decent rates of interest which are in a 'tax wrapper' so the interest is tax free. Help-to-Buy ISAs were available to prospective first-time buyers purchasing properties in the United Kingdom and are only paid when purchasing the first home (on purchases up to £250,000 outside London and £450,000 in London). Deposits can then be made of up to £1,200 when the account is opened followed by deposits up to £200 each month and you can continue saving until November 2029. The big benefit of help to buy ISA's is that the government boosts the young person's savings by 25 per cent, i.e. £50 for every £200 saved. So free cash which always gets the attention. The maximum free cash bonus is £3,000 on £12,000 of savings. You can transfer from the Help-to-Buy ISA to the LISA providing you meet the LISA conditions (aged 18 to 40) and you are also free to transfer it to another provider.

LISA: This is explained in more detail above so this is just a prompt that once they are 18 think about setting up a Lifetime Individual Savings Account to access the generous bonus paid, which can be put towards a first house or retirement.

Long-term lock-ups

Certain types of investment, mostly offered by insurance companies, provide fairly high guaranteed growth in exchange for your undertaking to leave a lump sum with them or to pay regular premiums for a fixed period, usually five years or longer.

Bonds

Bonds generally offer less opportunity for capital growth but they tend to be lower risk as they are less exposed to stock market volatility, and they have the advantage of producing a regular guaranteed income. The two main types of bonds are:

- *Gilts*: They are secured by the government, which guarantees both the interest payable and the return of your capital in full if you hold them until their maturity.

- *Corporate bonds*: These are fairly similar to gilts except that you are lending to a large company rather than owning a piece of it, as you do with an equity. The company has to repay the loan at some point, known as the bond's redemption date. If the company goes bust you may lose the lot.

Investment bonds

Investment Bonds are tax wrappers rather than specific investment instruments. They are a method of investing a lump sum with an insurance company over the long term. Available in both onshore and offshore variants, both offer life assurance cover as part of the deal, although this is usually only 101% of the fund value at time of death. The underlying investment of any type of investment bond will be retail unit trusts and OEICs – similar to those available under ISA or SIPP wrappers.

There has been much interest in offshore bonds from high earners looking for an alternative to pensions for their retirement savings. These can provide significant tax savings or tax deferrals but ongoing charges for offshore bonds are high – typically an extra 0.4 per cent per annum in addition to usual investment costs. Professional adviser charges on top mean that bonds are generally best for investments greater than £100,000. Chartered Financial Planner Martin Gorvett says:

"Investment bonds may seem friendly on the outside but they can pack a tax punch if not regularly reviewed by a professional adviser. Don't let investment inertia settle in. They are not tax-free (but are often promoted as such), they are tax-deferred. Returns in your hands are net of special rate of Corporation Tax. It may be that when other income ceases, freeing up your Personal and Basic Rate Allowances, investment returns 'live' to tax may offer greater 'net' returns."

Structured products

A structured product is a fixed-term investment where the payout depends on the performance of something else, typically a stock market index (egg FTSE 100 or S&P 500). They are complex and can carry hidden risk because they can appear on the surface to be an alternative to cash. The use of the word 'guaranteed' in the literature does not mean what you may first think! It means you are 'guaranteed' to get the returns stated *only* if the stock market index performs as required in the product's terms and conditions – noting that fees and charges may ultimately mean you get back less than you put in. Professional advice would be recommended for anyone seeking to make this type of investment. Martin Gorvett, Chartered Financial planner advises:

> "There are plenty of allowances for you to utilise to create 'tax-free' income in retirement. Indeed, these can be doubled if you involve your spouse in the planning phase. You each have a Personal Allowance of £12,500, a savings allowance of £1,000 (£500), the dividend allowance of £2,000 and a Capital Gains Tax Allowance of £12,300 (all are 2020/21 amounts). That's £27,800 each a year, doubled to £55,600 per annum if planned correctly between two people. When you add in the tax-free element of your pension (25 per cent of the fund value), investment bond withdrawals of 5 per cent (or original capital) and income from your ISA (tax-free), the payment of tax in retirement could be a preventable obligation with an investment in knowledge and planning."

Protection products

Protection products in financial services have been designed to pay out in the event of death, serious illness or accident. Different products have different names and costs and eligibility criteria and a knowledge of the main ones may help you shore up your protection.

Life assurance policies and endowments

Life assurance can provide you with one of two main benefits: it can either provide your successors with money when you die or it can be used as a savings plan to provide you with a lump sum (or income) on a fixed date. There are three basic types of life assurance: whole-life policies, term policies and endowment policies.

1. *Whole-life policies* are designed to pay out on your death. You pay a premium every year and, when you die, your beneficiaries receive the money.

2. *Term policies* involve a definite commitment. If you die during this period, your family will be paid the agreed sum in full. If you die after the end of the term (when you have stopped making payments) your family will normally receive nothing.

3. *Endowment policies* are savings products with some life cover. You pay regular premiums over a number of years and in exchange receive a lump sum on a specific date. If you wish to surrender an endowment policy before the date of the agreement you can request a 'surrender value' from the product provider but shop around as you may be able sell the policy for a sum that is higher than its surrender value. See the Association of Policy Market Makers website: www.apmm.org.

The size of premium varies depending on the type of policy you choose, the amount of cover you want and any health underwriting that may be required (medical checks may be involved). Under current legislation, the proceeds of a qualifying policy – whether taken as a lump sum or in regular income payments – are free of all tax.

Top tip

If you have assets above £325,000 and potentially another £175,000 if you have a house being left to a child you may be able to avoid significant Inheritance Tax by having your life insurance policy or endowment written into a trust so that the payment falls outside your estate on death. Instead payment will be made to the trustees to distribute to the beneficiaries of the trust. Your solicitor or financial adviser should be able to arrange this for very little cost.

Income protection and critical illness benefit

These can assist if you are still earning and do not have sick pay from your employer as they will pay a monthly income (income protection) or lump sum (critical illness benefit) if you suffer a serious illness and/or can't work due to a serious illness. There may be age restrictions although cover can last to 75 with some providers and medical screening questions will be required. If you have a challenging health history the premiums will increase. In return for regular monthly premiums it may provide added peace of mind. If you stop paying the premiums the cover stops. The payments you receive are normally tax free under the current rules.

Simple accident protection

This cover usually is very restricted in the events it will pay out for but it can give some peace of mind in the event of an accidental injury. It is fairly cheap, can be arranged with immediate effect and you may find insurers who will cover you up to 81 years of age. It does not require you to attend a medical and no medical questions are asked although UK providers do usually require your main place of residence to be in the UK. It is often overlooked but in the event of an accident and injury or death it could provide you or your partner with vital funds at a time of need.

Investor protection

Most financial transactions involving banks, investments, pensions and insurance take place without any problems but sometimes things go wrong. This is where the UK's regulatory regime steps in. As it is vitally important to your protection, part of that chapter is repeated here.

The **Financial Conduct Authority (FCA)** is accountable to the Treasury and aims to make sure the UK financial markets work well so that consumers get a fair deal. It registers individuals and companies that are suitable to work in the industry, checks that they are doing their job properly and fines them if they do a bad job. The FCA has a range of helpful guides and factsheets to help consumers understand the UK financial markets and the role of the FCA. More at www.fca.org.uk.

The **Financial Ombudsman Service (FOS)** is a free service set up by law with the power to sort out problems between consumers and registered financial businesses. It is an impartial service and will investigate your complaint if you have been unable to resolve matters with the registered individual or company (i.e. registered with the Financial Conduct Authority as above). If the ombudsman considers the complaint justified it can award compensation. More at www.financial-ombudsman.org.uk.

The **Financial Services Compensation Scheme (FSCS)** is the body that can pay you compensation if your financial services provider goes bust. The FSCS is independent and free to access. The financial services industry funds the FSCS and the compensation it pays. There are limits on how much compensation it pays and these are different for different types of financial products. To be eligible for compensation the person or company must have been registered with the FCA. The FSCS website outlines some key limits and criteria and more information is available at www.fscs.org.uk.

- Should the bank or building society get into serious financial difficulty up to £85,000 (double that if in joint names) of your money will be protected under the FSCS and the cover can increase for up to 6 months to £1 million for certain life events (for instance moving home).
- If a company that you own shares in goes bust there is no FSCS cover as FSCS does not protect investment losses arising from poor investment performance (however see negligent advice below).

In addition, the £85,000 per person limit also applies to the following:

- If your claim is about negligent advice, the advice must have been given on or after 18 August 1988, the firm must have been authorised at the time, and you must have lost money after acting on the advice you were given. You must be owed a civil liability in relation to regulated activity (e.g. the advice was negligent).
- If a firm fails holding client money or assets in connection with a regulated activity that FSCS can cover, they can compensate if there is a shortfall in your client money/assets. The activity and product must have been regulated and you must be an eligible claimant. Generally, individuals and small businesses are eligible.

Top tip

If you are unsure about how FSCS cover applies to your savings and investments review the FSCS website for more information and discuss any perceived risk with your financial adviser. Then consider options to mitigate any identified risk and follow through with relevant actions. I would say that this is one of the most urgent and high priority tips in this book due to expected financial fallout arising from the Covid-19 pandemic. This flows from my direct experience of dealing with the fall-out of the 1989 to 1993 recession which I have outlined elsewhere in this book.

Useful reading

For further help and information the following should prove useful.

- Martin Lewis's website, www.moneysavingexpert.com, which helps you weigh up the best deals on interest rates.

- The Financial Services Compensation Scheme ('FSCS') to check on how your savings or investments are covered if things go wrong. www.fscs.org.uk

- The Financial Ombudsman Service if you need to complain about a registered firm or individual. www.financial-ombudsman.org.uk

- The government funder Money Advice Service for free impartial information on saving and investing www.moneysavingexpert.com.

Reminder: Take any action points or follow up points to Chapter 12, Your Plan For A Better Retirement

Chapter Five
Tax

"I like to pay taxes. With them I buy civilization."

Oliver Wendell Holmes Jr

Benjamin Franklin said the only things certain in life are death and taxes. So there is no avoiding this chapter especially as tax in the UK is unnecessarily complicated and, therefore, it is a tough job making sense of it all in one chapter. For years I've been highlighting the overly complicated UK taxation system in my books and pleading for a simpler system. Back in 2018 I was pleased to see Carol Lewis of the Times highlighting this issue by placing a full page banner headline *"Tax rules now 'impossible to fathom'"* on an article about stamp duty and inheritance tax with Carol adding as a sub headline:

"Solicitors and accountants can't follow complicated tax guidance so what chance do we have"

Carol Lewis, The Times, 11 August 2018

Readers who work their way through this chapter will find that I shine a light on the complexities and then try and break things down into digestible content. I provide tips and pointers on retirement and tax planning where I may have been able to fathom out what on earth is going on. This knowledge will give you an advantage and you will, as part of the second essential step of retirement planning set out in this book, save more and achieve a better retirement. But time is running out on some actions as we can expect 'tax pain' later in 2021 to help pay for the debt that has arisen in the UK economy to pay for the Covid-19 pandemic.

But could we also find that a simpler taxation system starts to evolve in 2021 where the tax book is slashed down and simplified and tax is collected fairly and transparently to help 'buy civilisation' as per the headline quote at the top of this chapter? Let's start with the four basics on tax.

Firstly, taxes are necessary. Oliver Wendell Holmes Jr (one of the most widely cited US Supreme Court Justices and quoted at the beginning of this chapter) famously said *'I like to pay taxes. With them I buy civilization'*. Surely very few would want to disown the NHS that has saved so many of us, schooling, roads, security and rescue services that our taxes pay for (in one way or another). This is even more important this year as the Covid-19 pandemic measures implemented by the Government will need to be repaid and the consensus amongst financial commentators is that taxes will rise in the future. Throughout this book I talk about the 'tax pain' that is coming our way later in 2021 to help the UK start to repay the gigantic national debt it has taken on.

Secondly we currently have a low-interest-rate environment and, therefore, financing your retirement from savings has been difficult ground on which to find crumbs of comfort. However, there has been some good news in recent budgets for savers and imminent or new pensioners. Tax relief on interest and dividends has been introduced for most people; the tax-free limit on ISAs has risen to £20,000 per annum and there is the relatively new Lifetime ISA (LISA) introduced in April 2017 for adults aged under 40. There is also some useful tax free money for those earning £1,000 or less from small business income or property letting. And recent changes in inheritance tax mean that only a small minority of married couples will end up with the massive 40% inheritance tax charge eating into their estates.

Thirdly one of the biggest tax opportunities for future retirees lies in the world of pensions and flattening your tax bands by deferring income received today to some point in the future and too many people just miss this point or find out too late. This opportunity may be removed or reduced as part of any future Government measures to increase taxation and therefore time is running out to act on this.

Fourthly the UK has one of the longest tax books in the world and, therefore, tax knowledge and planning can save you money. This is not 'dodgy' – it is simply knowing the rules and applying them. The problem is not in this planning activity; it is in the long and complicated rule book. It is not the effect; it is the cause that is the real problem. I'm repeating myself from above now but surely there is a better way?

Related to this is the split between tax planning, tax avoidance and then tax evasion. Tax evasion is the easiest to define and remember because E is for evasion, which is 'E-legal'. That is the work of the tradesperson who takes cash above the £1,000 income exception per year and does not declare it to the taxman. It is also the individual who deliberately hides wealth in some offshore tax jurisdiction to try to evade tax on the interest they were earning or trade they are undertaking. HMRC's own definition of tax evasion is: *'When people or businesses deliberately do not pay the taxes that they owe'* (source: www.gov.uk). Then there is 'tax avoidance' and this is HMRC's own definition:

> *"Bending the rules of the tax system to gain a tax advantage that Parliament never intended. It often involves contrived, artificial transactions that serve little or no purpose other than to produce tax advantage. It involves operating within the letter – but not the spirit – of the law."*

It is the person who resides in the UK and takes an income and routes it round the world, writes it off through loans and puts it in and out of trusts and (somehow?) ends up spending the very same money in the UK and pays little or no tax. Hey presto, there is a rich lifestyle and no tax paid. The individual concerned would probably dismiss Oliver Wendell Holmes Jr's quote at the head of this chapter while still enjoying the free benefits their society provides. HMRC are targeting this sort of person with increased resources and commitment (and powers) – more later.

Planning is easy to illustrate. It's taking a planned route with your wealth and paying less tax as you've been able to work your way through the overly complex rules or paid someone to help you do this.

Importantly, this chapter is only a guide and it is neither legal nor taxation advice. Any potential tax advantages may be subject to change from the position in Autumn 2020 and will depend upon your individual circumstances, so individual professional advice should be obtained. The information outlined in this chapter may, however, assist you in understanding some of the issues you may face and the terminology used. Taking further professional advice or doing your own follow up (flagging this as you go along at the back of this book, Chapter 12, Your Plan) will help you 'save more' and achieve a better retirement.

This chapter at a glance

- The main income tax bands for zero tax, basic rate 20% tax, higher rate (40%) and upper rate (45%) are explained (as are the small differences in tax bands across the UK jurisdictions). National insurance, inheritance tax and capital gains tax are explained and the way they interact is outlined. This will help you get a broad understanding of the main taxes and the potential impact of tax planning.
- Potential opportunities are outlined to help you understand and then consider with professional help the use of your pension allowances to contribute to your pension pot and receive extra Income Tax relief. These may change in 2021 as

flagged up in Chapter 3, Pensions and thus could require urgent attention.

- A reminder on being careful about drawing down your pension pot too early as once you access the private pension pot taxable income there are rules that may restrict future tax relief to only £4,000 of contributions a year. This is to stop people recycling pension withdrawals and getting double tax relief.

- Reminders that you usually can't access pension pots before the age of 55 without incurring massive tax penalties so beware of anyone who says you can. Ensure any adviser is registered with the Financial Conduct Authority ("FCA") and call FCA to check that they are, indeed, registered.

- For 2020/21 'big earners' the loss of your tax free Personal Allowance is explained if your income is between £100,000 and £125,000. This is the tax 'kill zone' where income is effectively taxed at 60 per cent due to the gradual loss of the personal allowance. But did you know that you can shift the tax to being taxed at less than 20% if you make the appropriate pension contributions?

- If you do not use your £20,000 ISA allowance by 5 April 2021 the tax shelter for that amount will be lost forever. If you have a spouse or civil partner the amount doubles. Then open up and start funding your 2020/21 ISA and you can start saving more tax from 6 April 2021.

- Use capital gains tax breaks if you have shares or assets that have soared in value by selling some that have gained by £12,300 by 5 April 2021 without paying tax on the gain. This is especially important on shares that are not 'protected' from tax by one of the special tax wrappers (like an ISA or SIPP). Consider selling them and using the proceeds to fund, for instance, an ISA.

- Reduce your Inheritance Tax liability by gifting using the reliefs set out in this chapter. Larger gifts are normally inheritance tax-free if the giver survives a further seven years. Watch out for capital gains tax on the giver if they have made a large gain at the date they give the asset away (over its original cost or value at 31 March 1982). New Inheritance Tax rules can allow the IHT limit to increase from £650,000 to £1 million when a house is involved and money is left to your children.

- Tax reliefs allow you £2,000 of dividend Income tax-free and £1,000 of interest tax-free (for basic rate taxpayers and for higher rate taxpayers the amount reduces to £500 and nil for upper rate tax payers). If married or in a civil partnership you should consider how best to structure who holds investments and bank deposits.

- If you are both basic rate taxpayers you may be able to transfer part of your Personal Allowance to make you jointly more 'tax efficient' if you are a married couple or in a civil partnership.

- Tables of the main tax rates and allowances are set out as an annex at the end of this chapter.

Help! It's all so complicated – and I can't afford a tax advisor

The Retirement Planning Expert 2020/21 will try to help you cope with the challenges of the UK tax system and the main taxes and related issues are set out below step by step. I admit it's not a light read but I have tried to boil down a complex system into digestible chunks. If someone cannot follow the information in this chapter and cannot afford to pay for professional advice they are not alone. Here is the pick of free further help for those who may be elderly, recently bereaved (losing vital help and support) and find tax challenging.

Top Tip
Share information about these three organisations with older or vulnerable friends and relatives that may need free help with tax.

- *Tax Help for Older People* (TOP) is a charity that provides independent, free tax advice for vulnerable and unrepresented people on low incomes – www.taxvol.org.uk.

- *Tax Aid* is a charity that advises only those people on low incomes whose problems cannot be resolved by HMRC – www.taxaid.org.uk.

- *Citizens Advice* is very useful if someone does not meet the 'low income' criteria of the above two recommendations. It has a very useful website to help you understand tax and how it is collected and what to do if you have a tax problem. They can also provide face-to-face and telephone support – www.citizensadvice.org.uk.

Self-assessment

Self-assessment is the system HM Revenue & Customs (HMRC) uses to collect tax from individuals. Income tax is usually deducted automatically from wages and occupational and private pensions (but, significantly, not from the State Pension). Those people with other taxable income and capital gains must report it on the self-assessment return once a year. The tax you have to pay depends on allowances you have and the Income Tax band you're in; there are also different rates for Capital Gains Tax (CGT) and Inheritance Tax.

Self-assessment notices to complete the form are sent out in April each year. The details you need to enter on the form you receive in April 2020 are those relating to the 2020/21 tax year which is 6 April 2020 to 5 April 2021. Not everyone has to complete a self-assessment form but one is required from the self-employed who earn more than £1,000 and a partner in a business partnership. You may need to send one to HMRC if you are a company director; have income from savings and investments of £10,000 or more; have employment income on PAYE above £100,000 or have CGT to pay or have foreign income. If you don't receive a self-assessment request but owe tax to HMRC you are required to notify HMRC. Do this initially by writing to HMRC at: Self-Assessment, HM Revenue & Customs, BX9 1AX.

All taxpayers have an obligation to keep records of all their different sources of income and capital gains. These include:

- details of earnings plus any bonus, expenses and benefits in kind received;
- bank and building society interest;
- dividend vouchers and/or other documentation showing gains from investments;
- pension payments (state and occupational or private pensions);
- income and costs of any trading or other business activity;
- rental income from letting a property and associated costs;
- taxable social security benefits (for instance Jobseeker's Allowance and Carer's Allowance);
- gains or losses made on selling investments or a second home;
- payments against which tax relief can be claimed (egg charitable donations or contributions to a personal pension).

If you don't voluntarily disclose the fact that you may owe tax and HMRC finds out about untaxed income and launches an investigation into your tax affairs you could face stiff penalties as well as paying any tax due and interest (more on this later). Ignorance is no defence.

Income Tax

This is calculated on all (or nearly all) of your income, after deduction of your tax allowances. The reason for saying 'nearly all' is that some income you may receive is tax-free (a list of the main ones appears further on in this chapter).

The tax year runs from 6 April to the following 5 April so the amount of tax you pay in any one year is calculated on the income you receive between these two dates. The tax bands are as follows:

- The point at which most people start paying Income Tax will be the Personal Allowance of £12,500 (this should increase by 0.5% from 6 April 2021). Up to this level of income you will be paying no income tax and you are a 'zero rate taxpayer'.

- The 20 per cent basic rate of income tax is payable on income beyond the Personal Allowance up to a further £37,500 (this increase by 0.5% from 6 April 2021). The 'short hand' for a tax-payer who pays a basic rate of tax at 20% is a 'basic rate taxpayer'.

- The combined effect of the above measures is that the 40 per cent higher rate Income Tax threshold then starts at £50,000 for 2020/21 (and should increase by 0.5% to £52,250 for 2021/22). The tax-payer who pays a top rate of tax in this band is a 'higher rate taxpayer' but remember you only pay tax at 40% on the taxable income above £50,000 in 2020/21.

- The very top rate of 45 per cent is levied on incomes in excess of £150,000. This person is called an 'additional rate taxpayer' and again, remember, the 45% additional rate only applies to taxable income above £150,000.

The rates are slightly different in Scotland where there is a slightly lower 'starter' tax rate of 19% Income Tax for income between £12,500 and £14,585; the 20% 'basic' rate applies to income above £14,585 to £25,158 then there is a 21% 'intermediate' rate above £25,158 to £43,430. The rates then step up to 41% between £43,430 to £150,000 and over £150,000 is 46%. The cumulative effect of the changes seen in Scotland is to help lower earners pay a bit less tax and higher earners pay a bit more tax to balance the Scottish government's books.

A knowledge of the bands is vital to understanding some of the tax planning opportunities that lie ahead and which could help you save more and live better in retirement. So far so good? If so, you're ready for the next vital piece of knowledge.

Tax allowances

Personal Allowance and tax codes on your payslip

Your Personal Allowance is £12,500 for 2020/21 and is the amount of money you are allowed to retain before Income Tax becomes applicable. If you receive the full personal allowance you will see it as a tax code on your payslip as 1250L (one digit is dropped off the personal allowance of £12,500 to arrive at this 'code'- tax codes are as simple as that). Sometimes this basic tax code is amended by HMRC for various reasons and if appropriate the reasons will be set out on the tax code notice you receive from HMRC. Again it's as simple as that but you should check you tax code notices you receive and if something seems incorrect just call HMRC self-assessment and they will explain things and adjust any errors they have made. For big earners there is one big snag with the Personal Allowance as is reduced by £1 for every £2 of income over £100,000. The Personal Allowance will therefore disappear completely if your income in 2020/21 is above £125,000 in the tax year 2020/21.

For 2020/21 'big earners' you may still be able to preserve part or all of your Personal Allowance if your income is between £100,000 and £125,000 by making pension contributions as such contributions (subject to certain allowance limits) can, effectively, preserve the personal allowance. This can extend the £100,000 income 'barrier' and is worth considering as income in this tax 'kill zone' is taxed, effectively, at 60 per cent. The effect can be positive as income deferred into a pension may then be accessed more tax efficiently and, if you get your planning right, it may be 25% tax free and the remainder taxed at 20% basic rate. So put in very stark terms it's either tax of 60% or about 15% on that slice of £25,000 and the difference is just a bit of knowledge and then some planning.

Top tip

For 2020/21 'big earners' you may still be able to preserve part or all of your Personal Allowance if your income is between £100,000 and £125,000 by making pension contributions if your pension allowances allow this.

In much the same way individuals that end up as higher rate tax-payers can also make pension contributions to shift income from being taxed at 40% (or higher) to receiving 25% tax free and the remainder taxed at the 20% basic rate if you get your planning right.

Top tip

For 2020/21 higher rate tax payers may still be able to shift income being taxed at 40% to some being tax free and the remainder at 20% by making pension contributions. All this may change as part of future tax changes so act sooner rather than later and revisit again in 2021/21.

The other main tax allowances include:

- **Married Couple's Allowance** of £9,075 (2019/20 £8,915) is available if at least one partner was born before 6 April 1935. Tax relief is restricted to 10 per cent of £9,075 which is reduced by £1 for every £2 over £30,200 until you reach £3,510.

- A widowed partner, where the couple at the time of death were entitled to Married Couple's Allowance, can claim any unused portion of the allowance in the year he or she became widowed.

- Registered blind people can claim an allowance (the **Blind Person's Allowance**) of £2,500 per year. If both husband and wife are registered as blind, they can each claim the allowance.

- Marriage Allowance. Transferable tax allowances between married couples and civil partners could reduce your tax in 2020/21 where you have a basic rate tax payer that is married or in a civil partnership to someone who does not use up all of their tax-free Personal Allowance. This is called the Marriage Allowance and works by the partner who is not earning above £12,500 transferring £1,250 of their Personal Allowance to their partner. It is the non-taxpayer that must apply and you do this online at www.gov.uk (go to 'marriage allowance') or call HMRC on 0300 200 3300. One final thing – you both must have been born on or after 6 April 1935. If you were born before that date your own extra tax break is found at the Married Couple's Allowance, as above.

Same-sex partners

Same-sex couples in a civil partnership are treated the same as married couples for tax purposes.

Tax-free income

Not all income is taxable and the following list indicates some of the more common sources of income that are free of tax:

- Attendance Allowance.
- Child Benefit: there is a partial tax clawback if one parent earns more than £50,000 and it all becomes repayable if one earns £60,000 or more.
- Child Tax Credit.
- Disability Living Allowance and Personal Independence Payment.
- Housing Benefit.
- Industrial Injuries Disablement Pension.
- Income-related Employment and Support Allowance.
- Income Support (in some circumstances, such as when the recipient is also getting Jobseeker's Allowance, Income Support will be taxable).
- Pensions paid to war widows (plus any additions for children).
- Certain disablement pensions from the armed forces, police, fire brigade and merchant navy.
- The Winter Fuel Payment (paid to pensioners).
- Working Tax Credit.
- National Savings Premium Bond prizes.
- Winnings on the National Lottery and other forms of betting.
- Income received from certain insurance policies (mortgage payment protection, permanent health insurance, creditor insurance for loans and utility bills, various approved long-term care policies) if the recipient is sick, disabled or unemployed at the time the benefits become payable.
- Income and dividends received from savings in an ISA.
- The bonus on contributions to a LISA.

- Dividend income from investments in Venture Capital Trusts (see Chapter 4, Savings and Investments).

- Virtually all gifts (in certain circumstances you could have to pay tax if the gift is above £3,000 or if, as may occasionally be the case, the money from the donor has not been previously taxed).

- Certain redundancy payments up to the value of £30,000.

- A lump sum commuted from a pension.

- A matured endowment policy.

Top tip

If you are still in doubt about whether income is taxable take professional advice on any 'unusual' income that you have received or find further free information at the Citizens Advice website: www.citizensadvice.org.uk – taxable and non-taxable income.

Income Tax on savings and investments

Savings

Most people can earn some interest from their savings without paying tax due to the **Personal Savings Allowance** of £1,000 for basic rate taxpayers (£500 for higher rate taxpayers). There is no allowance for additional (45 per cent) rate taxpayers.

So far so good, but it then gets complicated. For 2020/21 there is a £5,000 tax-free (0 per cent) savings income band on top of the Personal Allowance so if you earn less than £18,500 a year in income plus savings interest you won't have to pay tax on the interest paid on saving. This comes from the £12,500 Personal Allowance (increases a bit if you have Blind Person's Allowance or Married Couple's Allowance), £5,000 savings income band and then the £1,000 Personal Savings Allowance.

Top tip

There is a tax-planning opportunity for a husband and wife (or partners in a civil partnership) on different tax bands (i.e. zero rate, basic rate, higher rate or additional rate). Review who holds the money and, therefore, who earns the interest and who can therefore benefit the most from the personal savings allowance.

Investments

There is a £2,000 dividend allowance in 2020/21 which allows dividends up to this value to be taken 'tax-free'. Dividends are basically a return of income each year from the profits made by a company that you have invested in. Higher dividend taxes would then be levied on amounts above £2,000. Dividend tax then increases from 7.5% to 32.5% as you move from the basic rate tax band to higher rate tax band. It increases further to 38.1% for additional rate taxpayers.

Top tip

Check out any opportunities to invest in your employer. Shares acquired under share incentive plans or sharesave schemes usually provide price discounts and tax breaks for taking part. Think about and plan your annual contribution limits so that there could be a steady flow of share sales in the future and you can maximise your Capital Gains Tax exemption.

Reclaiming tax on savings income

You can reclaim tax paid on savings interest within four years of the end of the relevant tax year by filling in form R40 and sending it to HMRC. It normally takes about six weeks to get the tax back.

Mistakes by HMRC

HMRC does sometimes make mistakes. Normally, if it has charged you insufficient tax and later discovers the error, it will send you a supplementary demand requesting the balance owing. However, a provision previously known as the 'Official Error Concession' and now labelled 'Extra Statutory Concession A19' provides that, if the mistake was due to HMRC's failure 'to make proper and timely use' of information it received, it is possible that you may be excused the arrears.

Undercharging is not the only type of error. It is equally possible that you may have been overcharged and either do not owe as much as has been stated or, not having spotted the mistake, have paid more than you needed to previously. If you think there has been a mistake, write to HMRC explaining why you think the amount is too high. If a large sum is involved it could well be worth asking an accountant to help you. If HMRC has acted incorrectly you may also be able to claim repayment of some or all of the accountant's fees (your accountant will be able to advise you on this). If the amounts involved are large this could justify the need for and cost of a professional tax advisor. If you can't afford one see the recommendations above at the section above 'Help - it's all so complicated'.

As part of the Taxpayers' Charter, HMRC has appointed an independent adjudicator to examine taxpayers' complaints about their dealings with HMRC and, if considered valid, to determine what action would be fair. Complaints appropriate to the adjudicator are mainly limited to the way that HMRC has handled someone's tax affairs (perhaps undue delays, errors and discourtesy). Before approaching the adjudicator, taxpayers are expected to have tried to resolve the matter with HMRC directly and the Charter contains details of how complaints can be raised with HMRC .

Important dates to remember

The deadline for filing paper self-assessment forms for the 2020/21 tax year is 31 October 2021. Those filing online will have until 31 January 2022. The penalty for breaching these deadlines is £100.

If your return is more than three months late an automatic penalty from 1 May of £10 per day commences up to a maximum of £900 in addition to the initial £100 penalty. If your return is still outstanding after a year another penalty arises based on the greater of £300 or 5 per cent of the tax due. In serious cases of delay a higher penalty of up to 100 per cent of the tax due can be imposed. You have 30 days to lodge an appeal with HMRC against a penalty if you believe have a reasonable excuse and if you remain dissatisfied with HMRC's review of its decision you can ask a tax tribunal to hear your appeal.

In addition if the payment is 30 days late from 31 January following the end of the tax year there is a further penalty of 5% of the tax due and then a further 5% if 6 months late and a further 5% if 12 months late.

If you are in financial difficulties engage with HMRC and request a formal 'time to pay agreement'. Additional support and more understanding is currently available from HMRC as a result of the Covid-19 pandemic including the ability to defer paying the second payment on account that was due by 3 July 2020 until 31 January 2021. The late payment penalty is suspended but the taxpayer will become liable to the penalty if the agreement is broken. If it is your first instance of requesting a 'time to pay agreement' you should find that HMRC are approachable albeit they will want to know how you got into the situation and something about your assets and debts.

One final key date – you can amend your self-assessment at any time in the 12-month period after the latest 31 January deadline.

Top tip

Submit a 'best efforts' self-assessment tax return rather than a late one. Explain any figures that are provisional in the additional notes section, apologise and explain that you will rectify matters as a priority (and do so!).

The late payment penalties can be worse than the late filing penalties and start just 30 days after 31 January. If you can't pay your tax do contact HMRC and see if you can enter into a 'time to pay agreement'- and then stick to the agreement.

Tax rebates

When you retire, you may be due a tax rebate because tax has been collected using PAYE assuming you will earn your salary for a whole year. Rebates can often arise for summer or autumn retirees. The tax overpayment would normally be resolved automatically, especially if you are getting a pension from your last employer or move into part-time employment. The P45 (tax form for leavers) should be used by the pension payer or new employer and, normally, the tax sorts itself out. If not, and the potential reclaim is for a previous tax year, HMRC may be ahead of you as they may spot it (usually by the end of July following the tax year) and send you a P800 tax calculation if they know you have paid too much tax. You will then get your refund automatically within 14 days of the P800.

If you have not received a P800 or can't wait to the end of the tax year you may make a claim to HMRC for any of the four previous tax years. You will need to know your National Insurance number and have your P45 if you have one and details of the jobs or state benefits you were getting at the time. HMRC will process the payment or explain what further information they need. Use this address for all Income Tax correspondence: Pay As You Earn and Self-Assessment, HM Revenue & Customs, BX9 1AS.

Corporation and business taxes

Refer to the Chapter 7, Starting Your Own Business.

Capital Gains Tax

You may have to pay Capital Gains Tax (CGT) if you make a profit (or, to use the proper term, 'gain') on the sale, exchange or other disposal of an asset and this includes giving it away. The usual assets are a second home, a valuable painting or a share investment that soars in price. CGT applies only to the actual gain you make after deducting a significant tax break known as the annual exemption from CGT. This is currently £12,300 for 2020/21. This means that in 2020/21 a married couple or a couple in a civil partnership can make gains of up to £24,600 that are free of CGT. However, it is not possible to use the losses of one spouse to cover the gains of the other. On the other hand, transfers of shares or assets between husband and wife or civil partners usually remain tax-free so should you be rethinking how your investments are held in this situation so that future gains are spread between the two of you?

Any gains you make are taxed at 10 per cent for basic rate taxpayers and 20 per cent for higher rate and additional rate taxpayers; however, sales of a second interest in a residential property (mainly aimed at people with second homes) remain at older rates of 18 per cent for basic rate taxpayers and 28 per cent for higher rate and additional rate taxpayers. Additionally, since 6 April 2020 it has become necessary for taxpayers realising a taxable gain on the sale of residential property to make an electronic tax return and tax payment to HMRC within 30 days of the sale, a significant acceleration compared to all other capital gains which are reported on the normal end of year tax return. The CGT rates of tax can appear generous and, therefore, may be subject to change as part of the expected 'tax pain' regime coming later in 2021. **Could, for instance, gains be charged instead at income tax rates to increase the tax receipts of the government and go towards the national debt arising from the Covid-19 pandemic?**

Following the same logic as immediately above, remember, transfers between husband and wife or civil partners usually remain tax-free so should you also be rethinking how your investments are held in this situation so that more of any future gains (after the annual exemption) are taxed as a basic rate rather than higher/additional rate tax payer? If your husband, wife or civil partner later sells or otherwise disposes of the asset, they will have to pay the tax on any gain made over the total period of ownership (after 31 March 1982, see below for more on this 'special' CGT date). The following assets are not subject to CGT and do not count towards the gains you are allowed to make:

- your main home (see below);
- most private use cars;
- personal belongings up to the value of £6,000 each, such as jewellery, paintings or antiques;
- proceeds of a life assurance policy (in most circumstances);
- profits on UK government loan stock issued by HM Treasury;
- National Savings certificates;
- gains from assets held in an ISA (and older PEPs);
- Premium Bond winnings: the maximum holding is £50,000 per person aged over 16 and under that age they may be held in the name of under - 16s by parents or guardians;
- betting and lottery winnings and life insurance policies if you are the original owner;
- gifts to registered charities;
- usually small part-disposals of land (limited to 5 per cent of the total holding, with a maximum value of £20,000 (but the amount you receive is taken off your cost for any future disposal);
- gains on the disposal of qualifying shares in a VCT or within the EIS and Seed Enterprise Investment Scheme provided these have been held for the necessary holding period. These are complex and tax-efficient investment schemes and they carry risk and are outside the scope of this book so professional advice should be sought. Find further information at www.gov.uk and go to 'enterprise investment scheme' and 'venture capital trusts'.

You work out the profit on disposal of an asset by comparing the sale proceeds with the original cost of the asset. If it was bought before 31 March 1982 you use the market value at that date. If you dispose of an asset left to you by the will of a relative you use the market value on the date of death of the relative. If you give away an asset to a child or other close relative you use the market value on the date of the gift as the proceeds instead of any amount received. To bring clarity to potential complex situations you can agree the valuation with HMRC before you submit your tax return by completing form CG 34 and professional advice may prove beneficial.

You can add other allowable costs that were incurred when acquiring the asset- such as stamp duty, solicitor's costs and valuation fees on a second home. You add these to the original cost so remember to keep the receipts or go and dig them out now and keep them in a safe place. Improvement costs, such as adding a conservatory or converting a garage also can be added to the cost on, say, a second property that may be subject to CGT but not maintenance costs such as decorating and repairs.

Your main home and capital gains tax

Your main home is usually exempt from CGT and for that reason individuals who buy small and extend tend to be tax efficient in using their funds to build up a tax free asset if it remains their main residence. Perhaps the strategy of buying the smallest most run down property on an expensive or up and coming area makes sense now! There are only a few trip points. One is if you convert part of your home into a dedicated office with, for instance, a separate entrance. Or into separate self-contained accommodation on which you charge rent. Both of these examples show how you may taint part of the CGT exemption for the relevant portion of the house over the relevant period and some CGT may be payable when you come to sell it.

If you leave your home to someone else who retains it for a while (as a property speculation or to rent out) and later decides to sell it then they may be liable for CGT when the property is later sold (although only on the gain since the date on which they acquired it). If you own two homes, only one of them is exempt from CGT, namely the one you designate as your 'main residence'. There may be some overlap opportunities and, providing a dwelling home has been your only or main home for a period, the final period of ownership that qualifies for relief can be useful. The final period of ownership of a private residence that potentially could qualify for relief is currently 9 months. HMRC's helpsheet HS283, 'Private residence relief', available from www.gov.uk, provides more information.

> **Top tip**
>
> If you have two homes and have lived in both consider taking professional advice on whether to make a main residence election for your second home if it is standing at a large gain or you are thinking of selling it first. One of the tests used by HMRC when considering the availability of such reliefs is the actual period of residence and the quality rather than quantity of that residence.

Selling a family business

CGT is payable if you are selling a family business, and is 20 per cent for higher rate and additional rate taxpayers, but the reduced level of 10 per cent for basic rate taxpayers. There are a number of CGT reduction opportunities or deferral reliefs available including the potential to attain business asset disposal relief (previously entrepreneurs' relief) which could produce a tax rate of 10 per cent. This, however, is a complex area and timing could be vital, so well before either retiring or selling your business or shares you should seek professional advice. You will want to do so anyway as the buyer will probably be getting professional advice and you could find yourself down on the deal pretty quickly if you are not receiving good professional advice (irrespective of any tax advantages).

Inheritance Tax

Inheritance tax is the tax paid on assets (the estate) that are left when someone dies. It is at a high rate of 40% and applies to the value of assets on death (property, bank funds, investments, cars and payouts from life insurance companies) but there are many important exemptions and reliefs which may mean that no tax is payable on the estate. No one knows precisely what is around the corner so this should be talked about sooner rather than later to help manage, wherever possible, Inheritance Tax to be paid on your 'estate'. Above all else there is the straightforward wish of not wanting ambiguity about what should happen after you die. So, time to take a deep breath and read on and then promise to talk to those that matter to you or put a large circle around the above sub-heading 'Inheritance Tax and wills' and pass this book to them with two words 'let's talk'.

The tax threshold (the level at which you'll need to pay tax) is set at £325,000 and is currently frozen at this rate until 2020/21. The threshold amount for married couples and civil partners is twice this, so £650,000, and this can be stretched to £1 million with the Main Residence Nil Rate Band (more below). The value of estates over and above this sum are taxed at 40 per cent. So the starting point is for you and your partner to sit down and make a list of your assets and then deduct all outstanding liabilities.

Top tip

Many people underestimate how much they are worth and forget assets like pensions in a defined contribution pension pot - that is why this is a two-person job as it is easy to overlook assets acquired over a long time.

Some people mistakenly think that giving away your wealth gets around Inheritance Tax. This is where the clouds of confusion sometimes arise from casual conversations with friends. Yes there are some detailed points where this can be true, such as gifts for the national benefit. There are also other exemptions that have been brought into the debate, which are correct, such as servicemen dying on active service being exempt from IHT. There are then grey areas such as war service hastening a veteran's death, which found, upon challenge, that the estate could be exempt from IHT.

However, the root of the confusion referred to above is because there is no immediate inheritance tax on lifetime gifts between individuals – it is only deferred. The gifts can then become wholly exempt if the donor survives for seven years. So when the donor dies, any gifts made within the previous seven years become chargeable as their value is added to the estate for IHT reasons. For this reason, in the seven-year period they are known as 'potentially exempt transfers' or PETs for short. Where gifts exceed the nil rate band there is a tapering relief which begins to soften any resulting tax charge, on a sliding scale between years three and seven following the gift. Gifts with strings attached are treated as if they did not happen so if you try to 'give away' your house to the kids but still live in it the 'gift' probably won't be a gift in the eyes of HMRC so it falls back into your assets pot with IHT due. The basic rule is that gifts 'with strings attached' probably won't work. Extreme care must be taken here, as not only might you fail to secure the desired IHT saving, you might also inadvertently create a CGT liability which would otherwise not have existed. Linked to 'give away' tactics are various schemes that seek to lock away the home in some form of a trust.

Trusts

A trust is a relationship between persons and property under which property is vested in persons known as trustees, who hold the property for the benefit of other persons known as beneficiaries. The settlor is the person who provides the property to be held on trust. The golden rule is that the terms of the trust must be certain and to be valid there must be three certainties: certainty of what was intended; certainty of what was going into the trust; and certainty of the beneficiaries (who they were). Trusts are complex and are usually created by family solicitors who are experienced in the relevant jurisdiction and can help with potential complexities such as conflicts of interest between generations and care around the settlor retaining sufficient assets to continue to live on to a standard that is acceptable. The jurisdiction point reflects England and Wales having a common system; minor differences in Northern Ireland and other differences in Scotland.

Certainly, some very old and established trusts have sheltered significant family estates from IHT as the occupier never actually owns the property; they are merely allowed to live there subject to conditions. This sort of thing was used by the wealthy to stop their children and subsequent grandchildren disposing of the main assets within a family estate and, instead, simply being allowed to live in or use the asset and receive some income. Trusts were also used to keep the family money within the bloodline (in the case of divorce and remarriage). This allowed the big family estate to be passed down intact from generation to generation.

In recent years, firms have tried to market tax saving schemes to 'protect your assets from the taxman' or schemes to shelter assets from 'claims for care home fees' based loosely on schemes involving trusts. These may include fancy seminars with free coffee and biscuits and smiling salesmen, but tread carefully. The ideal scenario is that you would want to be dealing with the trusted family solicitor regulated by the Law Society in your jurisdiction (for instance in England and Wales at www.lawsociety.org.uk) and you would want a solicitor accredited on their Wills and Inheritance Quality Scheme (WIQS). If you depart from this route the following questions may help your selection process:

- What are the specific legal and tax qualifications and regulating body of the individual that will be responsible for talking with you, understanding your position and then advising you? Check their name on that organisation's register. This could be one of the biggest transactions you make so obtain at least two quotations and seek recommendations from trusted family members or friends.

- Does the trust documentation provide certainty of what was intended; certainty of what was going into the trust; and certainty of the beneficiaries (who they were)? Ask what happens if the scheme does not work. How big is the firm advising you and how long have they been around? What professional indemnity insurance cover do they have?

- Extras? Have the total costs of all aspects from start to finish been set out in advance in writing so that you have clarity before proceeding? If changes are needed, what is the fee/ hourly rate? This avoids the issue of cost creep.

- What are the pros and cons? There will always be some risks to any scheme – how well are these set out and how prominent are they?

- What are the tax charges –what types of tax will the trust incur and when?

- What happens if the government rules change? Are the schemes amended and updated and at what hourly rate or other cost?

Notwithstanding the above the family trust remains a legitimate and useful tool in inheritance tax and family succession planning and when properly utilised can offer tax advantages, asset protection, retention or centralisation of control, and flexibility as to who in the family is benefitted, and how.

Top tip

There is no such thing as a magic wand that makes inheritance tax disappear on your main home if you continue to live in it or guarantees local authorities will not chase down assets deliberately given away to avoid claims for care home fees. Tread carefully if someone offers you a magic wand for a fee and satisfy yourself on the above questions.

Top tip

Proceeds from life insurance policies will form part of your estate unless you take steps to divert the proceeds, perhaps using a trust, directly to another party -

perhaps children or grandchildren. This is not a complex area of tax planning and many life assurance companies can provide simple trust forms for you to complete to shelter the funds from inheritance tax or consult a financial advisor or solicitor if you remain unsure.

Tax treatment of trusts

There may be IHT to pay when assets – such as money, land or buildings – are transferred into or out of trusts or when they reach a 10-year anniversary. There are complex rules that determine whether a trust needs to pay IHT in such situations so ensure you have clarity on the tax consequences and if unsure get further clarity on this with professional advice (usually a financial adviser, solicitor or chartered accountant could help). Further information is available on the website: www.hmrc.gov.uk – 'inheritance tax and trusts'.

Main residence nil rate band and IHT

The 'main residence nil rate band' is a relatively new and a very significant tax break that may remove the inheritance tax worry to the vast majority of UK married couples and civil partners. Here is how it works. Remember the £325,000 threshold allows married couples or civil partners to transfer the unused element of their IHT-free allowance to their spouse or civil partner when they die, giving an effective threshold of £650,000 before any inheritance tax will become payable. Then remember that IHT will be levied at 40 per cent above the IHT threshold (£650,000 for a couple or £325,000 on the estate of anyone who is single or divorced when they die).

And then along came the one of the biggest fanfares in the UK taxation system in the 2015 Budget with the announcement of the 'main residence nil rate band' which started being implemented on 6 April 2017. It is an extra relief available where the value of the estate is above the IHT threshold and contains a main residence that is being passed on to 'lineal descendants'. It will raise the IHT-free allowance to from £325,000 to £500,000 per person by 2020/21 where married couples jointly own a family home (worth less than £2 million) and want to leave this to their children. The joint IHT exemption between the married couple will be £1 million.

The key aspects are:

- The relief was introduced on 6 April 2017, for deaths on or after that date.

- It was phased in, starting at £100,000 in 2017/18, now rising to £125,000 in 2018/19, £150,000 in 2019/20 and £175,000 in 2020/21. For a couple, the £175,000 each plus the existing £325,000 each, makes up the £1 million maximum relief that will be achievable by 2020/21.

- The relief will then increase in line with CPI from 2021/22 onwards.

- The relief applies only on death, not on lifetime transfers.

- The amount available will be the lower of the net value of the property and the maximum amount of the main residence nil rate band. The net value of the property is after deducting liabilities such as a mortgage.

- The property will qualify if it has been the deceased's residence at some point.

- The property must be left to lineal descendants: children, grandchildren, great-grandchildren etc. or the spouses of the same. Children include step-children and adopted children.

- The relief is transferable, so the estate of the second spouse to die can benefit from the main residence nil rate band of their deceased spouse, regardless of when that spouse died.

- The relief will be tapered away for estates with a net value over £2 million, at the rate of £1 for every £2 over that limit, so will be reduced to zero on an estate of £2.35 million.

The Nil Rate Band (NRB) threshold is not *automatically* doubled for married couples and civil partners. If the deceased spouse left their entire estate to the surviving spouse, they did not use their own NRB and will instead have made use of their spousal exemption and there will be no IHT to pay on that basis. The surviving partner then 'inherits' their deceased spouse's unused NRB (or the portion of it which went unused), which combined with their own IHT NRB is a maximum of £650k. Married couples therefore need to ensure they maximise the transferable NRB by drafting wills accordingly and the advice of a solicitor is recommended (see Chapter 11, Sandwich Generation and 'Wills').

IHT and pensions

The transfer of pension pots from a deceased's estate can either be simple or complex and can be paid out tax free or taxed (sometimes at rates of up to 55% for unauthorised payments). There are complex rules depending on age at death, type of pension and whether it is a lump sum or an annuity and so on. Individuals or couples with an Estate (before taking account of any pension pots) worth more than the IHT exempt amounts should consider their pension pot strategy especially in the years up to age 75 and professional advice usually proves beneficial in such circumstances.

For basic information there is more at www.gov.uk and 'tax on pension death benefits'.

Top tip

The transfer of pension pots from a deceased's estate can result in tax anywhere between tax free to 55%. To an extent this is down to your choice and planning. The savings involved can be substantial for those who benefit from the wishes in your will so consider finding out more and then taking professional advice.

Other IHT planning

Other IHT planning includes the charitable donations exemption, with a reduced rate of IHT payable on estates that give at least 10 per cent of the value of their estate above the nil rate band (£325,000) to charity. The remainder is taxed at 36 per cent against the usual 40 per cent IHT rate.

Gifts or money up to the value of £3,000 can be given annually free of tax. If you didn't use last year's allowance you can carry it forward and use it this year to give £6,000 away to your children, for example. The allowance is per donor, not per child.

It is possible to make small gifts to any number of individuals free of tax, provided the amount to each does not exceed £250. You cannot combine this with the £3,000 allowance.

Gifts to mark a wedding or civil partnership. The limits for these gifts are up to £5,000 given to a child, £2,500 given to a grandchild or great-grandchild or £1,000 given to anyone else.

Perhaps the most generous of these reliefs, though, is that gifts made out of surplus income and which have a degree of regularity and do not detract from the donor's standard of living or capital worth may be made free from IHT without any fixed monetary limit. The greater your income and lower your living costs, the more can be given away in this fashion.

> **Top tip**
>
> **Planning and longevity go hand in hand, as most lifetime gifts to individuals (who are not covered by one of the exemptions mentioned) do not trigger IHT if you survive for seven years.**

Recent Budgets also created new and welcome provisions to enable the tax and other advantages of ISAs and pensions to be passed onto the deceased's spouse (for instance in the case of ISAs that funds could remain in the ISA tax-effective wrapper). Could it be tax-efficient to ensure that your spouse inherits your ISA under your will rather than the investments passing to other family members? Remember that the government can change the tax rules without notice and exemptions can be withdrawn or reduced.

Wills

Finally, as we draw this important section to a close, please remember the importance of a will and how it ties into IHT. Without a will in place it will be the intestacy laws that decide how your estate is distributed, not you. Having a will allows you to state precisely who your beneficiaries are and what they receive and allows you to appoint administrators who will administer the estate after your death. So make a will either through an online or postal service or, if your affairs are more complicated, with a face-to-face professional adviser, and consider a power of attorney. Keep them up to date so that they are effective and efficient from both a legal and a tax perspective. For further information, see 'Wills' in Chapter 11, Sandwich Generation, within this book and also find more at www.gov.uk (search for 'probate and inheritance tax').

What Tax Trends Should I Be Aware Of In 2020/21?

The way in which HMRC deals with taxpayers and the focus areas of the UK tax system evolve over time and I've asked Graham Boar, tax partner with UHY Hacker Young, to share his thoughts on current trends relevant to those approaching retirement. Here are his top 4:

Nudge Theory

"Under a system called common reporting standard (CRS) HMRC are now automatically provided with huge volumes of financial data relating to UK taxpayers from the tax authorities of overseas jurisdictions. Rather than trying to work through all this data HMRC have adopted a system of 'nudges', sending letters to those taxpayers to tell them HMRC have information about an overseas asset or income stream and encouraging them to check their tax compliance in that regard is up to scratch.

This approach has seen significant success and it extends beyond overseas income, recent campaigns including data suggesting the sale of second properties or data from tech platforms such as auction sites or property letting sites.

Recipients of such letters should give careful thought as to whether their tax affairs are up to date and accurate before responding to HMRC and should seek professional help if they think there is a disclosure needing to be made. There is also a consensus in our industry that completing the certificates enclosed with some of these nudge letters is not a good idea."

Pensions Contributions

"Over recent years the amounts which can tax efficiently be contributed to pensions has been steadily reduced, with high earners restricted more than others. Much has been made in the press of the tax charges facing senior NHS clinicians on their pensions funding and whilst that is the group which has made the headlines, experience in practice has shown many other professions being caught out by surprise tax charges thanks to their (usually) final salary type pension arrangements. Teachers are one group we've noticed getting caught out but civil servants, judges and a variety of other white collar workers with generous work based pension schemes are also potential candidates.

Anyone in a reasonably well paid job and with a defined benefit pension arrangement would do well to review their situation with the dual purpose of, firstly, checking there has been no inadvertent breach of allowances leading to an unexpected tax charge and, secondly, putting them in a position to plan to maximise the contributions their allowances permit."

Digitisation and Real Time Reporting

"More and more HMRC services are being moved to be online by default with a paper alternative only for those who are 'digitally excluded'. In other areas the timing of tax collection is being accelerated. 30 day CGT reporting for the sale of UK residential property is a good example that ticks both boxes, with the online return leading to tax collection acceleration of as much as 20 months compared to the pre-existing system.

Plans for 'Making Tax Digital' for income tax were kicked into the long grass a few years ago but have now reappeared on the radar and could be with us by 2023, obliging property landlords and the self employed to being making quarterly reports to HMRC. My advice in this regard is that taxpayers make an effort to keep up to date with developments relevant to them, in particular looking into the requirements for anything new or transactional before committing to it."

Buy Now While Stocks Last

"Tax rules change from time to time and with very few exceptions transactions will be taxed according to the laws in force when they were entered into even if those laws later change. The economic cost of COVID alone is enough to lead most commentators to imagine that future tax rises will be necessary, but even before the pandemic there were Office of Tax Simplification reviews commission in 2019 into inheritance tax and in 2020 into capital gains tax. There have also been other reports concerning these taxes, most notably the All Party Parliamentary Group report on inheritance tax published early in 2020.

In the same way that using allowances and reliefs for a tax year to avoid them being wasted, locking into planned transactions or structuring your affairs to lock into current known regimes is an important aspect of tax management. It's hard to imagine the tax landscape becoming more benign in the years that follow COVID and those who've proactively managed their affairs in the current climate might be viewed jealously in years to come by those who've adopted a wait and see approach."

I also asked Graham for his personal top five tax planning tips for a better retirement which were:

1. **"Get an early start**. *It's never too early to start planning for the future, but particularly in the four or five years preceding your retirement it might be possible to significantly change your behaviour towards savings, earnings, pension contributions and similar to achieve significant tax efficiencies.*

2. **Don't let the tail wag the dog**. *In other words, consider your tax position and take reasonable steps to mitigate charges that might arise. But don't let tax be the be all and end all, and certainly don't take tax-planning measures that risk leaving you struggling for money, worried or unhappy. Find a solution that ticks all the boxes, not just the tax box.*

3. **Keep it under review**. *Tax rules change all the time, and many of the measures affecting the retired are intended as a stimulus to behaviour. Don't just make a plan once and then rigidly stick to it; have a think about your tax position once a year (February is a good time) and consider any changes that could benefit you in the coming 12 months.*

4. **'I'm going to' and not 'I've just'**. *As a tax adviser, my heart sinks when a client calls me to ask about the tax implications of what they've just done and whether the position can be improved. Almost invariably the tax outcome of a transaction can only be improved in advance of committing to it and not once it is completed. So ask questions at the right time, especially where big life events are concerned.*

5. **Don't be pressured into things**. *Lifetime succession planning is a fantastic way of managing inheritance tax burdens, but it's disheartening when clients feel a guilty sense of obligation to provide an inheritance and worse still when children appear to be grasping after 'their inheritance'."*

Help in dealing with a tax investigation

HMRC is increasing its investigation capability, arming itself with more staff and more power. If HMRC believes your errors were deliberate they can go back 20 years. Add in interest on any late tax and further additional penalties of up to 200 per cent of the tax shortfall and you could be facing an eye-watering tax assessment.

HMRC will listen carefully to facts that may mitigate any penalty due – and if you are looking at serious amounts of tax due then early discussion with a professional adviser will assist you in dealing with the unwelcome situation you may find yourself in. You should also check whether any insurance or professional association memberships that you have could provide free tax investigation cover. This is a very useful piece of cover.

If HMRC discover an error during an investigation, they can re-open other closed years as well. For example, if a careless error is discovered, HMRC can include up to six years within any settlement negotiations. If a deliberate error is uncovered, HMRC can include up to 20 years in the most serious cases. Tax investigations can prove to be extremely stressful and very expensive so I would suggest the following.

1. **Engage an accountant.** If you are the subject of anything but the simplest of HMRC interventions, find an accountant who holds themselves out as a specialist in this area and take some advice, even if it's only some tips and help in dealing with the enquiry yourself, and ensuring that HMRC are playing by the rules.

2. **Get tax investigation insurance cover.** Many accountants will offer this type of insurance; specialist providers such as Markel do too, as well as trade membership bodies such as the Federation of Small Businesses. But if you get an enquiry and don't have a specific policy, it's worth checking things like your house insurance in case they provide some level of assistance.

3. **Keep good records.** When HMRC come knocking and you have contemporary written evidence supporting your position you will immediately be on the front foot and the onus will be on HMRC to undermine your stance. If you're relying on advice, get it in writing. And certainly don't think that a recollection of something an HMRC staff member told you on the phone will hold water if the inspector in front of you thinks differently.

4. **Consider disclosing interpretations.** If you're declaring your taxes based on an interpretation of a grey area or otherwise in circumstances which HMRC may not agree with, consider offering a full explanation in the tax return white space. The 'discovery' assessment provisions allow HMRC to look back six (careless) or 20 (deliberate) years, but a full set of details on your return may limit their enquiry window to 12 months post filing, giving you tax certainty a lot earlier.

Retiring abroad

A vital question for some readers is the taxation effects of living overseas. There are examples of people who retired abroad in the expectation of being able to afford a higher standard of living and who returned home a few years later, thoroughly disillusioned as they had not planned through the costs and implications – more in the 'Your Home and Property', Chapter 1 including notes of caution about the impact of Brexit on tax from 1 January 2021. Part of the plan has to be a consideration of tax.

Tax rates vary from one country to another. Additionally, many countries levy taxes that don't apply in the UK and complications can usually be expected from wealth taxes and estate duty on overseas property, and localised and national property taxes can also combine to trip up well-laid plans.

The starting point is therefore the free and quality information available on most countries from our own Foreign and Commonwealth Office – access via www.gov.uk and search for 'living in [country]'. The World Factbook by the US Central Intelligence Agency is also a useful source of quality information on every country in the world. As things advance, independent and appropriately qualified legal advice is absolutely essential when buying property overseas.

Many intending emigrants cheerfully imagine that, once they have settled themselves in a dream villa overseas, they are safely out of the clutches of the HMRC. This is not so and your first step is to work out your residence status. Whether you are a UK resident usually depends on how many days you spend in the UK in the tax year which runs from 6 April to 5 April the following year. According to HMRC: 'You're automatically resident in the UK if either you spent 183 or more days in the tax year or your only home was in the UK – you must have owned, rented or lived in it for at least 91 days in total – and you spent at least 30 days there in the tax year.' On the other hand, HMRC state that you're automatically non-resident 'if either you spent fewer than 16 days in the UK (or 46 days if you haven't been classed as UK resident for the three previous tax years) or you work abroad full-time (averaging at least 35 hours a week) and spent fewer than 91 days in the UK, of which no more than 30 were spent working.' In the year you move out of the UK (or back in) the year is usually split into two – a non-resident part and a resident part. More information is at www.gov.uk – go to 'statutory residence test' – and you can also use HMRC's tax residence indicator toolkit and go to 'check your residence status'.

So why is this 'residence' status so important for tax? Well, residents pay UK tax on all their income, whether it's from the UK or abroad. Non-residents only pay tax on their UK income and they do not pay UK tax on their foreign income. In addition, non-residents only pay UK Capital Gains Tax either on UK residential property or if they return to the UK.

The usual scenarios that may require non-residents to complete a self-assessment tax return include:

- if you are in receipt of UK rental income;
- if you make capital gains from the sale or disposal of assets in the UK;
- if you are a director of a UK company or
- if you receive profits from a UK partnership;
- if you earn an income in the UK through self-employment;
- if you do not live in the UK, but you do some or all of your work in the UK.

In addition, HMRC's Non-Resident Landlord Scheme requires landlords with a usual place of abode outside the UK to have the tax on their UK rentals collected by their UK letting agent or tenant and the tax is due for payment within 30 days of each quarter ending 30 June, 30 September, 31 December and 31 March. Where property is owned jointly, the share of each joint owner is considered separately. If you want to pay tax on your rental income through self-assessment, fill in HMRC form NRL1 and send it to HMRC. You must tell HMRC if you're either leaving the UK to live abroad permanently or going to work abroad full-time for at least one full tax year. You do this by HMRC's Form P85 and send it to Self-Assessment, HM Revenue and Customs, BX9 1AS, United Kingdom.

Double tax agreement

The country where you live might also seek to tax you on your UK income. This is where a double taxation agreement between the country you live in and the UK may save you being taxed twice by claiming a tax relief in the UK for foreign tax paid. The conditions for tax relief vary from agreement to agreement; find more at www.gov.uk and go to 'double taxation treaties: non-UK resident with UK income'.

Top tip

Tax is one of the most complex twists of moving overseas. Don't guess or listen to pub talk. Research the issue thoroughly or get professional advice both in the UK and the country you are moving to.

Important wealth warning

This chapter is only a guide on tax and it is neither legal nor taxation advice. Any potential tax advantages may be subject to change from the position as at Autumn 2020 and will depend upon your individual circumstances, so individual professional advice should be obtained.

Further information

- HMRC general enquiries number: 0300 200 3310 and Income Tax correspondence is sent to Pay As You Earn and Self-Assessment, HM Revenue & Customs, BX9 1AS.
- Complaint about HMRC: www.adjudicatorsoffice.gov.uk.
- Tax Help for Older People (TOP): free tax advice service for vulnerable and unrepresented people on low incomes: www.taxvol.org.uk.
- Tax Aid is a charity that advises only those people on low incomes whose problems cannot be resolved by HMRC: www.taxaid.org.uk.
- Citizens Advice has a very useful website to help you understand tax and how it is collected and what to do if you have a tax problem. They can also provide face-to-face and telephone support: www.citizensadvice.org.uk.

Useful reading

The Daily Telegraph Tax Guide 2020 by David Genders, published by Kogan Page.

Reminder: Take any action points or follow up points to Chapter 12, Your Plan For A Better Retirement.

Additional notes space for issues identified:

RETIRETMENT PLANNING EXPERT 2020/21   TAX ANNEX

INCOME TAX

Rates and bands (other than savings and dividend income)

Band £	2020/21 Rate %	Band £	2019/20 Rate %
£0- £37,500	20	0-37,500	20
£37,501- £150,000	40	37,501- 150,000	40
Over £150,000	45	Over 150,000	45

Bands in 2021/22 are expected to rise by 0.5%

Income tax rates in Scotland and Wales on income other than savings and dividend income have been devolved.

DEVOLVED INCOME TAX

Scotland rates and bands

Band £	2020/21 Rate %	Band £	2019/20 Rate %
£0- £2,085	19	£0- £2,049	19
£2,086- £12,658	20	£2,050- £12,444	20
£12,659- £30,930	21	£12,444- £30,930	21
£30,931- £150,000	41	£30,931- £150,000	41
Over £150,000	46	Over £150,000	46

Wales rates and bands

Band £	2020/21 Rate %	Band £	2019/20 Rate %
£0- £37,500	20	0-37,500	20
£37,501- £150,000	40	37,501- 150,000	40
Over £150,000	45	Over 150,000	45

Savings income	2020/21 and 2019/20
Savings allowance basic rate	£1,000
Savings allowance higher rate	£500

A starting rate of 0% may be available unless taxable non-savings income exceeds £5,000.

Dividend income	2020/21 and 2019/20
Dividend allowance	£2,000
Dividend ordinary rate	7.5%
Dividend upper rate	32.5%
Dividend additional rate	38.1%

INCOME TAX RELIEFS

	2020/21	2019/20
Personal allowance	£12,500	£12,500
Personal allowance income limit	£100,000	£100,000
Marriage allowance	£1,250	£1,250
Married couple's allowance	£9,075	£8,915
minimum amount	£3,510	£3,450
income limit	£30,200	£29,600
Blind person's allowance	£2,500	£2,450

Rates in 2021/22 are expected to rise by 0.5%

PROPERTY TAXES

Stamp Duty Land Tax
Land and buildings in England and Northern Ireland

Residential Band	Rate %	Non-residential Band	Rate %
£0 - £125,000	0	£0- £150,000	0
£125,001 - £250,000	2	£150,001- £250,000	2
£250,001 - £925,000	5	Over £250,000	5
£925,001 - £1,500,000	10		
Over £1,500,000	12		

Stamp Duty Land Tax Holiday 8th July 2020 to 31st March 2021*

Land and buildings in England and Northern Ireland

Residential Band	Rate %
£0 - £500,000	0
£500,001 - £925,000	5
£925,001 to £1,500,000	10

Over £1,500,000   12
* date correct as at Autumn
2020

Stamp Duty Land Tax for **existing** property owners

Land and buildings in England and Northern Ireland

You will be charged an additional 3% stamp duty on each portion of the price.

There are opportunities to reclaim this additional stamp duty where the
original home is sold within 3 years.

**Land and Buildings Transaction Tax in
Scotland**

Residential Band	Rate %	Non-residential Band	Rate %
£0 - £145,000	0	£0- £150,000	0
£145,001 - £250,000	2	£150,001- £250,000	1
£250,001 - £325,000	5	Over £250,000	5
£325,001 - £750,000	10		
Over £750,000	12		

Land and Buildings Transaction **Tax Holiday**

to 31st March 2021* in Scotland	Rate %
Residential Band	
£0 - £250,000	0
£250,001 - £325,000	5
£325,001 - £750,000	10
Over £750,000	12

Stamp Duty Land Tax for existing property owners

Land and buildings in Scotland

You will be charged an additional 4% stamp duty on each portion of the price.

There are opportunities to reclaim this additional stamp duty where the

original home is sold within 18 months (it was 3 years where the
second home was purchased between 24 September 2018 and 24 March 2020).
* date correct as at Autumn 2020

Land Transaction Tax in Wales	Rate %		Rate %
Residential Band		Non-residential Band	
£0 - £180,000	0	£0- £150,000	0
£180,001 - £250,000	3.5	£150,001- £250,000	1
£250,001- £400,000	5	£250,001- £1,000,000	5
£400,001 - £750,000	7.5	Over £1,000,000	6
£750,001- £1,500,000	10		
Over £1,500,000	12		

You will be charged an additional 3% stamp duty on each portion of the price. There are opportunities to reclaim this additional stamp duty where the original home is sold within 3 years.

Land and Buildings Transaction **Tax Holiday**

27 July 2021 to 31st March 2021* in Wales

Residential Band	Rate %
£0 - £250,000	0
£250,001- £400,000	5
£400,001 - £750,000	7.5
£750,001- £1,500,000	10
Over £1,500,000	12

The temporary holiday rates will not apply to the purchase of additional properties in Wales
* date correct as at Autumn 2020

INDIVIDUAL SAVINGS ACCOUNTS	2020/21	2019/20
Overall investment limit	£20,000	£20,000
Junior account investment limit	£9,000	£4,368

PENSIONS	2020/21	2019/20
Lifetime Allowance limit	£1,073,100	£1,055,000
Annual Allowance limit	£40,000	£40,000
Money Purchase Allowance	£4,000	£4,000

CAPITAL GAINS TAX

	2020/21	2019/20
Individuals		
Exemption	£12,300	£12,000
Standard rate	10%	10%
Higher/additional rate	20%	20%
Disposal of second homes/certain		
residential property	18%/28%	18%/28%
Trusts		
Exemption	£6,150	£6,000
Rate	20%	20%

Business asset disposal relief

The first £1m of qualifying gains are charged at 10% on or after 11 March 2020 (reduced from £10m on 10 March 2020).

INHERITANCE TAX

	Chargeable transfers 2020/21 and 2019/20
Death rate	
£0 - £325,000	Nil
Over £325,000	40%
Lifetime rate	
£0 - £325,000	Nil
Over £325,000	20%

A further nil rate band of £175,000 (2019/20 £150,000) may be available in relation to current or former residences.

NATIONAL INSURANCE

	2020/21
Class 1 (employed)	
Employee	%
Earnings per week	
Up to £183	Nil

£183.01 - £962	12
Over £962	2

Employer

Up to £169	Nil
Over £169	13.8

The employer rate is 0% for employees under 21
and apprentices under 25 of earnings uo to £962 per week

Class 1a   13.8

Employers - on employees taxable benefits

Class 2 (self employed)

Flat rate per week	£3.05
Small profits threshold	£6,475 per annum

Class 3 (voluntary)

Flat rate per week	£15.30

Class 4 (self employed)

Between £9,500 and £50,000	9% on profits
Over £50,000	2% on profits

Chapter Six
Cut costs and debt, Complaints and Scams

"A fool and his money are soon parted."

THOMAS TUSSER

The knowledge in this chapter will give you an advantage and you will, as part of the second essential step of retirement planning set out in this book, save more and achieve a better retirement. This is the final chapter of the 'save more' parts of this book. Combine chapters 2 to 6 together (the five 'save more' chapters) and the actions you have identified will make a massive difference to achieving a better retirement. Indeed this chapter alone will save some readers an absolute fortune as you will read in the scammer tips towards the end.

We have a problem in the UK as we can be complacent and over-pay for things when we could save more and have more to spend on other things when it comes to the active retirement years. This has come more sharply into focus this year as we deal with the various financial forces bearing down on us from the Covid-19 pandemic. More and more of us are looking to cut costs and debt and reshape our finances as we get through an emerging recession which could be the worst we have faced in 300 years. This chapter takes you through many opportunities to retune your finances and also points to a further British habit which can make matters worse

- we are not very good at complaining – or should we say complaining effectively and then upping the ante if we feel we are being fobbed off. Sadly there are predators out there who want a slice of our cake. It also seems that the recession is bringing out the worst in the scammers and even more of them. Scammers are basically clever crooks who deploy sleight of hand, fast talk and clever technology and a few back-up techniques such as vanity and knowing that people never want to admit to being stupid. You may never spot what they have done, in the same way as a good magician really will leave you believing that they made someone 'float' on stage. The equivalent of smoke, mirrors and sleight of hand can make anything look plausible. This chapter underlines a common-sense approach to help you ignore the smoke and mirrors deployed by the scammers and stay safer. Overall this chapter will help you 'save more' and achieve a better retirement.

This chapter at a glance

- *There is not much law around over-charging*. Whilst internet online scams present threats, the flip side should be recognised, as there are now massive opportunities to use the internet to turn information into power for yourself. So why do we so often end up accepting the price and over-paying? But no longer – welcome to a cold wet Winter's day that can save you, potentially, hundreds of pounds on services that you may have been overpaying. You will save £££s.
- *How to recession proof your finances and manage debt.*
- *Inevitably in life things do sometimes go wrong*. If you do lose out and someone is clearly at fault you may wish to complain. The complaint process can be frustrating and some people and organisations may not have the time or ability to deal with your concerns. Tips are provided on how to be heard, how to spell out what you want and then what you can do to up the ante.
- *Five simple golden rules for staying safe from scammers.* Follow them and you will be safer.
- *Scams tend to follow a pattern and just get dressed up in different guises each year.* The common scams are set out and you will learn the pattern and spot the next one that comes along.

Cutting costs checklist

Let's face it, there is, in reality, little protection against over-charging, and the buck usually stops with you on what you choose to pay for utilities, insurance, phone and TV contracts, and even big transactions like estate agency fees and those university loans that we encourage our children to take out.

Quite often, suppliers rely on lethargy, as there just never seems to be enough time to sit back, start thinking straight and review your main financial transactions. The automatic renewal comes through and you pay up (yet again). Choose any cold, wet winter day and dedicate it to checking all your current deals and contracts and seeing what you can save. Sometimes it will pay for some nights out but if you get good at this it will pay for another holiday.

Insurance

This is potentially one of the biggest areas for a saving. Log your insurance renewal dates: home buildings, home contents, car, pet and any others. Contact them and ask what discounts can be applied to a renewal and then check out their biggest competitor with equivalent policies. Be careful, however, about life and health insurance policies and pet insurance so you don't lose any existing cover for pre-existing conditions.

Utilities

Check with your supplier if you are on their best tariff and compare this to other options via Ofgem-approved comparison sites such as uswitch.com.

TV and broadband bundles

So, who is paying more than £75 a month? This is a hugely competitive market, with Sky, Virgin Media and BT all bidding for your money and Amazon and Netflix providing great entertainment platforms. Compare the deals and make the switch, and there will be dramatic price drops when you tell them you are leaving.

Mobile phones

The costs can mount up if you are paying for the mobiles of yourself, children and/or parents and providers can rely on lethargy. So it is a case of holding back from the early upgrade offer and then just using someone like www.uswitch.com to compare all the current offers on handset, calls and that vital data package and then you call the shots. A simple 5 minute call explaining you have found a better deal will usually see you passed through to the business retention department and you may receive a matched or bettered deal. You should also check for mobile providers who offer data sharing facilities across several mobile phones if you find that children keep going over their data limits - some providers offer this facility which can save you money.

Cash back and air mile credit cards

A quick look at www.moneysavingexpert.com could find you cutting your existing card in half and shifting to someone who will reward you properly. Some even come with neat little complimentary extras.

Pensions, savings and investments

Revisit Chapters 3 and 4 and the pointers on pension, savings and investments and renegotiate fees and account charges. Consider these in line with the quality of the related advice you receive and the returns you receive of dividend, interest, capital growth or other income.

Lost premium bonds or other National Savings and Investment

These can be traced via mylostaccount.org.uk.

Overpay your mortgage

Mortgages usually cost more than savings interest can earn. Assess whether you can start over-paying on your monthly mortgage payments without penalty and save money. Another trick is to move your monthly payment earlier in the month and the effect can mount up to more money saved.

Estate agent fees

If selling your home compare and contrast the costs and benefits between an online estate agent and a traditional estate agent as the cost differences can be significant.

If you are selling in a sought after location a local agents knowledge and contacts should not be underestimated.

If you can't save ££ try a change and vote with your feet

Even if savings are marginal remember that business is all about making money and if you are dissatisfied with customer service vote with your feet.

Top Tip
The 'oops, I forgot about that direct debit' moment. This is a must do. Get your bank statements and credit cards statements together and sit down with your partner and check you recognise and can account for all those direct debits and standing orders. Most online banks/phone banking apps can generate a list at the press of a button. If you don't use that club or gym membership, stop paying for it. And definitely do this review with an elderly relative once a year – pounds will be saved.

Recession proof your finances and debts during the Covid-19 pandemic

This year has been a re-set moment for most of us as we deal with unimagined death tolls and the recession that has flowed from the Covid-19 pandemic. The Daily Telegraph devoted its front page on 15 April 2020 to the following headline and sub headlines:

> *"Biggest economic shock in 300 years*
> - *Budget watchdog warns of slump not seen since 1709 if lockdown lasts 3 months*
> - *Unemployment rate could hit 10pc with more than 3.4 million out of work*
> - *Grim forecast intensifies debate when restrictions should be eased."*

The recession and devastation of the hospitality, events, tourism and retail high street has touched most families and caused many to revisit our personal/family budget and take steps to recession proof our finances. This checklist will help you and yours whilst we await a vaccine that will help us redefine our lives again. These are the toughest of times for some of us that don't have any work and may have missed out on government help.

1. Revisit Chapter 1, Your Plan and the financial budget you created. The starting point is to ensure you do this annual budget and then work out what you 'need' rather than just want. Remember the budget needs the sanity check I mention at Chapter 1. It also must cover a full year as it's the 'one offs' that always spoil a budget and most people underestimate their spending if they try to 'guess this'. Follow my approach and you'll have a good budget and just take it from there.

2. Clear or reduce your credit card or loan debts and if you are in arrears agree payment plans with the lenders or 'payment holidays'. Don't borrow more to try and solve your problems. If you are worried about debt the concern is made worse by keeping the worries to yourself. Talk with Step Change, the national debt charity, to get help with your options via www.stepchange.org and things will start to get better. If you are on Universal Credit review this and, for instance, see if you can get a temporary uplift in your universal credit allowances. Check if you are eligible for any benefits or grants at www.turn2us.org.uk.

3. Look at ways of earning a bit more (see the 'earn more' chapters of this book) or maybe it's just having a big clear out and selling off stuff you don't need via ebay, facebook marketplace or local sales.

4. Don't make impulsive bargain buys. Ignore discounts and special offers. All that matters if you are in a hole is '*do you actually need it and is the end price worth it.*"

5. Try using cheaper retail stores.

6. Know your consumer rights. If goods are faulty or not as described, the buyer should take it back for a refund. If you buy online you usually have 14 days under the Consumer Contracts Regulations to return the goods provided you have not broken the seal or it is perishable/personalised. Keep your receipts. You can find out more at www.which.co.uk and their consumer rights section.

7. Later in this chapter you will read about Section 75 and chargeback protection if you use a credit card or debit card to make a purchase. There is

also some protection by using paypal. Try to stick to these payment routines for some added protection.

8. You can check if your redundancy is fair and get help with this traumatic event at www.citizensadvice.org.uk (leaving a job section).

Fobbed off - complaints and how to complain

Things in life inevitably go wrong and sometimes you lose out when it was not your fault. It is always satisfying when you explain your complaint and an organization says:

'We are really sorry for the inconvenience we have caused you. Thank you for taking the time to set out your concerns. We have now fixed the issue and it will not happen again and we would like you to accept a bunch of flowers as our way of saying sorry.'

This sort of response is rare and we find it irritating the way more and more companies hide behind websites and make it almost impossible to find someone to speak to directly. Perhaps some businesses will see the benefit of reverting to two-way communications and proper customer care. You should expect justice, fairness, equality and accountability – the mantra of the radical lawyer Michael Mansfield, QC and this chapter will help you achieve this.

You have the right to complain and expect justice, fairness, equality and accountability

When something goes wrong, contact the firm or organisation responsible straight away and give them a chance to sort out the problem. Clearly state your complaint. Spend time thinking about this beforehand so that you can be clear and concise about what has happened and, more importantly, what you expect. If you are vague and unclear when you complain then you can expect a vague and unclear reply. If you want an apology, say this and say why. If you want compensation, state how much and why.

Your first port of call for assistance and back-up is usually The Consumer Rights

Act 2015. It came into effect on 1 October 2015 and covers what should happen when goods are faulty, services don't match up to what was agreed, or the service was not handled with reasonable care and skill. It also covers unfair terms in a contract, and extensions to existing laws brought in coverage of digital content (such as online films and games). For more details, including summaries of your rights, use www.citizensadvice.org.uk and go to 'The Consumer Rights Act 2015'.

Some complaint process tactics used by some organisations

- *Ignore.* Your concern is not responded to.

- *Prevaricate.* This is delayed responses, being passed from person to person and having to go over the specifics of your concern again and again.

- *Avoid.* Any response merely states their position and avoids dealing with the specifics you have set out.

- *Deflect.* Where they seek to shift the issue to a different point/person.

This is all about you recognising the tactic and then dealing with it.

Up the ante - 'formal complaint'

When you complain, keep a note of who you spoke to, the date and time, and what they said will happen next and by when. Put your complaint in writing. If the issue is not resolved or you encounter the tactics employed as outlined above, take steps to make it a formal complaint. Ask the organisation for the name, address, telephone number and email of the person or department that deals with complaints. Write a letter or email and head it up 'FORMAL COMPLAINT' quoting any reference you have. Spend time getting it factually correct and attach supporting evidence. If it goes beyond two pages it sounds like you could be rambling. Don't worry – we all do this when we feel aggrieved. But it probably means you need to set it aside and come back to it with a clearer head, re-read it and relegate some information to an attachment. Send it by email and ask for confirmation of receipt by return, or send by recorded delivery and keep a copy, together with the post office tracking receipt.

Take the case further if the organisation rejects your complaint and you believe they have not addressed your concerns trying something like:

Dear [name]

FORMAL COMPLAINT: Your ref [reference]

X weeks have now passed and I am dissatisfied with the way you have handled my complaint. Please let me have a copy of your complaints policy and if you have not got one please let me know how I may escalate my complaint within your organisation. Please also let me know of any ombudsman scheme, arbitration service or suchlike that I may go to outside your organisation if I continue to remain dissatisfied about the complaint that I first put to you on [date].

Yours

[your name]

Some organisations will try to get rid of you by sending you a 'go away' letter saying that they have 'fully considered' your complaint and have now exhausted all opportunities to reach a conclusion. The punchline is that they will no longer respond to any further letters or communications from you and they will close their file. At this stage it is up to you to decide whether to give up (that is what they want) or take if further.

Up the ante again - 'obtain your complaint file'

There is a very useful route that few people know about and most big companies have to sign up to. This should help you exert pressure and probe a little further before considering the next step. And it really is simple. Just ask for a copy of your complaint file including all internal notes, telephone transcripts, manager review notes and any other document bearing your name. State the request is made under the General Data Protection Regulations (basically a new improved Data Protection Act 1988) and is a subject access request. State that your request should be passed immediately to their Data Protection Officer. The information has to be supplied to you within a month and provided for free. When you have your complaint file review how they have considered your complaint; have they gone back to get the other side of the story to ensure 'fairness' and is it correct; have the other side said anything that is unfair or untrue or made derogatory statements about you.

Sometimes firms may blank out (or 'redact') parts of their files and there are strict rules about what can and cannot be redacted. If you believe information has been unfairly redacted you have a right of appeal to the organisation that oversees fair play. The Information Commissioners Office (ICO) have lots of helpful information and template letters that can help you access your personal information at www.ico.org.uk – go to 'for the public'.

Up the ante again- 'pull in some free help with clout'

It is then time to consider some final routes if you feel you feel you are not receiving justice, fairness, equality and accountability. Some organisations have independent assessors and their service is completely free (for instance, Companies House and other quasi-government agencies). Some have a free ombudsman service (banks, financial advisers and estate agents as we have signposted below). Others have regulating bodies (solicitors, surveyors and chartered accountants) that may be able to intervene on your behalf. Others have oversight organizations such as Ofcom (mobile phones) or Ofgem (utilities). The route to accessing the relevant organisation should be in the firm's complaint policy. If not try googling complaints about [name of firm] to see if that can provide a pointer.

Other help

Another useful route is to consider if mediation, arbitration or conciliation services are possible. These routes are referred to as 'alternative dispute resolution'. For instance, the National Conciliation Service handles issues about vehicles (including service and repairs) and can be found at www.nationalconciliationservice.co.uk (there is also www.themotorombudsman.org for resolving motor disputes). Then there is the ABTA arbitration scheme which deals with alleged breaches of contract and/or negligence between consumers and members of ABTA, the travel organisation, and has been in operation for over 40 years.

These schemes are provided so that consumers can have disputes resolved without having to go to court and without having to go to the expense of instructing solicitors. It is important to understand that some are a legal process, which means that if you do go through the process but are not happy with the outcome you cannot then go to court. You have to choose one or the other when pursuing your complaint. Alternative dispute resolution is extending its reach following the Consumer Rights Act 2015 and if you are in dispute with a business they will now need to make you aware of the relevant certified alternative dispute resolution provider.

You are not alone; Citizens Advice may know if there is an alternative dispute resolution process available for your complaint and it also has very useful template letters and advice for complainants at www.citizensadvice.org.uk or give them a call on 03454 040506.

If there is no external organisation, you could choose to use a complaints management service. These charge a fee so make sure you understand the costs you will have to pay. You could also consider legal proceedings so remember the costs you will pay include the other side's costs if the court decides you are wrong. There is a 'do it yourself' service via the County Court online (www.gov.uk and go to 'make a court claim for money').

Finally - vote with your feet

The final tip is to consider whether or not your complaint is really worth the effort of pursuing or do you just vote with your feet and go elsewhere – and tell your friends about it?

Stay safe from the scammers

The scammers seem to be everywhere these days. At your front door, on the phone and everywhere on the internet. The following section will save you more and you will achieve a better retirement if you tool up with the tips below and stay safe from the scammers.

The five golden rules for staying safe from scammers

Trust your instincts

It's a simple common-sense approach: ignore the smoke and mirrors and sleight of hand that crooks and scammers are so capable of pulling off that are used to distract you from the real issue. Does it look, feel, and 'smell' like something is not quite right? Does it get your hackles up? If so, trust your instincts and walk away, put the letter in the bin or put down the phone, shut the door or make an excuse and walk away/leave. Instincts have been honed in the human species over thousands of years – if they have served you well in the past, learn to trust them.

Actions speak louder than words

Scammers, generally, are all talk (unsurprisingly, they are very good at it) and no action. It should also come as no surprise that they are also charming and 'nice and friendly'. So here's the nub of the issue as, quite simply, any reasonable person should be able to deliver against what they promise or apologise and explain before you have to ask, 'what's going on?' If the actions don't happen just walk away and don't give them a second chance to take advantage of you. If some reasonable questions (it's good to ask and ask) provoke a hint of aggression or anything to put you down then that should tell you all you need to know. Remember the motto - its actions that count not words.

Too good to be true?

Scammers know that greed often gets the better of many people and employ it to their advantage. If it sounds too good to be true, it is probably a scam. Put down the phone, shut the door or make an excuse and walk away/leave.

Thank you, but I'll just check with...

We have great financial institutions in the United Kingdom and this goes to the very heart of the UK economy. Our regulatory system is sound. You should therefore check precisely who you are dealing with, and if it involves big money or risk ensure you are dealing with a professional adviser. For anything to do with savings, investments and pensions you must check that the firm is regulated by the Financial Conduct Authority at www.fca.org.uk.

Sometimes individuals hide behind the cloak of a firm or a company. If the company is not a high-street name you can do some free and easy research at Companies House. Go to 'Companies House' then 'find company information', then 'start' and enter the company name or unique number in the 'search the register' box and then look at the filing history documents (which has lots of juicy detail). Check how long it has been in existence and whether it has filed its accounts on time. Both can flag up warning signs and accessing the service is completely free and really easy to do.

Also linked to the 'I'll just check with...' tip is the simple fact that crooks have one other objective in addition to taking your hard-earned cash – and that is not getting caught out. This is where nosy neighbours are brilliant – a stroll over, a smile, a look in the eye and a few questions (after talking about the weather for 10 seconds!) can be of great assistance armed with tip number one, 'trust your instincts'.

If in doubt, stay out

Over the last decade the online world has gained a reach into our lives, our information and our wealth. Regulation has not been able to keep up to date to protect us as, literally, anyone, anywhere in the world can reach us and interact with us online. We really must accept that, to a large extent, it's up to us how much we use the online world acknowledging that everyone (including the government) is encouraging us to use it. For safety follow the golden rule - if in doubt stay out. That means if your browser does not display the 'secure' green padlock on the site you are looking at you have no protection. It means you keep people out by knowing and checking your profile settings on social media.

Share this with Granny

If you only do one thing as a result of this chapter, do this: require any elderly friend or relative to learn the above tips and read this chapter as the scammers prey on those that are alone or vulnerable and giving them the knowledge and confidence of your complete support is one of best things you could give.

Some common scams

Amazing concert tickets, beautiful holiday cottage – and it's all make believe

We probably know the reputable ticket resale sites and bona fide sites where you can get holiday accommodation. So why oh why do folk think they have found a bargain and then just send some crook in a suit money. Hey presto and, just like a magician, the scammer, concert ticket and holiday accommodation has disappeared. Stick to the reputable sites and if you do think you have a found a bargain, and it really is too good to be true, the acid test is in the payment route.

The warning bells have a range of sounds. They range from a non-bank transfer overseas (the alarm bells are sounding so loudly we can't sleep) to a bank transfer (still not good and a very uncomfortable night's sleep) and we only really settle down when they take a credit card payment and it is over the value of £100 (great, a good night's sleep). This is because if you pay for something costing between £100 and £30,000 on credit then the credit provider is equally liable if something goes wrong. If you want the details this comes from **Section 75 of the Consumer Credit Act 1974** which gives us the shorthand of a 'Section 75 claim'.

Payments by debit card get an honourable mention due to a process called **'chargeback'**. It works by you contacting the bank and stating: 'I want to chargeback the (describe transaction, amount and date) of the original debit card payment'. Importantly the request must be made with 120 days of the original transaction (this may not work for holiday accommodation or tickets booked more than 120 days in advance and you find out it was all a scam too late). Chargeback is usually used where goods do not show up, are damaged or differ from the description (i.e. breach of contract-type claims). If the bank rejects your claim you can appeal to the Financial Ombudsman (details below) to have your case reviewed.

Hackers

Your bank, solicitor or other trusted professional will email you to finalise payment of a transaction you currently have in progress. You diligently follow their instructions but end up being scammed and losing it all – perhaps a six figure sum if it was a house deposit. So how did that happen? The world of the internet had been hacked and someone, somewhere in the world identified your transaction was in progress and the parties involved. They simply created bogus emails drawing on the bank, solicitor or other professionals publicly accessible information and with a bit of clever graphic design and amending their real email so that it somehow displays in your email account as having come from the bank, solicitor or other professional. In some case the individual's account has been hacked so it comes from their genuine account. You duly make the payment. Unfortunately the scammer has set up bank accounts in the UK with false ID and the payment is cleared out and 'gone' before anyone has worked out what has really happened.

A variant is a scammer impersonating a regular supplier (to you individually or to your business) stating that they had changed their bank details and requesting the recipient amend their records.

To counter these attacks ensure your anti-virus software is up to date, use extra secure passwords (see below for more on this) and, on emailed bank details, call the firm and secure confirmation from two different people.

Other Email scammers and 'hooks' on apps on your phone

The ingenuity and creativity of email and phone scammers is reaching new heights. Someone somewhere has gathered thousands of email addresses, including yours, and mass-mails them with a piece of information – designed with only one purpose in mind. That purpose is to gain your attention and engagement and a 'click' on their planted dodgy button/link etc. All scam emails end up the same way, which is you losing out. Maybe they offer a refund from HMRC or purport to be a bank indicating that the security of your account has been compromised. It could be a fairly credible-looking court summons or something that looks like a Facebook friend request (but you are already Facebook friends so that seems a bit strange). The emails all have one purpose and one purpose only and that is to get you to 'click on a link'. The same applies to pop ups and adverts you may see on your phone. Here the scammers know your browsing habits and lure you with a fake advert whilst you are browsing a site or an app. The site you are taken to may be fake even though it has been designed very professionally and looks like it is representing your cherished brand or interest. You are lured with an offer, click, enter your bank details and the rest, as they say, is history. Unfortunately, the reality is that the message you received or saw has been built by scammers and they want to steal your money.

Top tip

Never, never, never click on any links from strange email accounts, or offers you see whilst you are browsing on your phone unless you are sure it is the real thing. If in doubt check it out with the organisation directly – hover over the displayed email address to show the actual email account the scammer. 'If in doubt, stay out'. On websites check the padlock sign by the website address (secure site) and you will be safer.

Generally try to protect yourself by restricting yourself to known organisations and deal directly with their websites and look for the secure 'padlock' symbol in the browser. If it is a UK business they must clearly show the company or business operating the website (usually in the 'contact us' or 'about us' section), which you can then check out. If it is a company and it is not a high-street name check out the company at Companies House as suggested in the 'thank you I will just check with' section above – the service is free. The watchwords here are 'If in doubt, stay out'.

The surprise prize-ballot win

There is usually a premium-rate telephone number to call in order to claim the prize or a fairly small-value payment to make but at the end of the day, and after much excitement, the ultimate actual prize is probably worthless or trivial. File anything like this under 'B' for bin. It is, however, sometimes fun to read the small print in such 'prizes' in order to spot the scam or the impossibility of winning the supposed big prize. This is how it works: there will be a few flashy big prizes (always something eye-catching to get you excited) and then other prizes for which there may be 5,000 or more 'winners' and will probably take you more than £10 in phone or other 'processing' charges to 'win'. In reality your chances of winning are remote and cunningly the scammers do not state the odds of actually winning. Watch out for words such as 'your assigned numbers could match', which means you may not have won anything at all and what you have is just a chance to enter some sort of ballot. The scammers rely on you getting distracted by the official-looking paperwork and the mention of prizes - the equivalent of the magician's smoke and mirror distractions mentioned earlier. As a final deterrent, if you are foolish enough to reply to something you didn't enter in the first place you are likely to be put on a 'suckers list' (the term the scammers use) and will be bombarded by even more junk ballots and scams.

Credit and bank card cloning or snatching

This can be the jackpot for the scammers, but how can they actually get your credit or bank card? The cloning devices that they attach to a bank's cash machine are not so far-fetched these days. But how about the scammer who calls you and pretends to be from the police, explaining they have just arrested someone who 'apparently' was caught with a clone of your card? They arrange for a courier to call and collect your actual card as part of their investigations. Unfortunately, it is all just another scam and the supposed police officer is just another scammer. These guys really do have guts but the bottom line is never, ever, be worried about feeling made to look silly.

Top tip

Don't be worried about being made to look silly and just act confused; ask them to write down exactly what they want so you can show it to your daughter/neighbour etc. If they won't and they tell you it's a secret then they are lying.

Advance fee fraud

This is one of the scammers' favourites and has been dressed up in a hundred different guises. The scam is remarkably simple. A payment is made by you with the promise of a bigger payout in return. Perhaps it is cloaked in terms of funds left to you by a mystery relative, where you pay a processing fee of £50, then maybe you are asked to pay another release fee of £150 and on it goes with a promise of £10,000 sucking you in (which, of course, you will never actually receive). Walk away.

Doorstep scams

National Trading Standards tell us that 85 per cent of victims of doorstep scams are aged 65 or over. These scams follow a regular routine. A knock on the door and a stranger. There is a request (Can I use the phone as it is an emergency? I noticed a broken window/broken roof tile/there is a gas leak or water leak etc.). Once inside the crook will distract you whilst their sidekick steals something, or else they provide some emergency service and then overcharge you. Remember you don't have to answer the door and always use a door chain and fit a spy hole on solid doors. Trust your instincts, ask for ID and if unsure ask them to return at a later time when someone will be with you. Again, this is where 'nosy neighbours' are brilliant so look out for each other.

Romance, dating fraud and sextortion

The new lover, or someone showing you interest, gives you attention you crave just when you may need it (maybe you are at a low point – remember, these scammers are clever crooks in suits). After a while the sob stories start – maybe money for a sick mother or child. Scammers know how to manipulate you to get the response they want. They usually want you to keep things 'secret' as they know that any friend you confide in will tell you to run a mile. Sadly, emotional involvement and shame prevent some people from acting rationally – and the scammers know this. Charming chat, sleight of hand and, just like a magician, your money is gone before you know it. A more extreme version is sextortion where blackmailers (organised crime, sometimes using entrapment) believe they have information on you which they threaten to disclose to compromise you. They want cash or a favour in return.

Top tip

Romance scams – trust your instincts when you smell a rat. Be brave and confide in someone you really trust and call in the Police. The Police have specialist teams to deal with organised crime based blackmail.

Call in the police

If you spot a scam or have been scammed, report it and get help. Contact the Police Action Fraud contact centre on 0300 123 2040 or online at www.actionfraud.police.uk, or contact the police in your area. If a crime is in progress or about to happen, the suspect is known or can be easily identified, or the crime involves a vulnerable victim, then dial 999 if it is an emergency or 101 if it isn't. For more information, take a look at the Police guidance the *Little Book of Big Scams*: visit www.met.police.uk and go to 'The Little Book of Big Scams' – I think it is an absolutely top piece of work. Advice about scam mail can be found at www.thinkjessica.com.

Keeping safe from telephone cold calls and online fraud

Cold callers on the telephone can be irritating at best and sometimes downright scary. They may not take 'no' for an answer. The way these calls are intruding into our life is becoming a real problem. The Telephone Preference Service (TPS) is a free service. It is the official central opt-out register on which you can record your preference not to receive unsolicited sales or marketing calls. It is a legal requirement that all organisations (including charities, voluntary organisations and political parties) do not make such calls to numbers registered on the TPS unless they have your consent to do so.

Premium rate phone call scams

A text message, email or even a missed parcel note or debt collector note through the door (clever eh!) asks you to call a phone number (and then insert some words that lure you... take your pick - a threat (debt collector), a prize, free holiday, free meal, free shopping voucher, missed parcel etc.). Always google the precise phone number as thankfully folk report scam numbers and log why and what happened on the internet and you will get the answer fairly quickly and you can then put it in the genuine pot (rare) or scam bin. The scam numbers are at extortionate rates and you'll lose out. They sometimes leave partial messages on your phone to lure you into being intrigued and you then call their premium rate number - clever eh?

Anti-virus software

Keep your anti-virus software up to date. There are free options such as AVG free (www.avg.com). For free online security advice, visit www.getsafeonline.org.

Have a backup

What happens if your laptop/other device is stolen or you get hacked and your data is stolen and then wiped. Take a secure back up on devices such as Apple's icloud or external hard drives or a USB flash drive.

Review and change you social media profile settings

We expose a massive amount of personal information on social media without locking out the bad boys and girls. Ensure your privacy settings are as you would want - usually friends only. Don't overlook this in Chapter 12, Your Plan, especially if you are about to post photos online showing you are thousands of miles from your home on holiday.

The worst passwords

This almost beggars belief, but Nordpass report the worst passwords each year, and the worst and most-used nightmare password in 2020 was 123456. Your password should be, where allowed, at least 12 digits long, contain a mix of upper- and lower-case letters, numbers and a character. Remember to password-protect your smart phone as there is probably more information on that device than can be obtained from breaking into your house. Only download apps from trusted sites such as Apple (www.apple.com/uk). If you sell or dispose of your phone, always clean it by restoring factory settings to blank it and remove media cards (younger relatives can show you how to do this if need be), or smash it to pieces.

Top tip

The easiest way to spot that you've been scammed is to know your finances inside out. Watching what goes in and out of your bank and credit cards will show up a problem quickly.

Top tip

Trust your instincts. If something doesn't feel right it's probably because it isn't.

Useful reading

Martin Lewis's website, www.moneysavingexpert.com

There are many useful template letters and advice for complainants at www.citizensadvice.org.uk or give them a call on 03454 040506.

The Little Book of Big Scams, published by the Metropolitan Police Service at www.met.police.uk – go to 'The Little Book of Big Scams'.

BBC's *Rip Off Britain* – go to www.bbc.co.uk, search for 'Rip Off Britain'

For free online security advice visit www.getsafeonline.org.

Citizens Advice: www.citizensadvice.org.uk and their 'scams' section.

Reminder: Take any action points or follow up points to Chapter 12, Your Plan For A Better Retirement

Chapter Seven

Starting your own business

"Screw it – let's do it!"

S<small>IR</small> R<small>ICHARD</small> B<small>RANSON</small>

More and more people are setting up their own business and becoming their own boss for reasons of personal freedom but in the current Covid-19 pandemic more people may turn to this as an option as the job market contracts. Running a business can carry additional risk and if things go badly wrong you could, at worst, lose your home. But on the other hand it can be rewarding, or a release route from a corporate environment or maybe it's just the opportunity to earn £1,000 per annum tax free to supplement your pension income. It can also keep you earning and occupied for years to come beyond your intended retirement date and, therefore, it is the first chapter within the 'earn more' essential step of retirement planning in my book. As a brief recap the core of this book is based around the four essential steps to achieving a better retirement: plan more, save more, earn more and live better.

If you have dived straight into this chapter looking to find your first piece of inspiration the biggest message of reassurance is, simply, you are not alone. According to the Department for Business, Energy and Industrial Strategy there were 5.9 million private-sector businesses in 2019, which is a massive 2.4 million more than in 2000. 59% trade as sole proprietorships (sometimes called the self-employed), 33% trade as companies and 7% are partnerships. These terms are explained in more detail in this chapter to help you decide which could be right for you. But for now the main message is that one or two person businesses are the absolute back-bone of the UK economy and are growing in number. Even better there is plenty of help out there – you will not be alone and this chapter will signpost you to free help and support (it is just a matter of knowing where to look to find the quality material!). This chapter goes to the heart of this book as prosperity is not just about material wealth it's also about what we get out of everyday life through the social and emotional benefits. It may also be a route to escaping corporate structures when there is still time to learn a new trick or two and, therefore, could be another option to help you save more / earn better in this section of the book.

Importantly, this chapter is only a guide and it is neither legal nor taxation advice. Any potential tax advantages may be subject to change from the position as at summer 2020 and will depend upon your individual circumstances, so individual professional advice should be obtained. The information outlined in this chapter may, however, assist you in understanding some of the issues you may face and the terminology used, helping you in planning for and achieving a better retirement.

This chapter at a glance

This chapter will give you the confidence to get started and provide plenty of straightforward advice. The key issues covered are:

- A one page quick-start guide (you can get going today if you want!).
- Understanding the differences between starting a small business and employment, especially if both options are still open to you.
- Help with the question: 'Do I really need to bother with a business plan?'
- Administration, finance and tax – keep on top of the paperwork or it will keep on top of you!
- Filling the diary with work, and some clever tips for marketing that will make a difference.
- The trading format and understanding personal risk – should you set up your own limited liability company, work as a sole trader or maybe go into partnership?
- Other ways of getting started and some operational issues.
- Where you can go for further help – remember you are not alone and these are enterprising times in the United Kingdom.
- A summary checklist to help you get started in business.

How to start a small business today in 1 page

This one page will get you on the way to starting a small business:

- Find something you enjoy doing that you know you can sell.

- Grab all the free help you can from your local enterprise partnership or equivalent (signposts are in this book).

- Register as self-employed with Her Majesty's Revenue & Customs (HMRC) via www.gov.uk (then go to 'working for yourself'). Complete HMRC's self-assessment form each year and declare your business taxable income (if it is above £1,000).

- Acquire some files and keep a list of your income and costs and all receipts. If it 'proves' your business transactions, you must keep it for six years.

- The big lesson: HMRC don't like people evading tax (it is illegal!). If you can't prove your transactions then you will be charged the tax that HMRC believe they were due, plus a penalty of up to an extra 200 per cent plus interest.

- Think really carefully about risk – as a self-employed person your personal wealth is backing your business and anything that goes wrong. If you are worried about risk then investigate and take out appropriate insurance and don't start trading until this is in place. If risk is potentially significant don't trade as self-employed but do look into the benefits of having a limited company (more in this chapter).

- Take a deep breath and start living your new business. Involve yourself with other people who run their own businesses and listen and learn from them. Join the best business club or organisation that you can find; a Federation of Small Business membership should be on your short list but listen to other recommendations from other business owners who you know and respect.

- Make sure that you can sell your product or service for more than it costs – do the numbers and remember to think about marketing, packaging and transport costs/postage and then 'administration/office costs'. To help your business grow further just jump to the marketing section in this chapter. The tips should take you to the next level and, in time, you may benefit from delving into even more of this chapter and its hints and tips.

The secret ingredients

There is a one great big secret ingredient for starting your own business and potentially bringing in a vital extra income and it's actually quite simple: it is the 'belief/can do' and positive attitude of the business owner. They have the ability to press on with their ambition and deliver on the goal they have set themselves. They involve others and are good at listening to those who can help (usually those who have experience of running their own successful businesses and professional advisers (their accountant and solicitor). However, they recognise, at the end of the day, that it's 100% down to them and get on with it using a timescale plan. The businesses that falter seem to do the opposite of this and never quite reach their potential. There are then three other secret ingredients, as follows:

Understanding and accepting the differences between starting a small business and employment

In some cases where there is an opportunity to start a small business there could be a similar opportunity to take a full- or part-time employed position. Make sure you are content with the route you are going down and that it's the right route t for you?

Here are some of the main reasons for starting a small business:

- focusing on what you are best at or enjoy;
- being your own boss and therefore benefiting from very rapid decision making;
- flexibility (around other interests/responsibilities);
- freedom to organise things your way;
- no commuting;
- less involvement in internal politics and no more attending meetings that you have started to believe were becoming a bit pointless;
- being able to work on your own;
- developing a unique idea or delivering a better solution/product;
- providing a legacy for your children;

- the more you put in, the more you get out.

On the other hand, here are some of the reasons for seeking a part- or full-time employed position:

- having a local employer with known travel requirements;
- security of income;
- benefits of holiday pay, pension, paid sick leave, and perhaps private health and life cover;
- bonuses;
- having a team and the friendship of colleagues;
- no personal liability if things go badly wrong;
- staff discounts or other perks.

Having a decent written business plan

There are thousands of success stories about those who took the plunge to build a business that provided involvement, enjoyment and a new or extra income. However, for every three success stories there is a business that does not work out and your money could disappear fast if you set up in the wrong way or overstretch yourself. Worst of all, you could lose your home if things go badly wrong. So, yes, you need some form of a plan and information below and tips throughout this chapter should help you plan and also help you understand and deal with the risks.

Learning from history on why businesses fail

Businesses can fail for many reasons. Learn from the mistakes of others. From my experience working in Corporate Recovery and Insolvency in the 1989 to 1993 recession I see many factors that remain the same today as we enter another recession. The first one is simply that *the market dries up or moves on and you are left behind*. Just look at fashion retail where many of the big traditional stores can't complete with the more agile online new entrants. Covid-19 and locked shops, high rents and reduced takings will take their toll on the traditionals whilst their more agile competitors adapt and thrive. The basics remain the same as in 1989 to 1993 - take time out to think and keep abreast of what your customers really want (have you tried asking them?). Then where are your competitors and what are they doing to keep on top of or ahead of the market and, overall, how is the market moving?

A second reason (and one that will continue to increase in 2021) is the *failure to deal with tax affairs properly*. The implications of penalties and interest levied by HMRC are often ignored and only hit home when it is too late. Keep your books properly and retain all records for six years after the year end – in brief, if you can't prove it, you may lose the tax benefit and pay additional tax, penalties and interest. If there is a problem, HMRC can go back and inspect previous years' accounts (for up to six years or even longer). There are currently opportunities to postpone paying some of your business taxes due to the impact of the Covid-19 pandemic but if, ultimately, you fail to pay your tax fully when it is due, HMRC will pursue you vigorously and you are giving them a reason to have a closer look at you and your business. On the other hand, if you have genuine cash flow difficulties and cannot pay your tax on the due date, talk to HMRC and you may find their attitude refreshing (especially if it is your first time of asking).

Other reasons include a failure to plan and also bad debts – if a customer goes bust and cannot pay your invoices, this will come off your bottom-line profit and can really hurt. There are a few simple steps that you can take to reduce the potential of taking such a hit. What are your credit terms and have you encouraged all customers to pay electronically? Do you contact them as soon as your invoices become overdue? Require cash on delivery or prepayment if there are some worrying signs emerging and do trust your instincts here. PayPal and mobile credit card machines are transforming payment services. In some cases it is worth remembering that a bad customer is sometimes worse than no customer at all.

In today's environment and if struggling financially it is also about doing *a top down cost review* based on your expenditure pattern- do you absolutely need to spend the money? Is there a better or cheaper option and talk things with your accountant and any advisers. Let's return to the question: 'Do I really need to bother with a business plan?' The answer is usually 'yes', even if it is just one page, as you are improving your chances of succeeding and may even do rather better than you first thought.

Covid-19 pandemic help and support

During the current Covid-19 pandemic the hospitality, events and tourism sector has been severely damaged with high street retail also taking the hardest of hits. Writing in Autumn 2020 there is no clear pathway to exiting the state of lockdowns and tiers. Various government packages have been implemented to help business owners. At the moment you need to understand and source free money (grants), assistance and tax payment extensions. It's all about trying to make the best of a tough time and adapting until things improve. The main headline issues and help are as follows:

1. Making your workplace Covid secure.
2. Furlough pay for staff unable to work.
3. Job retention scheme.
4. Kick-start scheme for creating jobs.
5. Self-employed income support scheme
6. Deferring your 2nd payment on account of self-assessed tax that was due on 31 July 2020 until up to 31 January 2021.
7. Deferring part of your VAT due.
8. Reduced rate of VAT (5%) on hospitality, holiday accommodation and attractions (presently until 31 March 2021).
9. Deferring corporation tax payments.
10. Business rates relief.
11. Grants for certain closed businesses (due to national restrictions)
12. Discretionary grants from local authorities
13. Coronavirus Business Interruption Loan Scheme
14. Coronavirus Bounce back loans (up to £50,000 or 25% of your turnover if lower).

All of the basic information as a national level is at www.gov.uk/coronavirus/business-support where there are then pointers to help within England, Scotland, Wales and Northern Ireland. After that search for support at your local level for other help especially discretionary grants which appear to pop up and may just help you get through until Easter 2021 when I hope we will all be in a better place.

Covid-19 pandemic – stop and start doing list

During the current Covid-19 pandemic some agile businesses will prosper and others will decline or fall away. The key is to adapt and thrive and think about how you can be a better business once a vaccine is available and distributed. I think this points to assessing what you need to stop doing and start doing. Here are my 10 suggestions based on three decades of experience in helping small businesses.

Stop doing

1. Worrying too much about some apparent discrepancies in government support. Grab what you can and keep watching for up-dates and announcements on the pointers I have listed above at the sites I've signposted.
2. Paying for things you don't need.

Start doing

1. Review and act on all government and local authority grants (free money) or support via tax deferring or loan assistance as I've signposted.
2. Check what your Local Enterprise Partnership (in England) can do for you. Regional or country-specific support is available at:

   - England: The Local Enterprise Partnership at www.lepnetwork.net;
   - Northern Ireland: www.nibusinessinfo.co.uk;
   - Scotland: www.mygov.scot/business;
   - Wales: www.business.wales.gov.uk.

3. Turn old stock into cash by offers/discounts and deals.
4. Form a plan and review it with your accountant and any advisers.
5. Provide more training for your staff so they are more tooled up and agile when (and as) things pick up.
6. What new technologies can you adopt to deliver better goods/services?
7. Recheck what your customers really want and adapt your business to this.
8. Re-appraise your products/services- how can they be differentiated to add more value or strip out cost and provide a cheaper option. How can they be delivered faster/ more efficiently? Use the time you have to adapt and

thrive and then become a better business.

What goes into a business plan?

'I have always found that plans are useless but planning is indispensable.' This is a quote from General Eisenhower and is about planning for battle. Pause and take in the wise words 'planning is indispensable', as too many people run a mile when the subject of a business plan comes up. Or, armed with confidence gained from a book on setting up a business, you may start a plan but never get it finished. The reason for this 'block' is usually fear of the planning process or feeling intimidated by daunting business plan templates and spreadsheets seen in some books or banking literature.

So try this. If you want to travel somewhere you use a map. In business it's just the same except you get yourself a *plan*. Do write it down and don't expect to get it right first time (no one does!). A few pages are fine to start with based on objectives, your market research and a budget for the year (accountants call this a profit-and-loss forecast). Review it with your accountant and/or a trusted friend who runs a business, then build it up.

Top tip

Have some sort of thought-out plan when you start and keep refreshing it. With experience you can tweak it and make it that bit slicker but you must put it down in writing.

Stage 1 of the plan: Objectives

What, financially, do you need to set as objectives to bring you in that £2,000 or £20,000 or £60,000 you need to help reach and attain the lifestyle you desire? This takes a bit of thinking through but you should be able to come up with two or three simple objectives based on income, gross profit (if you sell stock) and overheads.

As an example for someone who sells advice-based services and who does not sell stock it's easy and you only need two objectives.

Objective 1: I aim to invoice £30,000 in my first year of trading based on working at least 100 days at an average billing rate of £300 per day. I will review my billing rates quarterly and my performance monthly.

Objective 2: I aim to keep my overheads (after expenses recharged to clients) in my first year to £5,000.

Then, for the more complicated businesses, for example one that trades in buying and selling stock, you will need a further objective based around the difference between sales price and purchase price.

Objective 3 will be something like: I aim to achieve the following gross profit percentages:

- product line A: 30 per cent;
- product line B: 40 per cent;
- product line C: 50 per cent;
- gross profit percentages are calculated using (sales price less cost of materials/product sold ÷ sales price) × 100.

The key point with objectives is that less gives more: you don't want a long list of objectives and try and ensure each objective is Specific, Measurable, Achievable, Realistic and Timed (or S.M.A.R.T) and you will improve your chances of success.

Stage 2 of the plan: Your market research

The next page of your plan should be all about your marketing effort: this is a topic that is often misunderstood and mistaken for advertising. Think about approaching this section under the following three headings: products, customers and competitors.

Products

Start with your main product or service and think about the features and benefits of what you are selling. Understanding these and discussing them with your trusted advisers will allow you to start thinking about other related services or goods that you could offer.

Customers

For each main product area ask lots of questions to tease out your research. Who are my customers? Where are they based? When do they tend to buy? How and where do they tend to buy and at what price? How should I contact them? Keep asking those important questions of who, what, why, where, when and how – they tease out all sorts of quality research information that you can action.

Competitors

Again, ask yourself who, what, why, where, when and how? This should lead to a series of activities that you can do to help secure new quality work and customers (note that the marketing section later on in this chapter has further tips). If you end up with a jumble of unfocused ideas try ranking each idea on the basis of priority, impact and cost (free is good!).

Stage 3 of the plan: Your income and expenditure forecast

This third stage is the tricky one but hang in there as it is worth pushing your plan to include this: your income and expenditure forecast for the year. It is your financial map and will allow you to check your actual performance against the plan. You can then do something about it when you are off target. You should be able to do this yourself, but if it becomes a struggle ask your accountant or a friend who has their own business to help.

Is there more?

Once you have completed your first plan keep it alive and keep reviewing how you are doing against it and you should find that the planning process itself teases out things that will make things that little bit better – guaranteed!

Practical and emotional tips

Your partner's attitude is crucial. Even if not directly involved, he or she may have to accept (at least initially) the loss of some space in the house to give you an office. Do you have space available to work from home initially? Or as an alternative would you need/prefer to rent accommodation? The rental market has transformed in the last decade with many 'serviced' office providers opening up and renting out space by the hour, day or month on flexible and economic rents. These offices can be great places to meet and network with like-minded small business owners. If you are selling products or crafts google for craft and market events and try negotiating on a first attendance rate so you can try it out as attendances, site pitch and quality can vary.

If you work from home will you need to spend a bit of time managing the expectations of neighbours and/or friends about your new life and 'work hours'?

There will be the added distractions of out-of-hours phone calls and, perhaps, suddenly cancelled social engagements, depending on your business. Can your family/partner cope or help?

Can you cope without the resources/back-up provided by an employer (IT/HR/training/marketing/legal and/or administrative support)? You will have to do it yourself or buy it in at a cost (a potential overhead cost for your business plan).

Running a small business means developing new networks and the network that provides vital practical and emotional support is other like-minded individuals that run their own business, so join the best trade or professional association you can find (there are some listed further on in this chapter).

Keep on top of the paperwork/accounts

Generally, this one topic causes the most groans! But simple bookkeeping, if done properly, is just a by-product of your business and flows naturally from raising sales invoices or receipts to tracking income and tracking what you pay for, when and how. As a bonus, you will never miss an unpaid sales invoice if you are on top of your bookkeeping.

An even more compelling reason for doing your own bookkeeping is the HMRC 'prove it or lose it' viewpoint when enquiring into an aspect of your tax return. Under the system of self-assessment, HMRC relies on you completing your tax returns. In the case of an enquiry, HMRC tells you precisely what part of your tax return is under investigation and you are expected to be able to validate sample payments or receipts. If you are unable to prove the expenditure, you lose it as far as HMRC is concerned, resulting in, for example, fewer purchases being accepted as a deduction from your profits and more tax to pay. There will be penalties and interest to pay and the scope of HMRC's enquiries will be widened, which means more time, distraction from your business and, probably, stress.

Basic bookkeeping

All incoming and outgoing payments need to be recorded throughout the year. Records of outgoings need to be categorised according to type, and examples of some categories you might need to consider are stock, subscriptions/meeting fees, office equipment, office supplies, post and courier costs, travel fares, parking and subsistence, telephone and internet, sundry, accountancy and professional fees, and insurance.

Many small business owners opt to do their own bookkeeping, with or without the help of computer software. If you opt for software choose one that your accountant understands as their fees should be lower. For many small businesses your accountant should be able to provide some Excel spreadsheets that will do the job, together with a bookkeeping guide to help get you started.

If you are really averse to bookkeeping yourself, consider hiring a bookkeeper. Bookkeepers currently charge between about £15 and £25 per hour, depending on geographical location and experience, and can be found by recommendation from your accountant or business network contacts.

Finding a good accountant

Depending on qualifications and experience, accountants can charge from £35 to £120+ per hour (plus vat) to assist you in setting up in business and to prepare your accounts and tax. But as anyone can call themselves an accountant it can be a bit hit and miss, with very variable quality when things go wrong. Unreturned calls and not dealing factually with enquiries and questions, vague verbal assurances, and not dealing with formal complaints are all part of the 'deal' when you choose wrongly. If there are mistakes in your accounts and tax you will also find that you are very much on your own when it comes to dealing with HMRC enquiries.

> **Top tip**
>
> **Don't end up with the wrong accountant. What should you look for? The letters ACA or FCA, ACCA, CIMA after the accountant's name mean that you can be assured that you are dealing with a highly qualified accountant used to commerce but the key is that qualifications, professional indemnity held, any regulating body and complaints procedures should all be set out in writing for you at the start and before you sign up. If not, start shopping around.**

Some accountancy firms offer a combination of bookkeeping, accountancy and tax services and, if so, you can expect to pay a premium on the bookkeeping hourly rates quoted above.

So how can I find a good accountant? Ask your trusted family members or friends if they can recommend one. Then ensure you get clarity on four things:

1) confirmation of the accountant's qualifications (the type of qualifications);
2) the professional body you would complain to if there is ever a problem;
3) confirmation that they hold professional indemnity insurance; and
4) confirmation that they know and understand your business area.

It is advisable to meet at least two accountants and, importantly, see how you feel about rapport and the availability of proactive hints and tips. Make sure you believe you can get on with the accountant you select as it is likely to be a long and mutually beneficial relationship. Ask if the person you meet will be the person who does your accounts and tax and whether they will provide proactive advice. Get written confirmation of hourly rates plus an estimate of fees for the year, and get clarity on what happens if you decide to change accountants halfway through the year if fees are paid up front or monthly. Most accountants should be used to providing clients with a 'retainer', clarifying the above and what you and the accountant will do and by when. Best of all is a good accountant who knows your industry area as they will be able to help with general guidance and offer input to your plan on marketing and pricing, drawing on experience beyond accounting and tax.

Finally, there is sometimes some confusion over the term 'audit of accounts'. Many years ago, smallish companies in the UK had to have an audit of their accounts. The turnover threshold (one of three thresholds) for being required to have an audit has been increased and currently stands at £10.2 million, so the vast majority of start-ups need not concern themselves with audited accounts.

Taxes and National Insurance

There are quite significant differences in the taxes you will pay if you run a small business and, therefore, the different options are worth thinking through before getting started.

Sole traders

Self-employed individuals running their own businesses are usually called 'sole traders'. Nearly all new small businesses that trade as sole traders need to register as self-employed via www.gov.uk (then go to 'working for yourself').

First the good news if you just want to earn an extra £1,000 by doing odd-jobs or gardens in the warmer months to help pay for a holiday. From 1 April 2017 HMRC introduced a new 'trading allowance' for individuals with trading income and you can keep the money and don't have to tell HMRC providing the total income (before costs) is £1,000 or less.

If your trading income is above £1,000 you must register for self-assessment with HMRC and complete a self-assessment tax form and submit this to HMRC each year (www.gov.uk and search 'register for self-assessment'). While tax can be daunting, some sole traders with relatively straightforward billing and overheads do their own self-assessment and pay Income Tax on their profits. With Income Tax, you first have a Personal Allowance, which gives you a tax-free amount, and then any excess income (including your profits) is taxed at 20 per cent, then over a certain limit at 40 per cent and then 45 per cent. In very broad terms you currently (summer 2020) have a tax-free allowance of £12,500.

You are then taxed on the *next* £37,500 at 20 per cent, so for 2020/21 an individual will be able to earn £50,000 before having to pay tax at 40 per cent (i.e. £12,500 Personal Allowance at 0 per cent tax and then £37,500 at 20 per cent). Then 40 per cent tax applies to further taxable income up to £150,000. Anything above £150,000 gets taxed at 45 per cent. The rates are slightly different in Scotland (see the tax chapter).

Many sole traders choose to run their bookkeeping for the year to 5 April to coincide with the tax year end (or 31 March, which HMRC effectively accepts as equivalent to 5 April).

If you are past the state retirement age there will be no National Insurance Contributions (NICs) to pay. Subject to this, sole traders are liable for Class 2 NICs (currently a nominal amount of £3.05 per week). You are also liable for the much more significant Class 4 NICs that are assessed and collected by HMRC at the same time as assessing your Income Tax on profits. Currently (Autumn 2020) these are at 9 per cent on profits between £9,500 and £50,000 reducing to just 2 per cent on profits over £50,000.

The payment of sole-trader Income Tax is reasonably straightforward but there is a twist in your first year of trading. Assuming that you have a year end of 5 April 2021, the first payment will be due by 31 January 2022 so you have a long period of (effectively) interest-free credit, as some of the profits on which the tax is due may have been earned as long ago as May 2020. With the first payment, however, you get a 'double whammy' as you also have to pay on 31 January 2022 a payment on account of your second year's trading. Then on 31 July 2022 you have to make a second on-account payment of the second year's trading. Both on-account payments are set by default on the basis of your year 1 profits. Under-estimate this cash flow impact at your peril as it can hit hard if you don't 'get it'. You can 'claim' a reduction if year 2 is proving to have lower profits than year 1; your accountant will help you with this if it is appropriate.

After the initial tax famine, followed by (effectively) a double payment of tax, you will thereafter pay tax twice a year. Payments need to be made by 31 January (during the tax year) and then by 31 July after the end of that tax year, with any overpayment or underpayment sorted out by the following 31 January. Many sole-trader businesses set up a reserve bank account in addition to their current account, and place a percentage of their income aside, which is earning interest each month (albeit not amounting to much in the current climate). This tactic should help you resist the temptation to raid money that is not for spending – and ensure you can pay your tax on time.

Additionally, as a self-employed person you are allowed certain other reliefs. Ask your accountant, but the following expenses and allowances are usually tax deductible:

- *Business expenses*: These must be incurred 'wholly and exclusively' for the purposes of the trade. Office supplies that you buy will probably qualify; however, any business entertaining will not.

- *Partially allowable expenses*: These mainly apply if you are working from home. They include such items as the part of your rent (or mortgage interest), heating, lighting and telephone usage that you devote to business purposes, and also possibly some of the running expenses on your car, if you use your car for your business.

- *Spouse/partner's wages*: If you employ your spouse/partner in the business, his or her pay (provided this is reasonable) will usually qualify as a legitimate expense, in the same way as any other employee's, but must be accounted for through a PAYE system.

- *Pension contributions*: Tax relief is generally available for pension contributions at the higher of £3,600 (gross) or 100 per cent of relevant earnings up to a maximum of £40,000 (this is subject to a tapered reduction for taxpayers with 'adjusted income' in excess of £150,000). You can go above the £40,000 'maximum' if you have not used the £40,000 maximum in the previous three years and have not reached the lifetime allowance on your pension pots (for most people this is £1,073,100 for 2020/21). You will probably benefit from getting professional advice if there is the potential to make very significant pension contributions and obtain the associated tax reliefs.

- *Capital allowances*: This is a tax break for expenditure on equipment.

Partnerships

Partnership tax is broadly similar to the process described above for a sole trader, with the exception of there being some more paperwork due to submitting each partner's individual personal self-assessment tax return and a composite partnership tax return.

Limited company

Companies pay corporation tax on their profits (currently as of summer 2020 at 19%). Your company accounts need to be finalised and any corporation tax paid nine months after your year end.

The key point with a company is that the money coming in is not your money – it is the company's money – so how do you extract your money?

The first option is salary and this means running a Pay As You Earn (PAYE) system: another form of tax with a rigorous calculation regime and payments that have to be made to HMRC. PAYE carries the Income Tax rates as featured for the sole trader, but NICs (National Insurance contributions) are much higher as these are a composite of employee *and* employer NICs (as the company is an employer). Currently these are 12 per cent employee NICs on salary from £9,500 and £50,000 reducing to 2 per cent for amounts above £50,000 and then an additional 13.8 per cent employer NICs on everything above £9,500. The employer's national insurance is the killer blow if you are a one person company and seems unfair but, currently that's the way it is and drives many to look to a different route to profit extraction involving less salary and more dividends. Salary and employer's NICs are deductible when calculating corporation tax but dividends are not which complicates the scenario and doing the numbers.

The second option for extracting funds is dividends but, repeating for emphasis, these are not deductible when calculating your corporation tax. From April 2016, significant changes were introduced to the dividend tax regime. The change is designed to reduce what the government perceived to be an incentive for companies to extract profits through a dividend. The following was implemented:

- A new annual dividend allowance which has subsequently been reduced to £2,000 that is tax-free in 2020/21.

- The new rates of tax on dividends are 7.5 per cent if the dividend falls in the basic rate tax band, 32.5 per cent if it falls in the higher rate tax band (£50,000 to £150,000) and 38.1 per cent if it falls in the additional rate tax band (£150,000 plus).

For some contracting or consultancy-type businesses that trade as companies there is a 'tax trap' for the unwary known as HMRC regulation number 35 (IR35). HMRC is particularly interested in ex-employees setting up service companies that work exclusively for their former employer or for just a few clients (sometimes called 'personal service companies' to use an HMRC term). This is an extremely wide-ranging and difficult subject but, in very simplified terms, IR35 is to be avoided if at all possible; it only applies to companies (not sole traders). Most contractors/freelancers working on assignments with the public sector (or public-sector quasi-agencies) are likely to be caught by IR35.

There are many hints and tips and some urban myths about IR35, all of which are outside the scope of this guide. It is a big issue and one that you have first got to recognise and then, if potentially applicable, do something about. One of the key players in helping freelancers guide themselves through the minefield of IR35 is the Association of Independent Professionals and the Self-Employed (IPSE) at www.ipse.co.uk. This organisation, working in conjunction with a chartered accountant who understands IR35, is probably your next step if you are concerned. Briefly, if you fall foul of IR35, the tax inspector will seek to set aside the dividends you have paid and treat the dividend payment as if it were subject to PAYE and NICs (including employer NICs) and the tax advantage you thought you may have had could disappear.

Registering for VAT

Value Added Tax (VAT) was introduced in 1973 and it seems that many people have lost sight of the name of this tax and especially the word 'added'. You are adding a tax to your supplies, collecting it on behalf of HMRC and paying it over to HMRC. In effect you are an unpaid tax collector.

If your taxable turnover is likely to be more than £85,000 in a 12-month period (Summer 2020) you must register for VAT unless your supplies/services are outside the scope of VAT. Any expenses that you recharge to clients need to be included in the calculation of taxable turnover.

UK business clients are invariably registered for VAT so are not concerned about having VAT added to your invoice as they can reclaim it. For that reason, some businesses register for VAT before reaching the £85,000 compulsory registration limit so that they can claim VAT on their purchases - it's like buying equipment, supplies and services for 20% off. If your turnover is less than £85,000, before voluntarily applying consider whether registration will really be of benefit to you; whether reclaiming the VAT paid on items needed for your business (such as office equipment) is worth the trouble of sending in mandatory, quarterly VAT returns and keeping separate VAT records.

You can claim back VAT on pre-start/pre-registration expenditure incurred in setting up the business so keep those VAT receipts. If you elect for 'cash accounting' status, this means that VAT only becomes payable or reclaimable when invoices are actually paid. It avoids having to pay the VAT on your own sales invoices before slow-paying clients pay you, which creates cash-flow problems. One final positive note, if you do register for VAT it seems to give you added credibility with clients.

VAT flat-rate scheme

HMRC introduced the flat-rate scheme in 2004, with the aim of simplifying record keeping for small businesses. This allows you to charge VAT to your clients at the standard rate of 20 per cent and to pay VAT as a percentage of your VAT-inclusive turnover (instead of having to work out the VAT payable on your sales less purchases). You can apply to join the scheme if your taxable turnover (excluding VAT) will not be more than £150,000 in the next 12 months.

HMRC publishes a list of business categories from which you need to decide which best describes your business. A further bonus is that you can deduct 1 per cent from the flat rate that you use for your first year of VAT registration. As a tip, do not do anything without checking it out with your accountant as there are a few twists and turns that could make the VAT flat-rate scheme unsuitable, especially since the introduction of a new 'limited cost trader' category which many small businesses with low purchasing levels are forced to use.

Marketing

It is a sad fact that many new business owners believe that marketing simply means placing an advert in some well-known directory. This will achieve only a fraction of the sales of any comparable business with a decent grasp of marketing. So how can you generate sales for a new business? The following tips will get you started:

1. *Your own website and/or social media.* Business and the public now rely heavily on the internet and a presence is vital either through a website and/or harnessing social media. Is there a vital domain name that you need to secure and register? If this one question alone fills you with fear the solutions are nearer than you think – just try asking friends and don't ignore help that is right in front of your nose: young friends or relatives who may know more than you. It is also worth checking out websites run by trade or professional associations that may allow you to register and set up a profile. You can set up profiles on various social media networking websites such as LinkedIn. Depending on your business, Facebook and Twitter can provide the benefits of building your online contacts and allow you to showcase your expertise in a certain area. Social media (very like networking, below) is about building relationships and trust with an ever-increasing contact list.

2. *Personal contacts and networking.* Once you decide to set up your own business, your personal contacts, ex-colleagues or other small business owners are a potential source of work. Too many small businesses forget that behind every contact there is another layer of potential contacts who are just one introduction away, so ignore this multiplier effect at your peril. In your first year you should be re-educating your contacts to think of you not as 'Jane who used to work at IBM' but 'Jane who now runs her own

business advising small businesses on their IT needs'. Do not be afraid to pick up the phone or send business cards explaining your new business and what you can offer. Joining the best trade or professional association you can find will be a great way of developing your business contact network, with the added bonus of research facilities, information and other fringe benefits.

3. *Discounts and offers.* These can be used to great effect during seasonal dips, introducing a new service or clearing old stock. Whether it is 20 per cent off, a buy-one-get-one-free offer or the numerous variations of this basic approach, there are three golden rules:

    –   always state the original or usual price (to show the value in the offer);

    –   always specify an expiry date;

    –   always explain that the offer is subject to availability.

4. *Flyers and business cards.* Generally speaking, a response rate of 1 per cent to a flyer is considered fairly good, but with some clever thinking you can improve this. Have you targeted the flyer? A good example would be a wedding gown designer who neatly persuades a sought-after wedding location hotel to keep a flyer dispenser in their foyer. Are you able to include your professional or trade association logo on your flyer and business cards? Have you asked if this is possible? There are two sides to a flyer and business card – have you thought about putting information on the blank reverse side? Could this contain some useful tips or, perhaps, a special offer or discount? Anything that ensures the card or flyer is kept rather than dumped will help your business to edge ahead.

5. *Testimonials.* People generally buy on trust, and testimonials show prospective customers that you have done a good job and can be relied upon. Positive testimonials can be powerful and should never be underestimated.

6. *Agencies.* Agencies will be especially important for prospective consultants or contractors, as many recruitment agencies also place full- and part-time contracts (as opposed to employed positions). The contract market is growing and offers dynamic and fast-moving industries the opportunity to hire (and fire) swiftly. When marketing yourself through an agency the same rules apply as when marketing yourself to a potential employer. Good

personal and written presentation will help the agency to sell you on to its clients – and it is in their interest to find you work, given the fee they receive for placing you.

7. *Advertising*. There are many options for advertising yourself and your business, such as website banners, and free and paid-for directory listings. Another approach could be 'free' advertising through a press release that you forward to local or trade press with an interesting story. A clever variant is advertising yourself and your skills by writing articles in professional or trade journals – what do you have that is new or novel or leading edge?

8. *Sponsorship*. Another subset of advertising is sponsorship. The driving instructor who sponsored the playing shirts of the local under-17s football team is a great example of cost-effective and rather clever sponsorship.

9. *Awards*. Business awards can offer new businesses an opportunity to make a splash in the local area, introduce you to other vibrant businesses, and there may even be a category for mature business owners newly starting up. These are often sponsored by local press and the Federation of Small Businesses (www.fsb.org.uk) where more information can be found.

Learn when to say 'no'

This is one of the hardest lessons to learn and comes with experience. The fear of losing a sale to a competitor, or the uncertainty of where the next piece of work or sale will come from if you reject this one, may induce you to overstretch or undercut yourself. If you continually face this dilemma the resulting stress means you may not survive in business for long. So learning how to say 'no' in a way that does not burn bridges is important.

Business alliances

Business alliances can work well and when you first start up in business all sorts of folk and businesses may approach you. You will quickly learn that some are all talk and no action or seem more interested in accessing your contact network than building a mutually beneficial longer-term business relationship. Lord Alan Sugar's words on what makes an entrepreneur, in his book *The Way I See It*: *Rants, revelations and rules for life* (Pan Macmillan 2011, website: www.panmacmillan.com)

gives a clear and simple lesson on this: 'If you have partners, they have to bring something to the party.'

Trading formats

You need to choose a type of business format and each carries a different level of personal risk and a different level of bureaucracy. The following will help you decide which one is right for you.

Self-employed (also sole trader/sole proprietor)

A self-employed person is someone who works for him/herself, instead of an employer, and draws an income from their personally run business. If the profits from the work are accounted for on one person's tax return, that person is known as a sole trader. If the profits are shared between two or more people, it is a partnership (see below).

There is no clear definition of self-employment. Defining an employee, on the other hand, is slightly easier as it can generally be assumed that if Income Tax and NICs are deducted from an individual's salary before they are paid, then that individual is an employee.

Importantly, the business has no separate existence from the owner and, therefore, all debts of the business are debts of the owner, who is personally liable for all amounts owed by the business. This strikes fear into the hearts of many business owners. You only need to think of the number of business owners who go bust every time a recession comes around and lose their house. Should this be a worry?

First and foremost, you must consider the risk to you in any work that you do. Could it go wrong and could you be sued? Is that a realistic prospect or so remote that it does not even warrant thinking about? Or is it somewhere in the middle? Can insurance help? (More on insurance later.) Remember that such insurance is only as good as the disclosures you make and the levels of cover provided. At the end of the day you know your business, your customers and the work that you do, so the risk assessment can only be done by you.

How to start up as a sole trader

- You can start trading immediately.

- You can trade under virtually any name, subject to some restrictions that are mostly common sense, such as not suggesting something you are not (connection to government, royalty or international pre-eminence). A B Jones trading as Super Lawns, for example, is fine.

- The full name and address of the owner and any trading name must be disclosed on letters, orders and invoices.

- Register as self-employed by going to www.gov.uk and searching for 'working for yourself'.

Partnership

Two or more self-employed people who work together on a business and share the profits are trading in partnership. The profits from the work are accounted for on a partnership tax return and extracts from that partnership tax return are then copied into the partners' individual tax returns.

The business has no separate existence from the partners and, therefore, all debts of the business are debts of the partners, so they are personally liable for all amounts owed by the business. In addition, partners are jointly and severally liable for the debts of the business or, put more simply, the last person standing pays the lot. There is a saying that you need to trust your business partner better than your husband/wife/civil partner.

As with sole traders, the first consideration is the potential for business risk, since your personal wealth is backing the debts of the business. First and foremost, you must consider the risk to you in any work that you do and, given the 'joint and several liability' point explained above, the trust and faith you have in your business partner. Again, as with sole traders, can insurance help reduce the risk?

How to set up as a partnership

- You can start trading immediately.

- You can trade under virtually any name, subject to some restrictions that are mostly common sense, such as not suggesting something you are not (connection to government, royalty or international pre-eminence). As before, A B Jones and A B Smith trading as J & S Super Lawns is fine.

- You will need to consult a solicitor to assist with the preparation and signing of a partnership deed. The partnership deed is for your protection and is essential because it sets out the rules of the partnership including, for example, the profit or loss split between partners, what happens if one partner wishes to leave or you wish to admit a new partner.

- The full name and address of the partners and any trading name must be disclosed on letters, orders and invoices.

- Register the partnership with HMRC with form SA400 via www.gov.uk (then go to 'register a partnership for Self-Assessment').

Limited company

A limited liability company (often the shorthand of 'limited company' is used to describe this trading format) is a company whose liability is limited by shares and is the most common form of trading format. In the present Covid-19 pandemic the benefit of the limited liability status should not be underestimated as it could, potentially, protect your personal wealth if the company goes bust. The company is owned by its shareholders, and is run by directors who are appointed by the shareholders. This can be the one same person and indeed many companies in the UK are one person companies.

The shareholders are liable to contribute the amount remaining unpaid on the shares – usually zero, as most shares are issued fully paid up. The shareholders therefore achieve limited liability.

How to start up a limited company

- A company needs to be registered with Companies House and cannot trade until it is granted a Certificate of Incorporation. The registration process is quick and inexpensive using the Companies House web incorporation service (it currently costs £12 and is completed within 24 hours). Some people use a company formation agent (Google this term to find such an agent – there are plenty of them) and the process should cost less than £50.

- The company name needs to be approved by Companies House. No two companies can have the same name and approval is usually completed in a day. Names that suggest, for instance, an international aspect will require evidence to support the claim and certain names are prohibited unless there is a dispensation (for example 'Royal').

- You must appoint a director and this 'officer' of the company carries responsibilities that can incur penalties and/or a fine. The appointment of directors should therefore not be done lightly. The full range of responsibilities is set out in the Companies Act; further guidance is available from the Companies House section of www.gov.uk (go to 'running a limited company'). Some examples of responsibilities include the duty to maintain the financial records of the company, to prepare accounts, to retain the paperwork and to avoid conflicts of interest. Small businesses no longer need to have a separate company secretary but it can be useful to have another office-holder signatory and the risks associated with this position are relatively light. In addition you will need to appoint a registered office, which is a designated address at which official notices and communications can be received. The company's main place of business is usually used as the registered office but you could also use the address of your accountant or solicitor (there may be a charge for this).

Top tip

A limited liability company costs just £12 to set up. It provides enormous protection in managing the risk to your personal wealth due to limited liability.

Alternative ways of getting started

Umbrella company

This isn't really running your own business but it is a quick and easy way to get work and earn without all the red tape and time involved in running your own business. The downside is there are less tax planning opportunities. It is worth some description here as it may be an option for you or come up in conversation. Essentially it is a company that offers you a shelter (umbrella) from administration. You are employed through the umbrella company and the end firm that actually uses your services keeps you at arm's length. You don't accrue the usual employment rights that will be available to employed staff in that end firm. The umbrella company is very limited in its function - almost 'just' processing your payroll, deducting paye and national insurance and paying it over to HMRC and paying you the net salary. It can offer a win: win for both you and the end firm that uses your services. For example, for someone who wants flexibility and earnings – perhaps working ad hoc or a few days a week. It also offers firms that need staff a flexible labour pool that is easy to hire and fire as their only obligation is to pay the umbrella company a fee to cover your wages. The tricky bit is the administration charges levied by the umbrella company for running the payroll and who pays the employer's national insurance and you'll want to check out how that works - possibly in deductions and charges from what hits your pocket.

Overall the umbrella company is a useful route to earning some cash in a flexible way but if you have ambitions for earning over the longer term and over about £250 per day the other options for setting up your own business in this chapter could be more rewarding and tax efficient.

Buying a business

Buying an established business can be an attractive route to becoming your own boss, as it eliminates many of the problems of start-ups. The enterprise is likely to come equipped with stock, suppliers, an order book, premises and possibly employees. It is also likely to have debtors and creditors. Take professional advice before buying any business, even one from friends. In particular, you should consider why the business is being sold. It may be for perfectly respectable reasons – for instance, a change of circumstances such as retirement. But, equally, it may be that the market is saturated, that the rent is about to go sky-high or that major competition has opened up nearby.

Before parting with your money, verify that the assets are owned by the business and get the stock professionally valued. You should also ensure that the debts are collectable and that the same credit terms will apply from existing suppliers. Get an accountant to look at the figures for the last three years and have a chartered surveyor check the premises. A solicitor should be engaged to vet any legal documents, including staff and other ongoing contracts.

The value of the company's assets will be reflected in its purchase price, as will the 'goodwill' (or reputation) that it has established. For more information, agents specialising in small business sales have useful guides (for instance, see www.christie.com).

Franchising

Franchising continues to be a popular form of business entry route with attractions for both franchisor and franchisee. The franchisor gains, as their 'brand' is able to expand quickly. The advantage to the franchisee is that there are normally fewer risks than with starting a business from scratch.

A franchisee buys into an established business and builds up his or her own enterprise under its wing. In return for the investment, plus regular royalty payments, he or she acquires the right to sell the franchisor's products or services within a specified geographic area and enjoys the benefits of its reputation, buying power and marketing expertise. As a franchisee you are effectively your own boss. You finance the business, employ the staff and retain the profits after the franchisor has had its cut. You are usually expected to maintain certain standards and conform to the broad corporate approach of the organisation. In return, the franchisor should train you in the business, provide management support and give you access to a wide range of backup services.

The amount of capital needed to buy a franchise varies enormously according to the type of business, and can be anywhere between a few hundred pounds and £500,000 or more. The franchisee is normally liable to pay an initial fee, covering both the entry cost and the initial support services provided by the franchisor, such as advice about location and market research.

The length of the agreement will depend on both the type of business involved and the front-end fee. Agreements can run from three to 20 years and many franchisors include an option to renew the agreement, which should be treated as a valuable asset.

Many franchises have built up a good track record and raising money to invest in good franchises may not be too difficult. Most of the leading high-street banks operate specialist franchise loan sections. The franchisors may also be able to help in raising the money and can sometimes arrange more advantageous terms through their connections with financial institutions.

The British Franchise Association (BFA) represents 'the responsible face' of franchising, and its members have to conform to a code of practice. When considering opportunities, a good franchisor will provide a great deal of invaluable help. However, some franchisors may be less helpful and this will usually tell its own story. Make careful enquiries before committing any money; as basic information, you should ask for a bank reference, review several years accounts and appointments and resignations of directors (all available for free from Companies House), visit their head office and cost out and prepare a business plan and profit and loss forecast for at least the next year (see above on how to do this) and review this with the potential franchisor. Also check with the British Franchise Association whether the franchisor in question is a member and visit some of the other franchisees to find out what their experience has been. Before signing, seek advice from an accountant or solicitor. For more information, see the British Franchise Association website: www.thebfa.org.

Operational and other issues

Banking

If you operate through a limited company you have to set up a separate business bank account into which all income is paid and out of which you pay all costs. Most self-employed and partnerships will operate a separate bank account for their business as it can make the accounts easier and it can also help stop you muddling personal and business funds. Shop around for the best deal that suits your business (often a trade-off between the conveniences of a local 'bricks and mortar' branch accompanied by internet banking versus free or reduced charges for internet-only accounts) but often the convenience of maintaining business and personal bank accounts at one bank wins the day.

Inventions and intellectual property

If you have a clever idea that you would like to market you should ensure that your intellectual property is protected if you believe there is a special value in the name (trademark) or something special or unique about the product (patent). For information about patenting an invention, trademarks, copyright and much more, look at the UK Intellectual Property Office website at www.gov.uk (go to 'Intellectual Property Office').

Licences and permissions

Certain types of business require a licence or permit to trade; these include pubs, off-licences, nursing agencies, pet shops, kennels, minicabs or buses, driving instructors, betting shops, auction sale rooms, cinemas, street traders and, in some cases, travel agents and tour operators. You will also require a licence to import certain goods.

Depending on the nature of your business, other permissions may need to be obtained, including from the environmental health department, licensing authorities and the fire prevention officer. In particular, there are special requirements concerning the sale of food, and safety measures for hotels and guest houses.

Your local authority office will be able to advise you whether you require a licence, and in many cases your council will be the licensing authority. More information is available at www.gov.uk (go to 'licence finder').

Employing staff

Should you consider employing staff, you will immediately increase the complexity of your business. As well as paying salaries, you will have to account for PAYE, keep National Insurance records and conform to the multiple requirements of employment legislation. If you are worried or don't want the bother of doing the paperwork yourself, your accountant is likely to be able to introduce you to a payroll service, which will cost you money but will take some of the burden off your shoulders. Keeping personnel records will bring you into the scope of data protection: see ico.org.uk.

Employment legislation

As an employer, you have certain legal obligations with respect to your staff. The most important of these cover such issues as health and safety at work, terms and conditions of employment, and the provision of employee rights including, for example, parental leave, trade union activity and protection against unfair dismissal. Very small firms are exempt from some of the more onerous requirements, and the government is taking steps to reduce more of the red tape. However, it is important that you understand in general terms what legislation could affect you. You will usually find free support on this subject via membership of a trade association or organisation such as the Federation of Small Businesses (www.fsb.org.uk). The Health and Safety Executive also has a useful website: www.hse.gov.uk.

An employer, however small the business, may not discriminate against someone on the grounds of sex, race, disability, religion, marital status, sexual orientation or age. This applies to all aspects of employment, including training, promotion, recruitment, company benefits and facilities. More information can be found at: www.equalityhumanrights.com.

Disputes

If you find yourself with a potential dispute on your hands, it is sensible to approach the Advisory, Conciliation and Arbitration Service (ACAS), which operates an effective information and advisory service for employers and employees on a variety of workplace problems, including employment legislation and employment relations. It also has a wide range of useful publications, giving practical guidance on employment matters. See website: www.acas.org.uk.

Insurance

Insurance is more than just a wise precaution. It is essential if you employ staff, have business premises or use your car regularly for commercial purposes. Many insurance companies now offer 'package insurance' for small businesses, which covers most of the main contingencies in a single policy. This usually works out cheaper than buying a collection of individual policies. An insurance broker should be able to guide you through the risks and the insurance products available:

- *Employers' liability*: This is compulsory if you employ staff. It provides indemnity against liability for death or bodily injury to employees and subcontractors arising in connection with the business.
- *Product and public liability*: This insures the business and its products against claims by customers or the public.
- *Professional indemnity*: This is essential if a client could suffer a mishap, loss or other damage in consequence of advice or services received.
- *House insurance*: If you operate your business from home, check that you have notified your house insurer of this fact.
- *Motor risks*: Check that you have notified your insurer if you use your motor vehicle for your business.
- *Life assurance*: This ensures that funds are available to pay off any debts or to enable the business to continue in the event of your death.
- *Permanent health insurance*: Otherwise known as 'income protection', it provides insurance against long-term loss of income as a result of severe illness or disability by paying a regular income.
- *Critical illness insurance*: This provides insurance against long-term loss of income as a result of severe illness or disability by paying a lump sum.

- *Key person insurance*: This applies to the loss of a key person through prolonged illness as well as death. In small companies where the success or failure of the business is dependent upon the skills of one or two key executives, key person insurance may be demanded by lenders.

You should discuss these points with your insurance company or a broker. To find an insurance broker, see the British Insurance Brokers' Association website: www.biba.org.uk; or the Association of British Insurers website: www.abi.org.uk.

Top tip

If you work from home or use your car for work remember to notify your insurer.

Pensions

When you go out on your own a whole new opportunity opens up to you to manage your remuneration and pensions. A reasonably early review should be undertaken of existing pension provision against pension aspirations with a suitably qualified financial adviser. But remember there are also pension predators out there. More information on pensions is at Chapter 3, Pensions.

Top tip

Pensions planning can be dramatically effective and very tax-efficient but there are traps for the unwary. Get an early pensions review with an adviser regulated by the Financial Conduct Authority.

Useful reading

The government website (www.gov.uk) contains the government's online resource for businesses.

Regional or country-specific support is also available at:

- England: The Local Enterprise Partnership at www.lepnetwork.net;
- Northern Ireland: www.nibusinessinfo.co.uk;

- Scotland: www.mygov.scot/business;
- Wales: www.business.wales.gov.uk.

Business is Great has been set up by the government to help you with support, advice and inspiration for growing your business including advice on imports and exports, finance, employment, intellectual property and regulation. It includes a 'business support tool' and after answering a few questions you get a report of resources and schemes to start to support your business. Further information is available from: www.greatbusiness.gov.uk.

Start-up Britain has been set up by the government to help you find information about starting a business and contains offers and discounts available to new business start-ups. Further information is available from: www.startupbritain.org.

Other useful organisations

- *Solicitors*: Many solicitors offer a free initial consultation and advice can be sought on a range of issues. To find solicitors in your local area use the 'find a solicitor' section at the Law Society website: www.lawsociety.org.

- *The Federation of Small Businesses* (www.fsb.org.uk): The networking opportunities and benefits of the Federation of Small Businesses make it a 'must have' for most new small businesses.

- *Association of Independent Professionals and the Self Employed* (www.ipse.co.uk): Its *Guide to Freelancing* is free and can be downloaded from its website. The organisation's knowledge of and guidance on IR35 for freelancers and contractors is second to none.

- *Business start-up websites*: These are packed with free hints and tips and a useful one is www.bstartup.com; their exhibitions are free, well attended and have some excellent free workshops and guest speakers.

Reminder: Take any action points or follow up points to Chapter 12, Your Plan For A Better Retirement

---

Starting a business – checklist

When starting or running a business you will encounter a vast range of information and this can lead to you feeling swamped. This checklist has been developed to help you on the journey. Try annotating each item – N: not applicable; W: work on now; A: review with accountant; C: complete.

- If you want to travel somewhere you use a map. In business it's just the same except you get yourself a *plan*. Commit it to writing and don't expect to get it right first time (no one does!). A few pages are fine to start with. Then review it with your accountant and/trusted others.

- Choose your *trading format*, i.e. company (usually signified by 'limited'), sole trader or partnership or limited liability partnership. This is an important step and one to talk through with your accountant. You can set up a company for £12 at Companies House. Understand the personal liability risks of sole trader/partnership and, indeed, joint and several liability if trading in partnership ('last person standing pays the lot'!). If things go badly wrong your personal wealth could be at risk.

- Choose your *accountant.* Accountants are usually prepared to see you for an initial 'no obligation' meeting. Be clear about who your regular contact will be, their qualifications and knowledge of your industry, their hourly rates and whether they have professional indemnity insurance.

- Make sure you have a source of *legal help*. Could your local solicitor help? Alternatively, your trade association may offer a free legal helpline that may suffice initially. An early legal question that will usually arise is about your terms and conditions of trade or contracts and shareholder agreements.

- There is *free government help* that you can find at www.gov.uk. Also check out the government-backed initiatives www.startupbritain.org and www.greatbusiness.gov.uk for inspiration and ideas. Regional or country-specific support is also available at:

    - England: The Local Enterprise Partnership at www.lepnetwork.net;

    - Northern Ireland: www.nibusinessinfo.co.uk;

    - Scotland: www.mygov.scot/business;

-     Wales: www.business.wales.gov.uk.

- Join the best *trade or professional association* that you can identify and consider the extra benefits each provides in the areas of research information, networking events, helplines, tax investigation help and insurance offerings.

- Choose and, if appropriate, protect your *business name*. There is some useful free help available on intellectual property (patents, brands, etc.) at at www.gov.uk/government/organisations/intellectual-property-office.

- Choose a *business bank account*. Often a trade-off between the conveniences of a local 'bricks and mortar' branch accompanied by internet banking versus free or reduced charges for internet-only accounts.

- Combine business plans with your wealth and pension needs with a financial adviser regulated by the Financial Conduct Authority (FCA).

- Sort out your *tax and record keeping* (documents need to be kept for six years and you need to become a receipt/invoice hoarder with a logical 'system for filing'); as the taxman will say, 'Prove it or lose it.' Check first with your accountant before buying any bookkeeping system.

- Understand the implications of failing to deal with your *tax* affairs properly. Penalties can range from 30 per cent to 200 per cent plus interest. Some trade associations include 'free' tax investigation cover.

- Understand your key *tax obligations* and deadlines. For companies, you are obliged to file your annual accounts at Companies House nine months after your year end (your accountant will do this) and your *confirmation statement* on the anniversary of setting up a company each year.

- Understand your obligations on *VAT*. The current registration threshold for compulsory registration is £85,000. Consider VAT schemes, especially the VAT flat-rate scheme for small businesses.

- Set up your *premises* so that you can work effectively. If you work from home, manage the expectations of your family and neighbours – suddenly the phrase 'time is money' takes on a new meaning.

- Set up your *suppliers* (set up contracts and bills in the company or business name) and, if appropriate, set up stock control and delivery systems.

- Consider *insurance* policies for identified business risks (professional indemnity, public liability, product liability, etc.). An insurance broker can advise on this and you should also consider policies available via trade associations as these can provide increased cover at less cost (don't forget to notify your home and car insurers if you use these for business).

- Consider protecting the income you take from your business (especially if you have dependents) in the event of long-term *illness* or *death* and if in doubt take advice from a financial adviser regulated by the FCA.

- If you are not from a selling/marketing background, talk to trusted friends who run their own business and your accountant/adviser or mentor about your market research and marketing plan. Plan the *pricing* strategies for your product or service. A different package means a different price. How have you benchmarked your price and how have you differentiated your offering (features and benefits) to allow you to charge that little bit more? Conversely, what features and benefits have you stripped out to allow you to offer a price beneath the competition?

- Get paid promptly for your sales. What are your *payment terms* (terms and conditions)? Follow up on outstanding debts. If you sell stock, have you included a reservation of title clause if your client goes bust?

- Set up your *IT system* and support and have a system to back up your data securely. Check whether you need to notify the Information Commissioner under the *data protection* laws (ico.org.uk).

- Consider other *red tape*, especially if your area is a specialised sector (food, health and safety, etc.). Investigate and apply for the licences and permits that your business may need.

Top tip

Review and update your business plan in the light of experience and keep it a living, written document.

Chapter Eight
Working for others: Paid work and volunteering.

"We need to do a better job of putting ourselves higher on our own 'to do' list".
MICHELLE OBAMA

The first reaction of many people approaching retirement is often 'great, no more work' and they may be puzzled at the space I give to career transition and other paid work. High responsibility, high stress jobs with perhaps lots of travel within the UK or internationally can work right up to retirement. This may keep you busy and provide the finances you need. But is there another way perhaps starting about 10 years from retirement which provides more of a glide-path into retirement rather than a cliff-edge halt? Put another way, can you 'right-size' your employment?

Even if you enjoy your work and find it satisfying it may be restrictive in ways you don't see. You stick to the rules – specific tasks, regular timekeeping, keep going through thick and thin and limited personal freedom to do as you wanted. Have you heard folk explain that 'their life isn't their own' due to the demands of the job? So can the pressure be turned down or even off? Career transition describes the process of reassessing what you can offer, what you really want and exploring opportunities to achieve a better last decade of employment. Perhaps the employment may last beyond state retirement age if it helps you achieve a better retirement?

Alternatively your needs may be financial as, quite simply, having reviewed your retirement plans at Chapter 1 (Doing the sums) you now need to supplement your present anticipated or actual retirement income. This, therefore, sits as the second chapter within the 'earn more' essential step of retirement planning in my book. As a brief recap the core of this book is based around the four essential steps to achieving a better retirement: plan more, save more, earn more and live better. The other key readership for this chapter are those looking to retrain or just do some part time work to provide some interest and a bit of finance to pay for an extra holiday ('earn more'). Finally I explore the wonderful opportunities in volunteering where 'giving back' could be just the right thing for you and society.

This chapter at a glance

- Employment 'right-sizing' and using career transition to help you change career to provide a smoother glide path into retirement.
- How to assess yourself and find the right positions for you.
- Tips are provided to help you get that role.
- Tips are provided on redundancy situations.
- Help is provided on getting full or part time employment in retirement.
- There is also information and advice on training opportunities and other employment ideas, including finding public appointments.
- How to find volunteering opportunities.
- Some examples of volunteering types of work.
- A detailed look at one organisation that depends on volunteers who all make a difference, Citizens Advice.

Career transition

This comes down to blue sky thinking on a blank sheet of paper. You've worked for decades and probably have seen all sorts of positive and negative work experiences and your knowledge of work experiences of those close to you can be illuminating. This career review has five broad components: what type of job I'd like and where; what I bring; how I can make the best impression; what opportunities are out there and finally is the package sufficient?

What type of job I'd like and where?

It begins with a review of what you value in life - list it in importance. This is the big stuff in your life- your wants and desires. Is it remaining close to family and perhaps caring responsibilities, a location or community or more freedom to pursue your passion in life (sailing, riding, refurbishing a cottage etc.)? Conversely what do you want to avoid? Is the role to be full time or part time? What travel limits would you like to see?

Then assess how you respond best in a work situation and with what sort of management style above you. What causes you to thrive and what causes you stress? What really motivates you and conversely what demotivates you and learn from past experiences - both the best and worst? Is it team working that you enjoy and dealing with people or do you prefer to get on with things on your own?

Then think about the types of work you could do and whether they are in a declining, stable or increasing market. How does this influence the breadth of choice you should be looking at? Everyone is different and there is no right or wrong answer here. It's about reassessing what's best for you at this stage in life and as you move on from here.

What do I bring?

Then it's a case of identifying the skills you bring and especially how they are transferable to other roles and don't forget those learnt on hobbies or voluntary work. Discussions with people who know you and the potential jobs you could do can yield great intelligence here and some of those 'I'd never have thought of that moments.' Ignore the importance of these at your peril and try and set aside at least an hour for each and have a structure (maybe the points in this section) so you deal with specifics rather that vague notions. Generally the more experienced your confidants the better the output.

A trusted and structured form of career analysis is the 'Birkman method' which measures through a long questionnaire four main areas: your usual behaviour in the context of tasks and relationships; what you require in the environment and people around you to be at your best; the behaviours in stress situations when your needs are not met and, finally, your interests (that is the tasks and activities that offer you the greatest attraction and satisfaction). Your present employer may arrange for you to take this as part of a career review or you can access this via a number of HR type consultancies throughout the UK (just try googling 'Birkman method' and your location).

How I can make the best impression?

This is all about translating what you know about yourself into a credible statement that underlines your experience, skills and knowledge and how you can add value to the company or organisation in meeting the challenges they have.

Take care with application forms: In addition to your CV some firms may also ask you to complete an application form relating to the job in question. Read the questions they ask carefully and in your responses try to play to your own strengths and experience. Remember that in a competitive job market firms will use the application form to short-list those candidates they want to take a further look at through interview. Those short-listing decisions will be made solely on the quality of the application.

CV writing: This is so important, and presentation is key. If it's a few years since you've updated your CV, make sure it's current and contains the following sections: personal and contact information; education and qualifications; work history and/or experience and relevant skills to the job in question. Personal interests, achievements and hobbies can be covered briefly if relevant to the job. Use assertive, positive language, emphasising the skills you have gained from past work. The CV shouldn't run to more than two pages of A4 paper, attaching anything else as an annex to the CV.

Doing an interview: You may be called to do an interview. Take time to prepare for this and do research on the firm itself and the job vacancy itself. Study the attributes required for the role, you will find these on the job profile, and decide how you can show you meet these. You may be asked to do presentation and, if so, expect guidance on the subject, slide length and time allocation for the presentation and then the time for questions. Prepare a mental checklist of your own strengths and experience which might enable you to do the job in question – the interview panel will almost certainly want to explore this with you during the actual interview. Your decades of experience and loyalty will set you apart from youngsters so emphasise this with examples of achievements and extra work you did on the job and how you can add value. Prepare, prepare and prepare to do yourself justice and then, in the interview, just try to relax and be yourself.

Referees: These will not be required until you are at the point of receiving an offer. Have them ready: one should be a previous employer and the other someone who can vouch for you personally.

What opportunities are out there?

Get organised: Your career transition/job-hunting campaign needs planning. Don't leave something so important to chance.

Make use of your contacts: Within the network of people you know there are bound to be some who may not be able to actually get you a job, but can give some help with advice, information and possibly potential job leads.

Former colleagues and finder fees - a win-win: Introductions to prospective employers from a former colleague or a friend you know that already works for the target organisation can work well. It gives you a 'warm in' and may give the former colleague or friend a finder fee which can be significant. It cuts out the recruitment agencies and the fee they would otherwise get and can be a great win-win for all concerned. Tactically you may want to explore these routes before signing up with recruitment agencies.

Recruitment agencies: Identify the recruitment agencies who operate in your targeted career areas. These can vary in size and quality so ask around for recommendations on the good and the bad.

Is the package sufficient?

The numbers are important and will be dealt with in a moment but now that we are more experienced there are other vital factors:

- The new boss and prospective colleagues. Did you like and respect them?
- What is their spirit and ethos? Do they support volunteering and community work and from an ethics point of view did you feel they fit with you?
- You will be listening and looking during any interview and perhaps tour of the office. What do your instincts tell you? Trust them as they are usually well honed and tailored, of course, to you.
- What are the travel and overtime expectations - are these clear and understood?

- Do they offer a gym and other wellness activities?

Then onto the numbers. Are you clear on the package and what that means in terms of salary; any bonus expectations; health care, life cover; holiday entitlement, ability to buy extra days holiday (increasingly important as you glide into retirement); pensions (what you contribute and they contribute and the latter can be significant) and share purchase or option plans and other benefits.

Employment right-sizing

The traditional view is that folk press onward and upward in employment and in the old days of final salary pension schemes (see Chapter3, Pension) this had a logic. Today the model is turned on its head and the final decade or years of employment is more about a glide-path. So can you re-engineer with your current employer less stress, less travel and less responsibility for the same or similar headline pay but perhaps sacrificing some of the bonus by agreement? If not is it time to 'blue-sky' think and find that other role that meets your values and skills that provides a smoother glide-path into retirement? This is employment 'right-sizing'.

Redundancy

Managers feel that one of the worst jobs they will have to deal with is making someone redundant. Hopefully it will be handled with care and compassion with outplacement support ('outplacement' is the term the industry uses for the process to help move employees on when there is restructuring). The outplacement support can vary in length and quality but broadly may include a one to one relationship with a career counsellor who will assist you in the transition from one career into another or into early retirement. The process may include workbooks, seminars and workshops, webinars and the process should cover career research, the job application process, CV preparation and interview techniques. Other options such as early retirement or starting your own business may also be available.

Generally employers will want to handle this well as cost cutting and redundancies can involve several rounds as a business restructures. If the first round goes badly motivation and productivity can decrease and the business continues to decline. If redundancy is likely or if it strikes the following pointers may assist.

- If your employer's pension scheme allows it can you take your pension early in lieu of part or all of the severance package?
- Up to £30,000 of redundancy can be tax free and anything above that is taxed at your highest rate of tax so could it help if it fell in the next tax year if this was an option.
- Review with your Human Resources manager whether you can ask for part of any termination payment beyond the £30,000 tax free sum to be paid into your pension. This can be tax efficient and professional advice should also be sought.
- If you have share options these may lapse on the date you leave (your employment contract and options offer will clarify this point). If you feel the options are likely to increase substantially see if you can extend the period so that they are spread over two tax years or more. This may give you the more than one year of capital gains tax exemption if you can spread the sale of options.
- Check out your rights if you are feeling pressurised to 'exit' by processes that appear to be challenging your competence in your role. Follow this through with any legal expenses insurance that you have which can help you understand your rights. You may find that, instead, you are offered a 'compromise agreement' to move away from your role and the company rather than a formal redundancy. These are not exceptional and legal assistance should be sought to help negotiate any such 'package'. Remember legal expenses insurance often comes as an extra to home insurance or professional association membership so check your policies. If the business is insolvent and an insolvency practitioner is appointed in control of the business the rules are different and there is less protection (but a government safety net still exists for unpaid salary and redundancy payments).
- Don't agree to anything verbally and ask for all proposals to be put in writing and review via any legal expenses insurance you may have or consider taking legal advice.
- Check what happens to your benefits during any notice period that you are not required to work. What is the value of these and how will you be compensated?
- Check specifically if life cover and health cover can continue during any notice period that you are not required to work whilst you find a new job especially if you have a challenging medical history as these can be costly to implement for a short period and can take time to arrange in such circumstances.
- Ask about retaining office equipment you were been supplied with as it is usually more bother for the employer to gather these in. Ask about retaining mobile phone or laptop (restored back to original state to remove company information).

Training opportunities

Knowing what you want to do is one thing, but before starting a new job you may want to brush up existing skills or possibly acquire new ones. Most professional bodies have a full programme of training events, ranging from one-day seminars to courses lasting a week or longer. Additionally, adult education institutes run a vast range of courses or, if you are still in your present job, a more practical solution might be to investigate open and flexible learning, which you can do from home. There are a number of vocational education and training opportunities offering such training for individuals of all ages. You are more likely to be successful if you learn at a time, place and pace best suited to your own particular circumstances. You should try to find out what is available locally; the following organisations offer advice and a wide range of courses:

- free online courses from universities and specialist organisations: www.futurelearn.com;
- Adult Education Finder: www.adulteducationfinder.co.uk;
- Home Learning College: www.homelearningcollege.com;
- Learn Direct: www.learndirect.co.uk;
- University of the third age www.u3a.org.uk;
- National Extension College: www.nec.ac.uk;
- Open and Distance Learning Quality Council: www.odlqc.org.uk;
- Open University: www.open.ac.uk.

Other paid employment ideas

Consultancy and contracting

If the idea of hiring yourself out as a consultant or contractor appeals, you may be able to build up a steady stream of assignments and be recommended to other companies who could use your skills. There is more on this in Chapter 7, Starting Your Own Business or you may get placements through an agency; there is a vast choice through mainstream and niche agencies. If you're not sure about who's who in the world of agencies ask around (former HR colleagues and other contractors/consultants are the usual starting places). More research and information can be obtained from:

- Association of Independent Professionals and the Self-Employed: www.ipse.co.uk;
- Consultancy UK: www.consultancy.uk.

Interim management

Interim management is the temporary provision of senior or director-level management resources and skills. It is a short-term assignment of a proven heavyweight interim executive manager to manage a period of transition, crisis or change within an organisation. Assignments could be full-time or involve just one or two days' commitment per week. More research and information can be obtained from the Institute of Interim Management: www.iim.org.uk.

Non-executive directorships

A non-executive director, or external director, is a paid member of the board of directors of a company or organisation who does not form part of the executive management team. They are not an employee and they do not participate in the day-to-day management of the organisation. Instead, they are expected to monitor and challenge the performance of the executive directors and the management and give advice on broad strategic issues. Such appointments carry heavy responsibilities and people who are qualified to take on such a role are usually chosen for their breadth of experience and personal qualities. More at www.nedonboard.com.

Public appointments

There are a large number of advisory and other public bodies or quangos (quasi-autonomous non-government organisations) that have responsibility for a raft of public services at national, regional and local level. Those services cover a vast spectrum, including health, education, the environment, agriculture and food, defence, policing, legal/judicial, culture, media, sport, science and technology, and transport. The list is by no means exhaustive and further details can be found on the Cabinet Office website (publicappointments.cabinetoffice.gov.uk), which outlines opportunities throughout the whole of the UK.

Most of the bodies have a large staffing complement and a managing board or executive of senior administrative and professional staff. However, as public bodies, most are also required to have non-executive directors or board members drawn from the general public. The role of these external appointments is to bring outside experience and expertise to the table and also to bring a degree of external challenge to the work and decisions of the executive body or board. There are also purely advisory bodies designed to give external advice in a wide range of areas.

It is not necessary to have been in the public sector in order to be able to make a contribution. Indeed, in many instances the body will be looking for the sort of practical experience that people gain in business or commerce outside of the public sector. The skill set will vary from body to body and, in addition to a lay person's interest in the subject matter, experience in areas such as finance, human resources and change management, along, perhaps, with specialist knowledge, will often be seen as valuable.

The time commitment can vary, but on average it is probably one or two days per month. Likewise, the remuneration varies from body to body – from a very modest attendance allowance to several thousand pounds per year. But for some people the idea of being involved in an area of particular interest may be as attractive as any financial reward. For the post of chairperson, the time commitment is likely to be much greater, but so too will be the remuneration.

There is a rigorous and open appointments procedure for all posts, usually looking at the extent to which any candidate measures up to the specific competence-based criteria that the appointment requires. Full details of the appointment, the criteria relating to it and general advice on applying will be available to those who apply. It is important that this information is looked at in detail as the shortlist for final interview will be based on an objective assessment of the extent to which the information provided in the application form meets the specific criteria relating to the post.

Virtually all posts are now publicly advertised in the national, regional or local press – so anyone interested should keep an eye on this. Further information, including vacancies, is also available on the Cabinet Office website mentioned earlier or at a regional level from www.gov.scot/public-bodies for Scotland, and www.nidirect.gov.uk/public-appointments for Northern Ireland.

Paid work for charities

There are some opportunities to work for money rather than as a volunteer in the charity sector, although it might be helpful to work as a volunteer before seeking a paid appointment. Anyone thinking of applying for a job with a charity must of course be sympathetic to its aims and style and it is likely that you may have already been involved with the charity before seeking paid employment with it. You can also keep an eye on job adverts in that sector.

Jobs with tourism and travel

The travel and tourism sector comprises many different industries such as tour operators, tourist boards, passenger transport (coach, aviation, waterways and rail) and visitor attractions, such as museums, theme parks, zoos and heritage sites. This industry is not just for the young – mature and experienced people are also sought after. If you have stamina, enjoy meeting the general public and like travelling, working in the tourism sector could be interesting. Some people with specialist knowledge sign on as a lecturer with one of the travel companies offering special interest holidays; others specialise in tourist attractions nearer to home. Air courier jobs are also good for people who like travelling abroad.

Teaching and tutoring

If you have experience of teaching, there are a number of possibilities open to you, both in the United Kingdom and abroad. With examinations becoming more competitive many parents require private tutors to help their children prepare for public examinations. There is always a demand for people to teach English to foreign students at the many language schools, and most UK universities offer language courses during the summer.

House-sitting

There are opportunities throughout the United Kingdom and abroad to look after a house and maybe a pet whilst the owners are abroad. Companies who specialise in this kind of work include:

House Sitters UK: www.housesittersuk.co.uk.

Trusted House Sitters: www.trustedhousesitters.com.

Volunteering

Lots of volunteering is inspired by friends and relatives who have taken the plunge or been touched by a cause. That's a good starting point so ask around and you could be introduced sooner than you think. It's a two way process so expect some form of interview or chat and find out the benefits of working with the organisation, time expectations and flexibility. If it's not right don't waste each other's time and seek a different opportunity. Maybe you've been inspired by tipping your toe in the water? Do some more research thinking about the issues that really are important to you. Think about the skills that you bring and start your search.

Volunteering – finding opportunities

Finding opportunities are not as difficult as you may think. Community noticeboards, websites and the local library or Doctor's surgery notice board were the old fashioned ways but are still worthwhile. Then, as you would expect, there is the online noticeboard and www.do-it.org is a great starting point- try it now with your postcode and you'll be amazed at what's nearby. Regional focused websites include:

Northern Ireland: www.volunteernow.co.uk
Scotland: www.volunteerscotland.net
Wales: www.volunteering-wales.net
England: www.ncvo.org.uk

Why people become volunteers
The most frequently cited reasons why people volunteer include:

- It's their interest or passion:

- maintaining friendships, teamwork, status and a sense of belonging;

- wanting to 'make a difference' to other people's lives;

- enjoying using their skills in new and valuable ways;

- feeling better both physically and mentally;

- supporting local activities and neighbourhood organisations;
- being a committed member of social and charitable projects;
- actively participating in democratic institutions such as parish/community councils, boards of school governors, or neighbourhood watch;
- finding opportunities to help in education, sport, culture, leisure, conservation and the environment.

The type of volunteer work

There are so many types of work available to volunteers, depending on what you enjoy doing and what skills you have – you should be able to find something to suit. It is entirely dependent on you what you choose – the range is enormous, from the large international or national charities to much smaller organisations. Always play to your strengths; you should be able to find many opportunities in your local community to volunteer. Types of work could include:

- *Administrative*: Any active group is likely to need administrative and financial help, from stuffing and labelling envelopes to organising committees to keeping the finances in order. This may involve a day or so a week or occasional assistance at peak times. Many smaller charities are desperate for help from individuals with IT expertise and accountancy experience.
- *Committee work*: This can cover anything from very occasional help to a virtually full-time commitment as chair, treasurer or secretary. People with business skills or financial or legal backgrounds are likely to be especially valuable, and those whose skills include minute-taking are always in demand.
- *Direct work*: Hands on building and maintenance work, driving, delivering 'meals on wheels', counselling, visiting the housebound, working in a charity shop, gardening in a community garden, running arts classes or sports clubs, helping with a playgroup, respite care for carers; the list is endless. There are many interesting and useful jobs for those without special training.
- *Fundraising and marketing*: Every voluntary organisation needs money, and when donations are static or falling, more creativity and ingenuity are required to help bring in funds. Events are many and varied, but anyone with energy and experience of organising fundraising events would be welcomed with open arms as a volunteer.

- *Overseas*: Many more people in later life are now combining volunteering with travel. There are many in their 50s and 60s who are seizing this opportunity as they may have missed their 'gap year' when they were young. Each organisation has a minimum period of service. One of the better-known organisations involved in this area is Voluntary Service Overseas (www.vsointernational.org).

A case study: Citizens Advice

There are, literally, thousands of opportunities in volunteering but picking one allows us to penetrate in and explore the 'what they do, why and how a volunteer can help'. The case study is Citizens Advice but it could, quite literally, be any organisation.

Have you ever had a problem or crisis in your life when you needed advice? Citizens Advice provides people with advice for all kinds of problems without judging them and the organization is powered by an army of volunteers who make a difference and benefit from all that volunteering brings. There is probably a role for you at your local Citizens Advice outlet. But first some context. Citizens Advice provide a reliable and consistent service by sticking to a few key aims and principles:

- providing advice people need for the problems they face;
- trying to improve the policies and practices that affect people's lives by showing the people who make the decisions what people's experiences are.

Citizens Advice are independent and provide free, confidential and impartial advice to everyone regardless of race, sex, disability, sexuality or nationality. They are the largest advice-giving network in the United Kingdom, with over 3,000 outlets (there should be one near you) and 20,000 volunteers. They help people deal with nearly 6 million problems every year by phone, email and outreach sessions. The volunteers come from all walks of life and are committed to providing an independent advice service. The advice is based on four principles. It is:

- *Independent*: They will always act in the interests of their clients, without influence from outside bodies.
- *Impartial*: They won't charge their clients or make assumptions about them. The service is open to everyone and they treat everyone equally.
- *Confidential*: They will not pass on anything a client tells them, or even the fact that they visited, without their permission.
- *Free*: No one has to pay for any part of the service they provide.

Putting these principles into action enables them to provide a vital service to millions of people each year. They, and therefore you, can help make a real practical difference to people with problems in your local community.

What do Citizens Advice volunteers do?

There are lots of different roles and a few are summarised below – there really is something for everyone.

- *Caseworkers/advisers*: An adviser will assist clients at drop-in sessions, appointments in the outlet, over the phone or at outreach sessions explaining the choices and consequences clients face. They may refer clients to other agencies. They need to be good at listening, work as a team, be open-minded and non-judgemental and enjoy helping people.
- *Administrators*: Help ensure everything runs smoothly. There are many different roles that may match your skills and time availability. These can include developing administrative systems, helping to arrange events, receptionist activities such as greeting clients, and arranging appointments.
- *IT support coordinators*: Support training and troubleshoot hardware and software problems, develop networks, design spreadsheets and databases.
- *Campaigners*: Conduct research on local issues and manage media campaigning.

Each area is run autonomously as a separate charity. You should be able to make contact with the organisation serving your area through the website or by making enquiries through local churches or libraries.

What training is available from Citizens Advice?

You will initially receive a briefing lasting about two hours, which will explain more about your local Citizens Advice and the potential opportunities that are available. At this session you will be with six to ten other potential volunteers and have an opportunity to ask lots of questions (although numbers can vary regionally). It is a very comfortable session without any obligation. Following this session, if you do wish to volunteer, you then undergo the initial stage of training which lasts about eight weeks and takes about half a day per week. After that it's up to you what you want to give and how your new volunteering will progress. To find out more just check out www.citizensadvice.org.uk; in the volunteering section of the website you can search for opportunities by entering your postcode.

Top tip

Winston Churchill said "We make a living by what we get, but we make a life by what we give." You probably don't appreciate the talents you have and how wonderful they could be to one of our thousands of voluntary organisations or folk who just need a hand. Have a go and the real chances are that the art of giving will help you live better and achieve a better retirement.

Useful reading

Learn Direct: www.learndirect.co.uk

University of the Third Age www.u3a.org.uk

Northern Ireland: www.volunteernow.co.uk

Scotland: www.volunteerscotland.net

Wales: www.volunteering-wales.net

England: www.ncvo.org.uk

Reminder: Take any action points or follow up points to Chapter 12, Your Plan For A Better Retirement.

Chapter Nine
Personal relationships and health

"You don't develop courage by being happy in your relationships everyday. You develop it by surviving difficult times and challenging adversity."

EPICURUS

You can do so much to achieve a better retirement by following through on the preceding eight chapters in this book which have set out the first three essential steps of achieving a better retirement: plan more (Chapter 1); save more (Chapters 2 to 6) and earn more (Chapters 7 and 8). But all of your reading and all of your actions that have been developed are pretty pointless without the 4th essential step of 'living better'. Personal relationships and health go hand in hand and feature as must read parts of this 'live better' essential step. But do good relations promote good health or is it the other way around? Logic says that if you get your personal relationships right so much positivity will flow from them which should improve your overall health. Personal relationships within the family can make life much easier and more enjoyable but they can also make life more difficult if they become fractured.

Whether you are part of a couple or single having good personal relationships also provides you with a group around you for emotional support, advice, different viewpoints that challenge you, shoulders to cry on and folk with whom to share daft jokes, social occasions and transport. Don't forget the importance of having people around you who will take you down a peg or two if you sometimes tend to get beyond yourself.

More fundamentally it will be a rare person that is happy every day as there will always be difficult times and challenging situations so it is just as much about how you survive them as Epicurus said 2,300 years ago. His basic philosophy was about living a self-sufficient life surrounded by friends. Without getting too heavy about it he has a good point when he said *"You don't develop courage by being happy in your relationships everyday. You develop it by surviving difficult times and challenging adversity."* This seems perfect and is therefore chosen as the headline quote for this chapter.

This chapter at a glance

This is one of the shortest chapters but one of the most important in this book. If your personal relationships and health are maintained and improved you will have a better retirement.

- Retirement brings big changes to the dynamics of your personal relationships. If your life was your work and your friends were at work, the changes will be bigger than you could have realised.

- Adjusting to the new life balance with any partner will need care so that you do not get under each other's feet.

- Reminders about those other people who matter most to you – children, grandchildren, parents if you have them and other close relatives and good friends.

- Pointers to the new friends that will emerge from your new social groups in retirement and that good friends tend to stick around during the highs and lows of life.

- Some pointers on the key health focus points and help to recognise the issues and the action to take.

- Exercise is one of the greatest benefits to good health. This chapter shows you some options and choices, but then it's over to you and that willpower thing. Go on, you can change old habits.

- You are what you eat. Suggestions on how to eat more healthily. It's worth repeating here that action could add years to your life.

- Have you had a recent health screening check? If not, when new to retirement this may well give you some peace of mind. There are also sections on the NHS and advice about going into hospital.

Personal relationships

Reaching retirement age is something many people look forward to, but it is a major lifestyle change. According to Relate, 91 per cent of people aged over 50 in the UK said that a close personal relationship is as important as good health and financial security. This emphasises the fact that as we grow older we find that strong and healthy personal relationships count for even more. This covers the spectrum from former work colleagues to your partner, your children, your parents and other friendship groups. It may come as a big surprise but your retirement brings a change in these dynamics and this means that some may change, some may be lost and some new ones will be found. With some warning and preparation there shouldn't be too many bumps along the way but adjusting will take a little time.

Work

The chances are that most people will have spent a great deal of their time in a working environment where they will have established a whole series of relationships. Those will include work colleagues, fellow professionals, customers and suppliers; some of those colleagues may well have become close friends. Once retired some of those contacts will become much less significant in your life.

While individual circumstances can vary, the general advice on retirement is that you should not seek to return to your old working environment. You may initially be tempted to drop in to see how things are going and to have a quick chat with old friends, but generally it is not a great idea. Things can change very quickly, as can personnel, and life moves on. Whatever your previous role may have been and however important it was you will now be seen as an outsider. People in work will want to get on with the job in hand and will have little time for chit chat – just think how you may have reacted when you were actually working. So unless you have agreed some very specific role with your old organisation it is probably best to stay away right from the very start. That is not to say that you should not stay in contact with people with whom you were particularly friendly. But do so on the basis of an old boys' or old girls' or close friends' network outside the actual working environment.

Partner

The other major change will be with those nearest and dearest to you and you may have seen some relationships fracture after the age of 60 for the folk to go and join the ranks of the 'silver splitters'. If you are a couple you will now spend much more time together, and indeed this is something which you both may have been looking forward to. But you may need a little time to adjust to this new life balance and you need to be careful not to get under each other's feet. You may just need to give each other a bit of personal space and find or re-find activities that could keep you challenged and occupied. Also, if only one partner has retired you may need to sit down and work out how responsibility for undertaking all those everyday but necessary tasks might have to be readjusted.

These very personal relationships will be a key factor in how happy your retirement years are likely to be. So grab some time out and a cup of tea or glass of wine and sit down as a couple, talk through how best to work through what will be a new relationship, and be prepared to accept that it may take a little time to adjust to your new situation. But generally you should find that things eventually do fall fairly neatly into place. Should the need arise, the following organisations can offer help and advice:

- Marriage Care: www.marriagecare.org.uk;
- The Spark (Scotland): www.thespark.org.uk;
- Relate: www.relate.org.uk and in Northern Ireland www.relateni.org.

Children

You may also find that you have more time to devote to those wider family relationships. Your children may have moved on to start developing their own families, but it is likely they will continue to value whatever support you can give them. This may involve the occasional – or in some cases regular – babysitting duties. This can be a great bonus to both parties: you establish a closer bond with your grandchildren and your own children get a bit more freedom at an important stage of their own life. Also, if they are finding it difficult to get a foot on the property market, and you now find yourself with some available capital, you may want to discuss the possibility of giving or loaning them a helping hand to get started. But a word of warning: you should not impose yourself, your ideas of how things should be done or how to spend a gift –'give and let go' could be a useful phrase here. As in all things, a sensible balance is needed and don't forget that you need to retain your own freedom to do as you wish within reason. After all, you have worked hard for what you have now got and are entitled to enjoy it.

Parents

At the other end of the age spectrum your own or your partner's parents may now be getting to the stage where they may need some support or even just a little more of your time. Again, you need to tread carefully to avoid imposing your solutions on their problems and to ensure that they don't become overly dependent on you.

Sandwich generation

Those in their fifties and sixties are the 'sandwich generation' where dual pressures may influence the relationships. This could be caused by 'boomerang' kids who return home after University / College whereas, in previous generations, they tended to find their own independence at an earlier age. The same may apply if you have vulnerable or elderly parents that have needs and potentially care. More is set out in Chapter 11, Sandwich Generation.

Friends

You will probably already have a wide circle of social friendships and that is unlikely to change on retirement. Indeed, it is important to retain and even develop those links now that you have more time to do so. You should also take every opportunity to develop new acquaintanceships as you start to get involved with all of those activities you never had time to pursue during your working life. With more time there will be more opportunities to join new groups and if there is not a group around then take the lead and form one with the hints and tips provided in the Chapter 10, Leisure and Hoildays.

So the general message is every person and relationship is individual and will differ slightly from another. Usually things boil down to compromise and learning to work things out. An active social life, combined with building on those personal and family relationships is a sure-fire way of enhancing your retirement years and live better. Fractured relationships, on the other hand, usually have the opposite effect.

Some people may stay as friends and some may come and go but the true friends tend to stick around through the highs and lows of life; sharing these events and getting through them is all part and parcel of your personal relationship 'network' and as a species we can be a resilient bunch!

Health

The big picture- the truth about obesity

The NHS is clear in its advice: being obese puts you at raised risk of health problems such as heart disease, stroke and type 2 diabetes. Losing weight will bring significant health improvements. Achieving you targets can be tough and folk can, perhaps, be seen to give up too easily 'Ohh Peter is on another diet / health kick'. But face facts - it's actually simple and just requires a strength of mind to actually make and commit to a change of lifestyle.

Know exactly where you are on the Body Mass Index – visit www.nhs.uk and go to 'body mass index'. The body mass index is a measure that GPs like because it provides a relationship between your height and weight and then translates this into one of four categories: underweight, normal, overweight and obese. The worry points are the extremes of underweight and obese. If you are obese, start exercising more and eating better. The BMI calculator takes precisely one minute to complete by entering your age, height, weight and approximate activity level. There are also lots of advice, hints and tips on keeping healthy on the NHS website.

And did you know about the 'string test'? It's brilliantly simple, costs nothing and takes 1 minute and will help you know where you stand. It was promoted on the BBC programme 'The truth about obesity' screened on 26 April 2018. On the programme, Professor Steve Bloom, the Head of Division for Diabetes, Endocrinology and Metabolism at Imperial College London said

> *"If you manage to lose weight your cancer risk goes down to a half, your diabetes disappears, you live longer, alzheimer's disease is less and, of course, the long term effects in the human race of not having this tsunami of obesity is amazing. People will live longer, they will be healthier, they will be more effective."*

Here is how the string test works. Get a piece of string and measure your height with it and cut it off at your precise height level. Fold the string in half and now measure it round the widest part of your stomach. The two ends should touch and if you are left with a gap between the ends of the folded string you need to work on reducing the gap.

Keeping fit

Well this sounds simple and – you've guessed it – it is something easy that most of us can do. Staying physically active improves our health and quality of life, and can help us live longer. Among the advantages of keeping active are a reduced risk of developing a life-threatening disease, a better chance of avoiding obesity, maintaining or reaching a healthy weight, improved sleep and increased daytime energy, feeling happier, and keeping your brain sharp. The more physically active you are, the longer you are likely to remain independent. Exercise makes you stronger, boosts confidence and increases your sense of well-being. It is best to start slowly and build up gradually. Experts recommend 30 minutes of moderate exercise a day about five times a week and it can be something as simple as a brisk walk. It's easy to boost your physical activity by incorporating some of the following into your everyday life:

- avoid lifts and escalators – take the stairs instead;
- cycle/walk rather than drive;
- take up walking/rambling (get a dog?).

Top tip

If you do need to increase your activity levels get a step counter or use the app on your phone. It's simple – get your activity and steps up. Aim to eventually get over 5000 steps a day and the impact could be amazing. Just ensure you check your plan out with your Doctor/ health professional.

Organised activities

There are lots of ways of staying fit and in most local areas there are loads of classes to help you do it; some may even be free, or cut-price, at your sports or community centre or local park. Find out what's available in your area. There are all sorts of activities, including boxercise, Pilates, table tennis, circuit training, swimming, running, cycling, walking groups and even bowling, where your competitive streak can be let loose again. Getting fit as part of a group gives a social aspect to it and is probably more motivating but if you want to get started on your own try Fitness Blender, which offers more than 400 free workout videos, ranging from high-intensity interval training to yoga: www.fitnessblender.com.

Healthy eating

We need fewer calories in our 50s and 60s than we did in our 30s. Eating a balanced diet and not overeating is important. There are a huge number of special diets and the media are forever commenting on what we should and should not eat. Treat some of that with a great deal of caution and just stick to a sensible balanced diet and try to avoid overeating. To get the best from your diet, follow these suggestions:

- Eat more fresh fruit and vegetables a day;
- cut back on bread;
- drink plenty of water and reduce or cut out high sugar e.g. fizzy drinks;
- eat more fish;
- drink less alcohol and limit your salt intake.

Top tips

- **Buy some smaller plates – size is everything here.**
- **Colour is good - if your plate is colourful that means lots of vegtables and fruit.**
- **Willpower – it's not about a diet fad or joining a gym for a few months. It's all about a new lifestyle for a lasting impact. So what is that lifestyle you want to create and what can you do about it?**

Drink (alcohol)

There is so much reported about over-indulgence with alcohol that this topic may seem too obvious to mention. The more you drink, the greater the risk to your health. The NHS suggested limit is 14 units a week and a pint of lager or a 175 ml glass of wine count as two units. For people who suspect they may have a drinking problem, the first point of contact should be their GP. There are organisations to help those in need of support, such as:

- Al-Anon Family Groups UK & Eire: www.al-anonuk.org.uk;
- Alcohol Concern: www.alcoholconcern.org.uk;

- Alcoholics Anonymous: www.alcoholics-anonymous.org.uk.

Smoking

The only advice to give is that you simply should not smoke – and if you still do you should stop and improve your health and save more. The start point is the NHS stop smoking service and can massively boost your chances of quitting for good. www.nhs.uk and search 'stop smoking services'.

Health insurance

Health insurance or private medical insurance (PMI) pays out for private treatment if you fall ill; it also allows you to avoid long queues for treatment, receive fast-track consultations, and be treated privately in an NHS or private hospital. PMI is not essential and the cost of it can increase significantly as you get older. You do, therefore, need to look very carefully at the balance between cost and benefit depending on your own situation. If you have an accident or serious illness such as a heart attack or cancer then the NHS steps in and can be world class. But problems can arise from other conditions that may be debilitating but not life-threatening; the challenge may be in getting a timely intervention so that you are more comfortable and can get on with enjoying your retirement years. If you have disposable income and your finances are in order you may be able to buy in the help you need for extra peace of mind. Not every eventuality is covered by PMI, so it is important to check your policy details and review the cost and affordability from time to time. Take care before moving from one provider to another and find out if pre-existing conditions are covered – get this wrong and you could be in for a very nasty surprise. The main providers are well known but there are other options such as wwwbendenden.co.uk which is a membership organisation where you can access reduced fee consultations on a pay as you go basis.

Private patients – without insurance cover

If you do not have private medical insurance but want to go into hospital in the UK as a private patient, there is nothing to stop you, provided your doctor is willing and you are able to pay the bills from your savings. Start the process by asking your doctor, 'Can I get this done privately?' and they will guide you from there.

Medical tourism

The term 'medical tourism' refers to travellers who have chosen to have medical/dental/surgical treatment abroad. Cosmetic surgery, dental procedures and cardiac surgery are the most common procedures that medical tourists undergo. Since the standards of medical treatments and available treatments vary widely across the world, anyone considering undertaking medical treatment abroad should carry out their own independent research. Further information and advice can be found at www.nhs.uk/NHSEngland/Healthcareabroad.

Hospital care cash plans

A hospital healthcare cash plan is an insurance policy that helps you pay for routine healthcare treatment, such as eye tests, dental treatment and physiotherapy. They are totally different to private medical insurance and can be a cheap way of paying for everyday health costs. You pay a monthly premium, depending on how much cover you want. When you receive the treatment you pay upfront, send the receipt to the insurer and it reimburses you, depending on the terms of your policy. More information is available from the British Health Care Association: www.bhca.org.uk.

Income protection policies

Income protection insurance used to be known as permanent health - insurance. It is a replacement-of-earnings policy for people who are still in work (employed or self-employed). Critical illness benefit policies pay a lump sum on diagnosis of a critical illness (and some life policies may pay out on diagnosis of a terminal illness rather than awaiting death to make the payment – read the small print if you are unsure). Take advice on the appropriateness of these policies from a financial adviser and check that they are regulated by the Financial Conduct Authority (FCA). The FCA maintains a register of approved financial advisers. Find out more at www.fca.org and go to 'check the register'. In addition, help may be available through policies arranged by your work in the form of sick leave policies or stand-alone cover. If you are nearing retirement or have significant borrowings you may wish to revisit the adequacy of your cover from these sorts of products and check when they expire.

Health screening

Personalised health assessments are a wise investment because they give an overview of your current general health and aim to identify any future health risks. Private health screening, outside the NHS, can give people peace of mind that they are not suffering from a serious health problem. There are a number of health assessment options depending on your personal needs, covering key lifestyle and health risks. For more information see:

- www.bmihealthcare.co.uk;
- www.bupa.co.uk;
- www.privatehealth.co.uk.

National Health Service

Choosing a GP

If you need to choose a new GP for whatever reason, is there a way of checking on how good they are? If you live in England or Wales you can do this quite easily via the Care Quality Commission (www.cqc.org.uk); at the top of their website toggle the drop-down box to doctors/GPs and then search by postcode.

Assessments ratings of outstanding, good, requires improvement and inadequate are provided for each of the following:

- treating people with respect and involving them in their care;
- providing care, treatment and support that meets people's needs;
- caring for people safely and protecting them from harm;
- staffing;
- quality and suitability of management.

Otherwise the usual best way to find a good GP is to ask for recommendations from trusted friends or, if you are new to an area, from your new neighbours – it's also a good ice-breaker.

Changing your GP

Since January 2015 all GP practices in England have been free to register new patients who live outside their boundary area. These arrangements are voluntary; if the practice has no capacity at the time or feels that it is not clinically appropriate for you to be registered, it can refuse registration and explain its reasons for so doing. If you know of a doctor whose list you would like to be on, you can simply turn up at his or her surgery and ask to be registered. You do not need to give a reason for wanting to change, and you do not need to ask anyone's permission. A request will then be made to your current GP for your medical records to be transferred to the new GP surgery.

NHS 111 service

111 is the NHS non-emergency number. It's fast, easy and free. When you call 111, you will speak to an adviser, supported by healthcare professionals, who will ask a number of questions to assess symptoms and direct you to the best medical care available. NHS 111 is available 24 hours a day, 365 days a year, and calls are free from landlines and mobile phones. For further information, see www.nhs.uk.

Prescriptions

The current prescription charge is £9.15 (2020/21 and reviewed annually from 1 April each year) but both men and women aged 60 and over are entitled to free NHS prescriptions. Certain other groups are also entitled to free prescriptions, including those on low incomes, and they are free in, for instance, Northern Ireland and Scotland. Find out more at www.nhs.uk and go to 'prescriptions'.

> **Top tip**
>
> If you are under 60 and pay for prescriptions, a 12-month prescription certificate costs £105.90 or it can be paid in 10 instalments (at Autumn 2020); if you need two items each month you can save over £100 (and over £300 if you have four items each month). You can do this online via the NHS website or your chemist can help you arrange it.

Going into hospital

Going into hospital can cause people a lot of anxiety. You may be admitted as an outpatient, a day patient (day case), or an inpatient. Many patients are unaware that they can ask their GP to refer them to a consultant at a different NHS trust or even, in certain cases, help make arrangements for them to be treated overseas. Before you can become a patient at another hospital, your GP will need to agree to your being referred. Those likely to need help on leaving hospital should speak to the hospital social worker, who will help make any necessary arrangements. Help is sometimes available to assist patients with their travel costs to and from hospital. Remember to take your phone charger and headphones. If you go into hospital you will continue to receive your pension as normal.

Complaints

If you want to make a complaint about any aspect of NHS treatment you have received or been refused, go to the practice or the hospital concerned and ask for a copy of their complaints procedure. This is the same for GPs, opticians, dentists, hospitals and any care given in the NHS. Full details of how to do this can be found at www.nhs.uk – 'complaints'. You can take the matter to the Health Services Ombudsman should you be dissatisfied after an independent review has been carried out. For further details see:

- Parliamentary and Health Service Ombudsman for England: www.ombudsman.org.uk;
- Public Services Ombudsman for Wales: www.ombudsman-wales.org.uk;
- Scottish Public Services Ombudsman: www.spso.org.uk.

An alternative would be to get in touch with your local Patient Advice and Liaison Service (PALS) office in the event of a problem with the health service. Find out more at www.nhs.uk – 'Patient Advice and Liaison Service'.

Complementary and alternative medicine

Complementary and alternative medicines are treatments that fall outside mainstream healthcare. Although the terms 'complementary' and 'alternative' medicine are often used interchangeably, there are distinct differences between them. Complementary medicine is a treatment that is used alongside conventional medicine, whereas alternative medicine is a treatment used in place of conventional medicine. The best known of these practices are homoeopathy, reflexology, osteopathy, chiropractic, aromatherapy, herbal remedies and hypnosis. Information on the most popular forms can be found on the following websites:

- Association of Reflexologists: www.aor.org.uk;
- British Acupuncture Council: www.acupuncture.org.uk;
- British Chiropractic Association: www.chiropractic-uk.co.uk;
- British Homoeopathic Association: www.britishhomeopathic.org;
- British Hypnotherapy Association: www.hypnotherapy-association.org;
- National Institute of Medical Herbalists: www.nimh.org.uk.

Useful reading on common health issues

The NHS website is the go to source for more information and explains medical conditions and provides advice. It's best to keep away from other sites as they just make things look scary and that does not help you or deal with the issue.

There are also good sites for specific conditions such as Cancer Research UK that can provide detailed guidance. As a general rule avoid any non-UK sites and chat rooms.

Reminder: Take any action points or follow up points to Chapter 12, Your Plan For A Better Retirement.

Chapter Ten
Leisure and holidays

"For my part, I travel not to go anywhere, but to go. I travel for travel's sake. The great affair is to move"

ROBERT LOUIS STEVENSON

For many this may be the chapter they first turn to on opening this book as we wait for the easing of restrictions imposed by the Covid-19 pandemic. It's all the more frustrating if you are very close to retirement or recently retired as, after all, it's what you have been working towards for decades. A time of endless leisure and holidays? Is that the vision? Well it's each to their own but the big factors are what you have planned and aspire to and then what your financial planning allows. So this chapter is all about making the best of the increased free time that is available to you. For some it may involve splashing out £20,000 on a 120 day round the world cruise with all food and drink paid for and you just sit back and take it all in. For others it may be developing the good life of allotments, home grown food and devoting themselves to helping others less fortunate through volunteering. For others the early active years of retirement may involve bringing in some extra money through a part time job or small business, trimming costs a bit and then enjoying a mix of regular holidays four or five times a year combined with some new interests. See how the chapters of this book come together! Get it right and you will achieve a better retirement but remember we are all different and just to repeat the point - it is 'each to their own'. Importantly this chapter is where the good stuff happens - leisure and holidays, and hopefully we will start approaching the lifestyles we used to enjoy from Easter 2021.

Putting this into achieving a better retirement means planning the sort of retirement you want over the three phases of retirement. The active years of retirement (as outlined in Chapter 1) are going to potentially involve more holidays and leisure activities. It is very difficult to give standard advice because we are all different. This chapter is intended to get you thinking ahead about the sort of leisure and holiday activities you could tackle as you embark on your 'active retirement years'.

This chapter at a glance

- Keeping fit – some reminders of the easy starting points. Then just keep going.
- Sporting activities, watching sport and forming your own club. Don't sit around waiting for someone else to do it – it's easy and our three-step model will help get things going.
- Entertainment and hobbies – try something different, you just never know what you might ignite. This includes how to access free 'big name' entertainment by getting hold of TV/radio audience tickets – and we all like things that are quality and free (and those two words do not often go hand in hand).
- How to get started on writing that book you have had buzzing around your head and how to follow through on any study aspirations.
- Tips and pointers on holidays, cruises, short UK breaks and starting to tick off some more European city breaks (especially if you can buy a flight for £40 each way).
- In reading this chapter you might surprise yourself at finding a hidden talent that has lain dormant until now.
- Travel insurance and help if things go wrong on holiday – some essential tips. Don't leave home without them.

Keeping yourself fit

A good starting point is to look at ways of keeping yourself reasonably fit as it seems that the fairly basic rule is a simple one: the fitter you are the better and longer your quality of life. More at Chapter 9, Health and Relationships and remember to speak to your doctor / GP before embarking on a radical change / increase in exercise.

Walking and running

Walking costs nothing, doesn't require expensive equipment and is the best form of natural exercise. It keeps you healthy, prolongs your life and improves your mental health. There is walking (in the park), hiking (in the hills), rambling (across country), hill walking (in mountainous areas), fell walking (particularly in the Lake District and Yorkshire Dales – fell meaning high, uncultivated land) and scrambling (sometimes applied to mountain walking).

Why not join a small group, which may even have a side benefit of introducing a new circle of friends. Get onto the web and see what might be available locally or take a few soundings from friends and acquaintances. Failing that, try the Ramblers' Charity at www.ramblers.org.uk. If you are more enthusiastic, try running as a hobby. You can do this indoors (at the gym) or outdoors, by yourself as a solo activity, with a group or by joining a club. For those keen to get running try the 'Couch to 5k' app or the following websites for more information:

1. England Athletics: www.englandathletics.org;

2. Run England: www.runengland.org;

3. Association of Running Clubs: www.runningclubs.org.uk.

4. Your local area for park 'fun runs' or up a level to www.parkrun.org.uk for 5k community runs on Saturday mornings.

Swimming

Swimming is also one of the best forms of exercise; it builds strength and endurance and it is beneficial for your metabolism and the cardiovascular system. Swimming as a hobby, whether you are a beginner or a seasoned swimmer, is a great way to relax and get fit. For more information see British Swimming at www.britishswimming.org.

Sporting activities

The list of possibilities is virtually endless and popular leisure sports are golf, tennis, boating, cycling and fishing and there is a further endless list of activities. A bit of research and asking around friends could spark that 'oh, why not, I'll give it a try' moment!

Watching sport and forming your own club

There is excellent coverage of sport on TV but it is really enjoyable to get out and watch live sport. There are many different opportunities – you can watch your local football, netball or rugby team, and of course there are also the big international events which all provide a good day out with a bunch of friends. The main thing is to get off the couch and get out and support your favourite or local team in person or even try something new. Transport and cost issues can be solved by forming your own 'club' – just follow these three easy rules:

1. Find three or four like-minded friends – that is all you need to get started.

2. Agree the briefest of 'rules'– going to events, enjoyment, friendship and sharing the cost.

3. Manage the money. The rules require everyone to chip in £50, which the 'treasurer' keeps. You then top it up after each event so that the pot always comes back to number of members times £50. The 'secretary' identifies the event, date and cost and people decide if they want to go or not. If you don't go the £50 in the pot is rolled forward. Every group need a 'chairperson' who just makes the final decision if there is a split vote – then you get on with it. You'll soon find the group of four extends to six and then 10; at some point you'll have to call it a day on new members as part of the fun is the friendship of a smallish group.

Top tip

Don't wait for someone else to get your own club going. An informal club can apply to anything – sports followers, entertainment viewing or even a club that follows both! Just get on with it; agree a few simple rules, have someone trustworthy keep a tab on the money pot and off you go.

Entertainment

Approaching – and reaching – retirement means you will probably have increased opportunities to head off for a night's entertainment. Why not try something new?

Look beyond your local mainstream cinemas and then also try local drama groups.

A bit of culture – opera, ballet, concerts and museums

Love, hate or don't know? Some of the gems of the UK are its museums and music concerts (from punk to a full orchestra). If you have never tried a ballet or a night at the opera then why not give it a go?

TV and radio audiences

Participating as members of studio audiences and making contributions to programmes is entertaining and free. Tickets for very popular shows can be hard to obtain but you never know – and a new show could be the next big thing. Check out:
Applause Store (www.applausestore.com)
BBC Shows (www.bbc.co.uk/showsandtours/tickets)

Hobbies and other interests

Wikipedia has compiled a great 'list of hobbies' page which lists literally hundreds of possibilities along with their usual click-through facility to reveal more. They range from Acting to Zumba. If something in particular takes your fancy then do a bit more specific exploring on the web and then locally. Don't be worried if you then find it is not for you, just move on to something else – you have time to get it right and find something that really sits with your time, skills, values and beliefs. Below are seven selected as random examples and literally this book could have been filled with lists of hobbies. There is absolutely no limit on what you could do once we recover from the re-set moment brought about by the Covid-19 pandemic. Who knows where the hobby could lead and remember it's never too soon to start that new hobby if active retirement is years away and you are still in the planning phase.

Gardening

Views differ on where to classify gardening – is it a hobby, a pastime or a necessity? Whatever view you may take, most of us do have gardens and either enjoy looking after them or are forced to do so. If you are already a keen gardener who really enjoys working and relaxing in the garden then keep the good work going and you will enjoy the fact that you now have the time and opportunity to do even more. If you are amongst the less enthusiastic, perhaps due to a busy working schedule, now may be the opportunity to devote a little more time to it. Don't regard it as a chore, and just concentrate on the simple things at first. A nice lawn is the centrepiece to many gardens and the fact that you will now have the time to give it a weekly trim rather than a quick cut when time permits will work wonders for the appearance of your garden.

Jazz appreciation society - 'nice'

This is another randomly selected hobby just to illustrate the range and diversity of hobbies. This could be a group of enthusiasts that meet in a hall or bar to listen to jazz. At each meeting a member presents an hour of their choice of jazz followed by members playing music from their own collections based on a regular monthly theme. If there is not a club or if you want to change the genre and form your own just follow the tips in the watching sport section above to form your own club.

Mentor

You could help young people in your area. There are many government backed schemes and one is Mosiac a national charity mentoring network backed by the Prince's Trust (www.mosaicnetwork.co.uk).

Model railway clubs

Enthusiasts include Warren Buffett, Eric Clapton, Tom Hanks, Bruce Springsteen, Rod Stewart, Ringo Star and Pete Waterman. Clubs provide a social scene and new members can benefit from the experience and wealth of knowledge and good clubs always adapt to the needs of their members.

Museum volunteer

From the Imperial War Museum to the National History Museum to local museums. The opportunities are abundant for paid and unpaid roles. Check out your favourite museums for opportunities and if it follows one of your passions then even better.

Painting

Get those creative genes flowing onto canvas and try exploring those skills that may have lain dormant since those art classes in your school days. It's never too late to take up this hobby and find your preferred media (watercolour, pastel or ink etc.) and style. Local clubs can be found by an internet search or from your circle of friends where someone will know someone and can introduce you. New member events are usually held throughout the year where the novices can started in a nice friendly environment.

Zookeeper

Zoos depend on volunteers and training will be provided. It keeps you fit and will be sociable as there can be lots of interacting with the public. Enquire at your local zoo.

Write that book?

Why not write that book you've had buzzing around in your head? You might discover a hidden talent and write a bestseller, but for many it ends up as an unfinished project. If you are determined then just start at the beginning, with a fair idea of the ending, and take your readers on the journey. Your motto will be to write, read, rewrite (and repeat). It may end up being self-printed for family and friends or self-published for a wider audience. Or you may find yourself in the realms of working with a publisher, either with or without the help of an agent. As far as top tips go, you will find that lots of people have lots to say on the internet about writing. So we will leave you with just two suggestions. First, make writing a habit; it requires perseverance. Create a routine and write at the same time every day; if it just isn't working one day then give up that day and go and do something else. Then buy a guidebook to help steer you through the maze of options and opportunities – try the *Writers and Artists Yearbook 2021* (more at www.writersandartists.co.uk). Once you are established as a writer, and if you meet their criteria, the Society of Authors is the 'must join' organisation (www.societyofauthors.org). In the meantime a check online should find any local writers' groups in your area which is another good starting point.

More study?

You may well feel that during your working life you have done enough studying and attended enough courses and consider you are more than due a break from all of that. However, when the pressure of being almost forced to do something disappears, you can study what takes your fancy, and of course you now have time to do so. You may enjoy holidaying abroad in a particular area but miss out on a lot because of language barriers – now is the time to try to pick up the basics; your computer and IT skills may be a bit rusty – again, you now have time to put that right. Try www.learndirect.com for IT courses and help. You might want to tune up your home cooking skills. There are a wide range of part-time vocational-type courses available at local Further Education Colleges and other institutes of learning throughout the country. Take a little time to find out what is available in your own area. Your local community will offer various social and learning activities, so visit your leisure centre, church, community centre or library to find out what's available. Libraries are an endangered species these days so pop in – you never know what or who you might spot, see or meet.

Also worth looking at is the University of the Third Age (U3A). This organisation could almost be described as 'one size fits all' because it is committed to lifelong learning, can help combat loneliness with social interaction, and offers a huge range of activities and courses both cerebral and physical. There are plenty of U3A branches around the United Kingdom, so you should be able to find one near you. For more information, visit www.u3a.org.uk.

Holidays

This may well be the part of retirement that you are really looking forward to once we return to normal. With all that time now available you might be thinking about a world cruise, more overseas visits to relatives and close friends, taking an expedition to some remote corner of the world, visiting cities on your must-see list, or maybe just long, leisurely days somewhere in the sun. Retirement really does give you additional options. You are no longer stuck with set holiday dates, which has the additional bonus of allowing you to take advantage of last-minute offers and cheaper rates at off-peak times. Also, of course, you now have time to shop around for the best bargains. So get out there and start looking for your ideal holiday or adventure at the best price. If you are reasonably competent with computers and the internet you can do a great deal of your business in that way and it frequently represents good value for money. But don't ignore a tried-and-trusted travel agent, many of whom are very knowledgeable about locations and prices.

Here are a few examples just to get your mind working on the endless opportunities.

Bus travel and coach and rail holidays

You may be entitled to concessionary travel in England, Wales, Scotland and Northern Ireland with different rules in different countries and even regions. Just jump onto www.ageuk.org.uk and 'free bus pass and transport concessions and take whatever you get and enjoy! The Senior Railcard can save a third of the cost on standard or first-class fares (www.senior-railcard.co.uk) and National Express offer a Senior Coachcard that entitles you to a third off ticket prices (www.nationalexpress.com).

Cruising

The cruise market continued to break records up until February 2020 and the onset of the Covid-19 pandemic. It was driven by new and often larger ships constantly being launched. And, of course, cruising does tend to be particularly attractive to the older generation. Cruising may be reshaped as part of the re-set moment post Covid-19 but don't be put off and consider the offers that will start to come through again. It would seem obvious to say that there may be a reshaping towards smaller boats providing more personal space.

Cruising can take you to virtually anywhere in the world or around the British Isles and our wonderful coastline. The big advantage is that your own hotel travels along with you. You can simply relax in the sun of the Mediterranean or the Caribbean; explore a range of classic cities; get to know the Scandinavian countries or Alaska; explore the mysteries of the Far East; or visit Australia and New Zealand. The possibilities are endless, as can be seen from a quick browse of cruise brochures in any travel agents. Or get online and type in the names of a couple of cruise lines.

There are various reasons why so many people enjoy cruising: many operators have ships leaving from the UK, reducing air travel; seeing multiple destinations but unpacking only once; the wide choice, as cruise ships come in all shapes and sizes. Cruise holiday are easy to plan, they are social and there are activities and entertainments galore. If you want to take a closer look at the range on offer from cruise companies and what their individual ships are like, get hold of a copy of the Berlitz book on cruising, which is regularly updated and provides lots of valuable and dependable information on all aspects of cruising and cruise ships.

Top cruising tips

- *Inside cabins* can be an absolute bargain for those on a budget but wanting exceptional itineraries. However, there is no natural light, which can play havoc with your body clock and they can be in poor locations (corridor, lift, engine or other noise) – but don't dismiss them as an option.
- *Buy early or buy late*: Experienced cruisers know the form. Buy early to get the best cabins in the best locations and deep discounts or hang on to the last minute to get a bargain on an under-booked cruise. Shopping around or staying with the same agent (loyalty bonuses and trusted knowledge) can both help with the price you pay. Try negotiations around the amount of on-board spend they will credit to your room as part of any 'deal'.
- *How much!* Many cruises make deep profits on the price of drinks and that final day when you settle up your bill can be sobering. Think about pre-paid drinks packages; some cruises offer these free as an inducement.
- *Repositioning cruises* are made by all the major cruise lines where the ship moves between continents and seasons. There are more days at sea and less ports visited but they are cheaper.
- *How much (part 2)!* Cruise lines also make deep profits from excursions. The bonus is that their ship probably won't leave port if your coach breaks down and you miss the scheduled departure time. On the other hand you can probably halve the cruise excursion price by going with a local alternative, and enterprising organisations have set up 'shore excursion' companies offering trips that mirror the cruise company offering. A brief search on the internet will find these, but always check out the independent reviews and get back to the port on time as the ship may not wait for you.
- *Cruise from the UK or a European port?* We know our lovely UK weather but who has crossed the Atlantic or the Bay of Biscay when it's been rough? The passage to

warmer, smoother seas may eat up four or five days of your precious holiday, so is it worth it? Or do you fly out and pick up a cruise from a Mediterranean port in the more challenging months outside the May-to-mid-September window?

- Some useful websites are www.whatsinport.com for overviews and hints and tips on what is in and around the port area with maps and suggestions that may help if you don't want to go on excursions. Another useful website is www.cruisecritic.co.uk for port and ship overviews and user reviews.

Cargo ship cruises

Seeing the world by cargo ship doesn't offer the trappings of a conventional cruise, but being aboard a freight ship as a paying passenger is like being in another world. Many carry up to 12 non-crew members on routes from a week to months long. Securing a berth can be complicated, and periods in port tend to be brief, but life on board is uneventful – perfect for reading and writing. See Cargo Ship Voyages: www.cargoshipvoyages.com.

River cruising

This type of cruising has some similarities to ocean cruising but there are differences.

Riverboats are much smaller and tend to be more intimate, which some people prefer. Because of their size there tends to be less concentration on entertainment. They do, however, give an excellent opportunity to explore inland towns and cities. Frequently the mooring is very close to the city or town centre – just step off the boat and you are there.

Short breaks

The UK is a brilliant place packed with diversity and places of interest - that's why the world flocks here as a must see destination. So as a quick reminder and a starter for ten you could start planning those weekends:

- shop in London (as it's better than New York, Paris or Milan);
- take in the pretty gardens and villages in the Cotswolds;
- Caernarfon Castle;
- hit the Lanes and seafront at Brighton;
- take in the rugby, shops and restaurants in Edinburgh:
- have a titanic experience in Belfast;

- stride the Giant's Causeway;
- tackle the Lake District;
- drive Bwlch y Groes (Hell Fire Pass) in Wales;
- put a bet on at Newmarket racecourse;
- take a steam train to historic York;
- see and experience the world class museums in London.

The list is literally endless just google 'what's on' in different areas and start your own list. You may already have taken advantage of weekend breaks during your working life. A short trip of three or four days is attractive due to relatively low-cost air fares. If you book early and can travel mid-Wednesday afternoon with only hand baggage, you can nab some of those £40 seats when travel gets back to normal after the Covid-19 pandemic. Next best is to try starting your trip on a Sunday night – it's usually the cheapest time for hotel rates. Again, the list is endless and the budget airline websites carry decent overviews and tips. To get your list going try visiting or revisiting :

- Amsterdam – tulips, art, culture and wacky cafes.

- Barcelona – excellent flight connections make this a must-see city with its Olympic stadium, beach and Las Ramblas all combining very well. Gaudi's La Sagrada Familia Cathedral will stop you in your tracks (oh, and there is that football team as well).

- Belfast – according to the New York Times "an eye watering experience in the best possible way".

- Any island in the Canaries - for a long weekend and some proper Winter sun.

- The walled City of Dubrovnik – nearly every roof was replaced following the shelling it endured less than three decades ago but the city is standing tall again.

- Prague – exceptional value and perhaps one of the most beautiful places you will visit.

- Rome – culturally outstanding, if a little expensive.

- Venice – enchanting.

- Reykjavik – highlights include the Northern Lights and National Parks. Timing can mean lots of daylight or darkness and the cost of living when out there can seem expensive.

> **Top tip**
>
> Some city festivals are truly stunning and world class, leaving an indelible memory. Try La Mercè in Barcelona in September to see what I mean. Prices may go up so plan and book your flights and hotel early and enjoy!

Activity holidays

Holidays that involve your hobby can be a double bonus. Rambling, sport, war tours, history club tours, motor racing, art, reading, painting, yoga retreats – the list is endless. Check with your local contacts and look online.

Holidays for people with disabilities

Affordable, accessible and enjoyable holidays for the disabled are many and varied. Airlines, hotels and resorts are providing people with disabilities or mobility issues the opportunities to travel, enjoy holidays and see the world. Specially designed self-catering units are more plentiful and of a higher standard. Also, an increasing number of trains and coaches are installing accessible loos. An elderly or disabled person seeking a holiday must explain clearly what their care needs are, not only in terms of getting to and from, but also with regard to accommodation requirements. Some people take companions/carers with them. There is a great deal of information available on the internet, so do take time to research carefully. Organizations that can help you include:

- Age UK: www.ageuk.org.uk;
- Able Community Care: www.uk-care.com;
- Accessible Travel: www.accessibletravel.co.uk;
- Disabled Holidays: www.disabledholidays.com;
- Disabled Access Holidays: www.disabledaccessholidays.com.

Hotels and Airbnb

Airbnb (www.airbnb.co.uk) has come into everyday use and helps you find homes and rooms in holiday hotspots for much less than hotel room rates. The quality can be amazing but there has been an incidence of scam accommodation so check for a history or reviews (both quantity and quality) over a few years.

Big hotel groups have loyalty programmes that can stack up and beat price comparison websites prices and the 'loyalty' also helps ensure you don't end up with the nightmare room (above the kitchen, no sea view, beside the lift etc).

Top tip

Rock bottom prices from comparator websites without a room type guarantee usually means a rock bottom room without a view. Try the hotel direct and get a guarantee on the room class - generally the more you pay the better the room. Every hotel has some rooms that no one wants to end up in.

Holidays on your own

When it comes to travelling there are many single people who want to see the world but are daunted by the prospect. Many people travel solo; some may be single, others not. There are companies specialising in singles holidays, tour holidays, exploring holidays and relaxing escape holidays - try searching for 'holidays for solo travellers' and www.friendshiptravel.com for an idea of the offering. Singles holidays should help improve safety, security and the certainty of help and support when needed. There is advice for single travellers on the Age UK website – visit www.ageuk.org.uk and go to 'Tips for single travellers' (including tips on breaking the ice, making time for yourself and staying safe).

Home-swapping holidays

House-swapping with someone on the other side of the world is easy and saves money on accommodation and the bonus for those who dare to do this is the experience of living life as a local, not a tourist. Check with your insurance company in case they place restrictions or exclusions on either your home contents or buildings cover. Some broker sites are:

- Exchange Holiday Homes: www.exchangeholidayhomes.com;
- Home Exchange: www.homeexchange.com;
- Love Home Swap: www.lovehomeswap.com.

Travel insurance

As you age you are far more likely to have a pre-existing medical condition that needs to be declared and covered on travel insurance. Some tips on buying holiday insurance follow:

- If you are travelling solely to Europe, *don't rely on your European Health Insurance Card for protection*; it won't cover everything and may not be valid from 1 January 2021 and Brexit (check www.gov.uk and 'healthcare for UK nationals visiting the EU for updates).
- Adequate *personal liability cover is essential*; a minimum of around £1 million is advisable.
- For safety, *medical expenses cover* should be around £2 million and review conditions that apply to Covid-19.
- Your policy should have appropriate *cancellation and curtailment cover* in case you fall ill or cut your holiday short – read the small print for limitations and exclusions.
- *Don't leave arranging cover until just before you depart*, in case anything happens between booking and departure.
- If you're planning a few breaks over the next year, it could be more cost-effective to buy *annual worldwide cover*. Have a look at some of the comparison websites.
- *If you have a packaged (paid-for) bank account, check if it includes travel insurance*. Some bank accounts include a family travel policy, or winter sports cover.

A cost-effective idea may be to extend any existing medical insurance you have to cover you while abroad. Then take out a separate policy (without medical insurance) to cover you for the rest of your travel needs.

The basic advice is that it can be a complex field and you do need to shop around to get the cover that suits you at the best price.

Things can go wrong

For complaints and assistance when things go wrong, and for the framing of a complaint, see Chapter 6.

Plane delays and missed connections can ruin a holiday but if you are armed with information about your rights you might just save the day. Concise, well-written guides are hard to find but we like the Consumer Council for Northern Ireland's 'Plane Facts'. Download and print a copy and stick it in your baggage just in case. Visit www.consumercouncil.org.uk and go to 'Plane Facts'.

Your rights and translating those rights when travelling abroad in Europe can be difficult if your knowledge of the host country language is non-existent or rusty. Help is now at hand by downloading the app 'EEC-Net: Travel' for free. It provides a range of common problems you may encounter when travelling and the usual phrase that you would ask in English – at a press of a button the phrase is translated, with then further help prompted by yes/no buttons. And it works!

Top tip

Download, print and store 'Plane Facts' in your baggage and download the 'EEC-Net: Travel' app on your phone. Details of both are above.

Compensation for lost baggage and cancelled or overbooked flights

There is plenty of protection and we won't take up space here with the details of how to complain, your rights, appeals and the amounts you can expect – just download, print and keep 'Plane Facts' as mentioned above. Is the message getting through?

Some final holiday tips

- *Safety.* If in doubt, leave it out this year and trust your instincts on foreign travel where there is or is perceived to be an increased security or Covid-19 threat. For more official information check the Foreign Office's latest advice at www.gov.uk

and go to 'foreign travel advice' where there is detailed country-specific information and advice. Your travel insurance may not cover you if you travel against Foreign Office advice so ask 'is it really worth it?' before you go ahead.

- *When organising travel always pay by credit card* (if you have paid more than £100, credit cards give increased protection if things go wrong or a contract is broken). More information on these rights (known as 'Section 75 rights') can be found in Chapter 6, which also explains that a second-best route is to use a debit card because of the protection known as 'charge back'. Unless vital, don't transfer funds from bank account to bank account as this route offers no protection.
- *Always check the small print of your insurance.* Going for the cheapest option can come back to haunt you under the 'what you pay is what you get' rule of life. Check if your insurance covers anything Covid-19 related including if hospitalised or for repatriation.
- *Make sure that your carrier/travel company is ATOL (Air Travel Organiser's Licence) registered if your purchase involves a flight and a hotel.* E There is also the Association of British Travel Agents (ABTA), which deals with rail, cruise and self-drive holidays. Note that ABTA has an arbitration scheme for breaches of contract, which can be cheaper and more efficient than going to court. ABTA also has a mediation service for disputes about personal injury and sickness (see www.abta.com.
- Pack any regular medicines you require and take a copy of a prescription and any relevant medical history. Even familiar branded products can be difficult to obtain in some countries. In addition, take a mini first-aid kit with you. If you are going to any developing country, consult your doctor as to what pills (and any special precautions) you should take.
- *Have a photocopy of your passport tucked away and write an emergency contact name and number on it - just in case.*
- *Be careful of the water you drink.* If the local water has a reputation for being dodgy watch out for ice, salads, and any fruit that you do not peel yourself.
- *Have any travel inoculations or vaccinations well in advance of your departure date.*

Useful reading

The list of hobbies on Wikipedia and associated links.

The Foreign Office's latest advice at www.gov.uk and go to 'foreign travel advice' There is detailed country-specific information and advice.

Lonely Planet travel guides on all countries.

'Plane Facts'. Download and print a copy and stick it in your travel baggage just in case. Visit www.consumercouncil.org.uk and go to 'Plane Facts'.

Reminder: Take any action points or follow up points to Chapter 12, Your Plan For A Better Retirement.

Chapter Eleven
The sandwich generation

"Ageing is an extraordinary process, whereby you become the person that you always should have been."

DAVID BOWIE

The sandwich generation is the shorthand being adopted to describe the people that are looking after both dependent young adults and dependent elderly relatives. It's a growing issue in terms of the number of people affected and the scale of the financial and emotions involved. It is challenging because many in the sandwich generation who are in their fifties may have wholly or partly lost out on those gold-plated final pension schemes. Then just as the sandwich generation thought that things could not get any worse along comes the Covid-19 pandemic. If this all rings true then this final chapter is the one for you. It sits comfortably within the 'live better' essential step of this book as there are many things that you can retune things and help achieve a better retirement when we come through the Covid-19 pandemic.

One main driver is a debt-laden younger generation, with university leavers from the 2012 entrance year and beyond racking up £50,000 in student loans which have onerous interest rates. Buying a first house will be challenging for them and many sandwich generation parents may feel that their children still need a helping hand in the near future, even though they are well into their twenties and beyond. The prospect of helping shield them from some or all of the student loan impact may also create financial (and emotional) stress that increases if you have two, three or more children entering this phase of their lives.

Those same children may go on to get married with the sandwich generation parents looking to follow in their parent's footsteps and foot the bill or part of it. With the average price of a wedding running out at £32,000 the impact may make your eye's water if you have several children. I actually question this figure and think that beautiful, emotional and personal weddings can be achieved for a fraction of that cost and maybe the Covid-19 re-set moment may see things change.

Another pressure point on our younger people is unaffordable housing which has led to home ownership halving and, instead, our young people paying out 'dead money' in rent and not acquiring an asset base early enough. The size of the deposit is too much and the lending deal may simply be unaffordable, irrespective of help to buy schemes, and especially if you live in London or the South East or other property 'hot spots'.

Then we have the simple fact that Covid-19 has ripped the guts out of the hospitality, entertainment, events and retail sector upon which many of our young folk depend for early or part time employment.

The up-shot is boomerang kids who will be living with parents a lot longer than their parents lived at home with all the associated emotional and financial factors that arise from this fact.

Looking up a generation to the parents of the sandwich generation, the pressures are, again, both emotional and financial and both are interlinked as quality care has a significant cost (or put another way 'you pay your money and make your choice'). With residential care costs running at anywhere between £30,000 to £60,000 per year depending on location and the extent of medical assistance needed you can see the predicament. The sandwich generation may find the financial pressures of their children are compounded by the financial pressures of elderly relatives where the state funding or the relative's assets are insufficient. The third phase of retirement may be approaching for your relative when home maintenance issues and costs start to run away with themselves and perhaps even raise questions of safety and welfare. The garden may get to be too difficult to cope with. There may also be medical factors which are making things not as easy as they used to be. Their being alone in a house, however cherished, may also bring pressures of loneliness and depression. Of course it may not get that way but there could be an alternative way. It is the decision about moving into a care environment.

Well that's probably enough to set the scene and now it's time to work through things and find opportunities to 'live better' and achieve a better retirement.

This chapter at a glance

- Some facts about the retirement prospects of our younger people.
- Boomerang children returning back to home after University / College and the need for space.
- Helping millennials on the way with pensions planning and funding.
- Planning for the big events that may be just round the corner: university fees, weddings, house deposits and grandchildren.
- Planning for care home fees.
- Maintaining independence for as long as possible and the ways quality of life can be preserved, via help from local authority services, healthcare professionals and specialist services.
- Home repairs and adaptations, so that your loved ones can remain safely in their own home, retaining their dignity and independence.
- Accommodation, housing options and costs.
- Voluntary organisations that can help.
- Practical help and information on benefits and allowances and how to obtain financial assistance, if eligible.

Changes in intergenerational outcomes over 95 years

The Silent Generation (born 1925 to 1945) were disciplined and grew up expecting a hard life. The Baby Boomers (born 1946 to 1964) were part of a huge population increase and forged new conventions and broke down old ones. Generation X followed (born between 1965 and 1979) with Millennials (born 1980 to 1994) believing they could achieve anything and are very self-sufficient. Generation Z (born 1995 to 2012) are more tolerant of others. I'm not sure if they have come up with a label for those born in 2020/21- maybe it will be the Isolation Generation?

Millennials and Generation Z are a very relevant age group to 'sandwich generation' parents. The retirement outcomes of the Millennials and Generation Z put many of our own concerns into sharp focus and are worth thinking through as the sandwich generation may need to rethink priorities and retirement planning.

The Resolution Foundation undertakes research on living standards in the UK. Their research showed that millennials are only half as likely to own their home by age 30 as baby boomers were by the same age, and four times more likely to rent privately. Earnings progress has stalled for young adults today. Millennials are earning the same as those born 15 years before them were at the same age. There is pessimism about young adults' chances of improving on their parents' lives – pessimists outnumbered optimists by two-to-one. This marks a dramatic, and very rapid, turnaround in outlook. As recently as 2003, optimists outnumbered pessimists by nearly four-to-one. The resolution Foundation found that healthcare is the most pressing area of worry for British adults: 42 per cent place it in their top three concerns for the country, whereas internationally it ranks in fifth place. These concerns may partly be anchored in the increasingly parlous state of adult social care services, with the number of people in England who do not get the care they need having doubled since 2010 to 1.2 million. They found that baby boomers feel they are at risk of not getting the health and care they need in later life.

Boomerang children and the sandwich generation

The term boomerang children describes those who flew off to University or College and then return 'home' after completing their course or graduating. They may be saddled with debt and the employment opportunities in terms of income, security and pension and other benefits is eroding in real terms. Many can't afford to rent and can't afford to buy a house so the benefits of several years back home may assist. This allows them to save a deposit for a house or progress in their career to earn enough to rent. The issue for the sandwich generation of home owners may be gaining sufficient space for each other under one roof and sandwich generation parents may, therefore, be interested in home adaptions or home expansion as a way to a solution, more in Chapter 1, Your Home and Property.

Pensions for the millennials

Pensions knowledge and retirement planning is poor amongst millennials and disposable cash is limited. Government initiatives around automatic enrollment is finally starting to see decent amounts being saved into pensions as the employer is compelled to contribute as well as the employee. The amount of employer contribution has increased so it is a form of deferred pay rise. But it remains short of ideal levels and only impacts the employed and, therefore, the self-employed or unemployed millennials are still left struggling on pension funding. Could this be where grandparents, parents and close relatives help millennials with contributions into a pension or LISA (see Chapter 4, Savings and Investments). This is either to top up the employer / employee contributions or to kick start pensions for other millennials. This has half an eye on inheritance tax planning as gifting and surviving seven years can (under current tax rules) reduce inheritance tax and the question is whether those with large estates should be gifting earlier (seer Chapter 4, Tax)?

Planning for big events – university fees, weddings, house deposits and grandchildren

Let's take this one by one against the back drop of millennials and their stagnating earnings as shown above. How can sandwich generation parents help (and, indeed, cope)?

The first thing that will hit parents of younger millennials is the sharp increases in University fees from 2012. In very rough terms university fees soared overnight from around £3,500 to around £9,000 a year. Add on top off this about £5,000 a year for accommodation and about £3,500 for maintenance (basically food, drink, entertainment, travel and hopefully some books). So say about £50,000 over three years but less if you stay at home. At the same time the interest rate applied to the loans changed significantly and now sees a two tier system of interest. If your children started university after 2012 the interest on their loans will be charged at about 5.6% (Autumn 2020). The basic theory goes like this. If your children don't earn enough the loan will eventually be written off and the interest charged on the remainder partly reflects this 'bad debt' provision. But if it's likely your children are going to pay off their loans then should you look around at alternative forms of finance for part or all of the loan especially if you have the money or can access low interest rate finance of around 2% in alternative ways such as the equity in your home via a remortgage?

Then we have the wedding. The wedding website Hitched.co.uk states the average bill for wedding arrangements had risen to £31,974 in 2019. It also pointed out tips like picking a cheaper month, hiring a marquee and selecting your own caterers which all nibbled away at the headline cost. Alternatively could there be another way with the sandwich generation parents looking to help things out with clever use of pension tax free lump sum planning and playing the tax rate bands to ultimately provide more money at the right time (more at Chapter 3, Pensions)? Or maybe grandparents could think about anti-inheritance tax gifting into ISAs for the lucky couple as outlined in Chapter4.

Still struggling on limited earnings and having moved out of the family home the millennials and generation z will come to need to find a deposit for their first home as they become fed up with the dead money of renting. By dead money it means it is not part of their asset wealth that will, eventually, help finance their own retirement or their own children's 'big events' or their own nice care home. Again the sandwich generation parents could look to help things out with clever use of pension tax free lump sum planning and maybe even grandparents thinking about anti-inheritance tax gifting down into LISAs for the lucky couple as outlined in Chapters 4 and 5. This should be looked at sooner rather than later as some tax breaks (particularly around pensions) are likely to be tightened as part of a 'tax pain' agenda that we should see surfacing later in 2021.

Related to purchasing a home the sandwich generation parents could consider lending their names to the new home mortgage. These are called 'Joint Borrower, Sole Proprietor' mortgages which take the income of two borrowers into account (parent and child) but only puts the child's name on the deeds. This should avoid the extra 3% stamp duty that a property owning parent would incur if their name was on the deeds but the maximum age (maybe 70 to 75?) at the end of the mortgage term may limit the availability of this solution. A solicitor should be consulted to review what happens if the relationship does not work out and how everyone's interests can be protected. At the moment there is also additional and currently temporary stamp duty holiday regimes in place across the home nations and more is set out in Chapter5, Tax.)

The next big event will be grandchildren. The Times (Mark Atherton) reported on 28 April 2018 about getting to grips with the big financial events of your life and that "A newborn baby will cost £229,251 to raise to the age of 21, according to the Centre for Economic and Business Research. This includes childcare and education related costs but not private school... add £141,863 for a day pupil and £260,927 for a border." Sandwich generation parents may still be able to help at this stage but, if not, some of the best advice you can give is about having an emergency fund and to review their life cover.

Planning for care home fees

In managing potential care home planning for elderly relatives the potential positive is that there is likely to be some capital (in the form of a house) to fall back on and there may also be state help available. If you are in the position of caring for an elderly person, be that a parent, relative or loved one, you will contribute to make their remaining years happy, comfortable and meaningful. As the 'meat' in the sandwich between younger and older generations you can be that little bit more effective with some improved knowledge.

In terms of the main 'elephant in the room' issue it will be down to you, your relatives, close family and the family solicitor to determine policy and planning around the use of the home and care fees. As a reminder from the Chapter 5, Tax tread carefully if someone offers you a magic wand to 'protect your assets from the taxman' or schemes to shelter assets from 'claims for care home fees' based loosely on schemes involving trusts. The ideal scenario is that you would want to be dealing with the trusted family solicitor regulated by the Law Society in your jurisdiction (for instance in England and Wales at www.lawsociety.org.uk) and you would want a solicitor accredited on their Wills and Inheritance Quality Scheme (WIQS). If you depart from this route there are some questions set out in Chapter 5, Tax that may help you steer a safer course.

Maintaining independence

Being able to remain independent for as long as possible, and living in our own home, can be hugely important as you get older. The challenge is the cost, safety and convenience of the home as the years roll by. The cost is relatively straightforward if you face the facts – are the maintenance costs of the house and garden, insurance and council tax too high? On top of that, have you the time and ability to maintain both the house and garden or the funds to pay someone to do it? Perhaps more importantly, it is a simple fact that decent suitable housing underpins health and well-being, particularly in later life. The English Housing Survey found over a million homes occupied by those over 55 where there is significant risk to health (such as excess cold or injury from falling on poorly designed steps). These findings emphasise the importance of 'future-proofing' your home as you grow older so you can live safely and independently for as long as possible.

Local authority services

Local authorities have a responsibility to help elderly people and provide services that vulnerable people and those with disabilities may need.

After an initial discussion with your GP who may be able to assist with some local knowledge, hints and tips, you then need to approach your adult social services department, explaining you need to arrange a 'care assessment'. Find your local council at www.gov.uk – go to 'find your local council'. They will be able to advise you about what is needed and how to obtain the required help. Your relatives should be assigned a social worker who will be able to make the necessary arrangements or advise you on how to do this. Some of the services available include:

- practical help in the home, with the support of a home help;
- adaptations to the home, such as a ramp for a wheelchair;
- provision of day centres, clubs and similar;
- blue badge scheme for cars driven or used by people with a disability;
- advice about other transport services or concessions that may be available locally;
- assistance with preparing meals, bathing and washing, getting in and out of bed and cleaning.

There is a range of support personnel that you may encounter and they include:

- *Occupational therapists* have a wide knowledge of disability and can assist individuals via training, exercise or access to aids, equipment or adaptations to the home.
- *Health visitors* are nurses with a broad knowledge of health matters and specialised facilities that may be required.
- *District nurses* are fully qualified nurses who will visit a patient in the home, change dressings, attend to other routine nursing matters, monitor progress and help with the arrangements if more specialised care is required.
- *Physiotherapists* use exercise and massage to help improve mobility and strengthen muscles. They are normally available at both hospitals and health

centres.

- *Medical social workers* (MSWs) should be consulted if patients have any problems on leaving hospital. MSWs can advise on coping with a disablement, as well as such practical matters as transport, aftercare and other immediate arrangements. They work in hospitals, and an appointment should be made before the patient is discharged.

Following the assessment a care plan will be agreed and written out for you. Most councils charge you for care costs they provide at home; this remains an item high on the political agenda and costs are subject to both change and limits. Amounts, limits and caps vary depending on where you live. If you are over 65 you might be able to claim Attendance Allowance and if under 65 a Personal Independent Payment. Age UK advise:

> *"Most local councils charge for the services at home they provide. Some place an upper weekly limit on the amount you have to pay. Before charging you for services, your local council must work out how much you can afford to pay and this amount should leave you with a reasonable level of income. Check your local council's website for their charging information."*

Follow this advice and check back for updates at www.ageuk.org – go to 'finding help at home'.

Council Tax

There may be deductions available to you in the amount of Council Tax you have to pay (or in Northern Ireland the equivalent rates scheme). Typically these can include: 25 per cent reduction if living alone; if the property is empty as the resident is in a care home; disability deductions, including for severe mental impairments such as dementia. Contact your local council and enquire about help.

Special accommodation for the elderly

The time to start looking for appropriate accommodation for elderly parents or relatives is before they need it. A lot of research will have to be done, and there will be a better (and happier) outcome for all concerned if this process is not rushed. The earlier you make an assessment of their needs, the more choices and control you all will have.

At first glance, the loss of some level of independence can be overwhelming for many older people and thoughts may turn to feelings of shame, fear and confusion. But with your help and increased knowledge you may be able to tilt these initial feelings towards the opportunities and choices that may come with the change, such as increased safety, companionship, new views, closer proximity to a town's amenities and more. Brainstorm with family and trusted friends, and involve their medical team. Often the older person may listen more readily to their doctor or an impartial third party.

A good place to find information about options and funding is FirstStop Advice (www.firststopcareadvice.org.uk), an independent, impartial and free service provided by the national charity Elderly Accommodation Counsel (www.eac.org.uk). This service is for older people, their families and carers. It aims to get elderly people the help and care they need to live independently and comfortably for as long as possible. You will also find first-rate independent help from the Carers Trust via www.carers.org. You are not alone and are treading a well-worn path so start improving your knowledge and options on one of the most vital pieces of support you will provide in your lifetime.

Housing options

The following is a very brief overview of the different types of housing for elderly people.

Living with family

This might at first seem the simplest option, but will the elderly relative have friends and social amenities after moving in? What would happen if the family relationship broke down? Talk with the rest of the family and others that have done this (local networks at www.carers.org should be able to help place 'issues' on your list of things to think about). Sit down with your solicitor and consider any financial or legal implications that could arise before selling the person's home and building expensive annexes or extensions.

Sheltered or retirement housing

If your elderly relatives are able to buy or rent a retirement property from their own private means, the choice is entirely theirs. Prices and types of property vary enormously, from small flats to luxurious homes on sites with every amenity. The majority of properties are sold on a long lease (typically 125 years). It is advisable to check that the management company is a member of The Association of Retirement Housing Managers and therefore bound by its Code of Practice. There is usually a minimum age for residents of 60 or sometimes 55.

Some points to consider when assessing this option could include:

- Do they allow pets?
- Location and proximity to local amenities.
- Guest suites that can be rented (cost?) for visiting families and friends.
- Camera entry and 24-hour call system for added peace of mind.
- The availability of a home-owners' lounge for relaxing with other home-owners in a 'neutral' environment, which can also be used for events.
- Is there a house manager who takes care of the day-to-day running of the site and any organised activities? How accessible are they?
- Is there a complaints book – can you have a look at it?
- Quality of the communal gardens.
- If the property is rented what is the percentage cap on annual rental increases? 'Stealth' increases above the rate of inflation can seem very unfair once you are settled in. Ascertain the increases over the last 3 years
- And most importantly, what is the annual service charge for amenities and shared costs (and what has it been over the last 3 years)?

Home care or care at home

This is where the elderly person remains in their home and receives support during the day and/or at night. The time may come when elderly people are no longer able to cope with running their homes and caring for themselves without a bit of assistance. There are various options, some more expensive than others. If approaching agencies, it is well worth asking friends and neighbours for personal recommendations, as this can give a lot of peace of mind. Some of the agencies listed at 'other assistance' in this chapter specialise in providing temporary help, rather than permanent staff. Others can offer a flexible service and nursing care, if appropriate. Fees are normally paid by private funding but, depending on individual circumstances, public financial assistance may be available. There are some things to bear in mind when hiring a carer:

- Should you organise home care for your elderly relative, you or your relative actually becomes an employer, which brings obligations around administering a payroll and, potentially, a pension for the carer. Search 'payroll help' for local help on this or ask around for recommendations. Another alternative is to try it yourself by downloading HMRC's basic payroll tool (www.gov.uk – go to 'basic payroll tool'). If you employ the carer, undertake a DBS check. Criminal Records Bureau (CRB) checks are now called Disclosure and Barring Service (DBS) checks. Help is available with these at www.gov.uk – go to 'DBS checks'.

- Elderly people organising care themselves also have the responsibility for checking eligibility to work in the UK and conducting a DBS check.

- Carers need clear guidelines as to documentation, medication, care plans and dietary guidance.

- There must be a contingency plan should the chosen carer fall ill or be unable to work for other reasons.

Fees are around £15 per hour and you have the advantage of being in familiar surroundings. Find more information at www.thenationalcareline.org and www.carers.org.

Housing with care

This is a newer form of specialist housing, sometimes referred to as extra care housing. Properties can be rented, owned or occasionally part-owned/part-rented. They are fully self-contained homes, usually with one or two bedrooms. To find some options just google 'housing with care' and your region.

Care homes

Deciding whether a care home is right for an elderly relative is a difficult decision that sometimes has to be made in a hurry. All care homes in England are registered and inspected by the Care Quality Commission (CQC) and must display their CQC rating (outstanding, good, requires improvement or inadequate) throughout the home and on their website – see www.cqc.org.uk.

In Wales, the inspectorate is called the Care Standards Inspectorate for Wales – www.cssiw.org.uk.

In Scotland it is called the Care Inspectorate – www.careinspectorate.com.

In Northern Ireland it is the Regulation and Quality Improvement Authority – www.rqia.org.uk.

Top tip

The oversight organisations listed above provide thorough independent information and reports on each care home in the UK. You simply cannot do your relative any justice if you do not access, compare and review the information they have for the areas being considered for your relative.

The next step is to start visiting some care homes – possibly by yourself at first – and just doing a drive past to get a feel for a possible 'shortlist' from a longer list established from a review of the above websites and, of course, the care home's own website if they have one. Then download the Age UK care home checklist and start your visits (www.ageuk.org – 'finding a care home'). There are lots of invaluable hints and tips; use the checklist together with a few of our own tips:

- Overall, recognise that often it comes down to fees, and generally speaking rooms with a view and high-quality services and amenities all come with a cost – the better the standard, the higher the price.

- Recognise that all of your relative's belongings will probably need to fit into one room.

- Look at any entertainment schedule and pop along to see it for yourself.

- Is there free internet access?

- How do they meet religious/pastoral needs?

- Ask about special situations such as dementia – what is their approach for both those that have it and those that do not?

- Ask to see sample menus and, better still, ask to pop in to see the kitchens whilst mealtimes are in progress. Visit two or three times and reconsider this point; the quality of food reveals a lot. Can they cater for special diets?

- Ask about visiting times – are there restricted hours?

- Is contents insurance included in the fee?

- Ask about links to a hospital and any assigned doctor.

- Ask how personal care is addressed and at what cost – typically this is hairstyling and care of fingernails and toenails.

- Ask if you can bring your/their pet in to visit your relative.

- Trust your instincts about your overall feelings about the home and how it may be suitable for your relative.

There are two main types of care homes: residential and nursing homes:

- *Residential homes* can range from small in size with a few beds, to large-scale facilities. They offer care and support throughout the day and night. Staff are on hand to help with personal care. Rates vary but fees can be around £30,000 to £40,000+ per annum.

- *Nursing homes* offer the same type of care as residential homes but with the addition of 24-hour medical care from a qualified nurse. Rates vary but fees can be around £40,000 to £50,000+ per annum.

Care homes costs and help

There are currently over half a million older people living in residential and nursing homes in the UK. Care homes vary in cost, and fees rise depending on how complex the needs of the elderly person are.

The funding aspect is complex and can be subject to political pressure and change. Funding may be available for part or all of the nursing/medical care element of any fees. There are then fees for the 'accommodation aspect'; currently (Autumn 2020), if your savings and capital come to less than £14,250 you won't have to use any of this money towards care home fees. If you have savings and capital worth between £14,250 and £23,250 the council will contribute towards your care home fees, but you will also have to pay towards them at a rate of £1 per week for every £250 in savings and capital you have between £14,250 and £23,250. If you have savings and capital worth over £23,250 you will have to pay all your care home accommodation fees – this is called 'self-funding'. Your home counts towards 'capital' although, in some situations, your home may not be taken into account in the test. For instance currently (Autumn 2020) it may not be counted if your home is still occupied by your partner; a relative who is aged over 60; a child of yours aged under 18 or a relative who is disabled.

If you give your home away to a child or relative in an attempt to exclude it from the test on income and capital limits it may count as a deliberate 'deprivation of assets'. This is the technical term used by Councils it means that you still pay the same level of care fees as if you still owned the home.

Top tip

Take care if an organisation seems to be promising to shelter your home and finances from the grasps of the local authority with schemes and arrangements involving trusts and tax planning to remove your home from your ownership to avoid care home fees being paid by you. There are suggested questions and checks in Chapter 5, Tax in the section on Inheritance Tax.

Other assistance

In addition to the services provided by statutory health and social services for elderly people living at home, there are a number of voluntary organisations that can offer help, including:

- lunch clubs and day centres;
- holidays and short-term placements;
- aids such as wheelchairs;
- transport;
- odd jobs and decorating;
- gardening;
- good neighbour schemes;
- prescription collection;
- advice and information;
- family support schemes.

You will be able to find out more via your local Citizens Advice Bureau (www.citizensadvice.org.uk) but some of the key agencies are:

- Age UK: www.ageuk.org.uk;
- Age Scotland: www.ageuk.org.uk/scotland;
- Age Cymru: www.ageuk.org.uk/cymru;
- Age NI: www.ageuk.org.uk/northern-ireland;

- Care Information Scotland: www.careinfoscotland.scot;
- Centre for Individual Living, Northern Ireland: www.cilbelfast.org;
- Contact the Elderly: www.contact-the-elderly.org;
- Disability Wales: www.disabilitywales.org.

Practical help for carers

The UK has 6.5 million carers and while your elderly relative is reasonably active and independent – visiting friends, able to do his or her own shopping, enjoying hobbies and socialising – the strains of caring for them may be light. However, when this is not the case, far more intensive care may be required. Make sure you find out what help is available and how to obtain it.

Top tip

Download, review and follow through on the advice and information in the free guide 'Looking after someone: information and support for carers', available from www.carersuk.org

---

Laws of intestacy

If you die without leaving a will your finances are dealt with under the rules of intestacy. The rules differ slightly between England and Wales, Scotland and Northern Ireland but that should not detract from our key message. An intestacy is basically a great big mess that will take time, money and effort to sort out and even then things won't follow a smooth path. Rules set by the government (the laws of intestacy) will determine who inherits the deceased person's estate (possessions, property and money). There is no guarantee that the deceased person's wishes will be carried out or that their estate will go to those they intended. Promises made will count for nothing and may only cause confusion and perhaps upset. Only married or civil partners (actually married at the time of death) and close relatives can inherit under the rules of intestacy. An unmarried partner and stepchildren have no automatic rights. Possessions, including the home, may have to be sold to split the proceeds between the heirs and if there are no relatives the Crown gets the lot.

All is not bleak, as usually a close relative will have the legal right to step in, prove their position and relationship and seek to sort out the estate of the person who has died intestate. To administer someone's estate you apply to the deceased's local Probate Office for a 'Grant of Letters of Administration'. You can ask your solicitor to help you with applying for a grant or you can make a personal application. When you get the grant you become the 'administrator' of the estate. The grant provides proof to banks, building societies and other organisations that you have authority to access and distribute funds that were held in the deceased's name. If Inheritance Tax is due on the estate, some or all of this must be paid before a grant will be issued.

> **Top tip**
>
> **Intestacy is a mess so don't put your relatives through it. Make a will and use that as an opportunity to revisit your end-of-life plans and the other matters covered in this chapter. Bear in mind the motto "Tough discussions and decisions are often not so difficult once the subject is broached."**

Wills

A will is a legal document that sets out a person's final financial wishes. There are six main reasons why you should make a will if you have not done so already:

- The alternative is the mess of intestacy as above.
- It means your wishes are known with clarity (after all you won't be around to clarify things!).
- It helps avoid disputes between relatives. Some relatives may not agree and some may still seek to make a claim on your estate but the fact that you have clarified what you want goes a very long way to prevent disgruntled relatives disputing things.
- It can protect assets for future generations. If you are fortunate to have assets that can stay in the family and you wish these to be preserved for future generations the will can be directed to put certain assets or funds into a trust to help preserve them for the benefit of future generations. This may help prevent the next generation blowing the lot and can be useful in large

and complex estates or family situations that appear chaotic.

- Inheritance tax. If you leave your estate to your husband, wife or civil partner then no inheritance is paid. Anything left to a charity is also exempt from inheritance tax. Armed with some of the information on gifts from Chapter 5 (Tax) you will also see how you could be more tax-efficient with more knowledge and advice.

- Clarify the funeral that you would like and provide for the costs of the funeral and any after event (catering and venue hire) to be paid from your estate. This allows you to specify what you would like and also anything that you do not want, and removes significant stresses from those left to make the arrangements.

Having a will becomes absolutely essential if you live with an unmarried partner, have divorced, remarried, or need to provide for someone with a disability. You can write your will yourself or with the assistance of do-it-yourself will-writing kits available online or from stationery shops. Both routes can be prone to error and misinterpretation and therefore advice and assistance really should be sought.

There are several different types of wills, amongst which are:

- a *single will* relates to an individual;

- *mirror (or joint) wills* are designed for couples who have the same wishes;

- a *property trust will* places the estate into trust for beneficiaries;

- a *discretionary trust will* allows trustees to decide what is best at the time of your death.

There is no 'one size fits all' answer to deciding which sort of will is best. Specialist advice is essential and researching your circumstances (personal and financial) will reveal what kind of will is right for you. Your will should be stored carefully where the relevant people can find it and needs to be formally witnessed and signed to make it legally valid. If at any time you wish to update your will, this must be done officially, by means of a 'codicil'. If your circumstances change (divorce, death of a loved one, or new family members) you should review the position and decide if a new will is necessary.

Keep with your papers at home a list of your 'assets'. Where is the treasure buried? By keeping this information up to date you can save your executors hours of work pursuing wild goose chases. Ultimately, those you wish to benefit will get more if your paperwork is accurate.

Mike and Tom Bottomley of Ewart Price Solicitors share their top five tips for a successful will:

1. Think carefully about what you own (your assets); are there any unusual things about them that you need to consider?

2. Whom do you wish to benefit? People might have expectations, for example close family members. If you are not benefiting them, why not? Seek advice about whether a disappointed individual might have a claim against the estate.

3. Meet with a solicitor and instruct him or her to draft a will for you.

4. Carefully check the draft, and ask for an explanation about anything you do not understand. There is no point signing a document you do not understand.

5. Leave the original will with the solicitor and keep a copy. You can register the will with Certainty, the National Will Register officially recognized in the UK, who will be able to say from their database who has the will (www.nationalwillregister.co.uk).

Banks

Some banks offer a will-writing service. Make sure that you can choose your own executor or understand in advance the bank's charges for acting as executor as fees can be relatively expensive if banks undertake the executor service.

Professional will-writing specialists

A will-writing service can be cheaper than using a solicitor, and more reliable than a DIY will. A will-writing service could be a good choice if you understand the basics of how wills work, you wish to pay less than a solicitor would charge, and your estate is not complex. Before you instruct a will-writing service make sure they have professional indemnity insurance, because if they get it wrong there may be nobody to sue.

Solicitors

The best solution is usually through an appropriately qualified solicitor who will ensure your will is interpreted the way you want and may tease out tricky issues that you may not have anticipated. If you do not have a solicitor, ask friends for a recommendation, or ask Citizens Advice. You can budget for around £200 to £500 plus VAT for this help – more if you have very complex financial affairs.

What to include and terminology

Your will should explain the main assets you own (your 'estate') and indicate your debts (what you owe). This is not an exhaustive list but it will be helpful to detail any homes, significant assets, investments, savings and life policies, their location and the main debts owed (usually mortgages, loans and a listing of credit cards). Jointly owned property should be clarified and remember 'joint tenants' will see your share automatically passing to the other joint tenant(s) on death and 'tenants in common' means you can leave your share to someone else. 'Executors' are the vital people who make sure your will happens as you intended – more on them below.

'Beneficiaries' are the people you name to receive something in your will; remember to give their full names and precise relationship to you to make sure they are correctly identified. 'Legacies' is the name for gifts you make to beneficiaries. A 'residual beneficiary' is the person or charity that receives the remainder of your estate once specific gifts have been paid out.

'A letter of wishes' can often accompany a will as an annex and can be helpful in avoiding cluttering up a will with a long list of people who are to be given specific assets. It can be useful for clarifying desired funeral arrangements and some health matters (such as do not resuscitate, organ donation wishes, etc.) but it is not a legally binding document. Particularly where you have created a discretionary trust in your will, a letter of wishes can flesh out the bones of a dry legal document. Typically, where young parents are worried about their children becoming orphans, they wish to say how they would like their children to be educated.

> **Top tip**
>
> Ask for a quotation for completing the will and the costs of any anticipated extras (for instance lasting powers of attorney – see below). If using a solicitor, check that they are a member of the Law Society's Wills and Inheritance Quality Scheme and that anyone else entrusted to write your will is a member of the Society of Trust and Estate Practitioners (STEP).

Deeds of variation

A deed of variation can be used to change a will up to two years after the date of death where all those affected by the alteration agree to the change. Typically it is used to redirect the stated benefit in a will from, say, a child to, say, a grandchild to keep down the inheritance tax potential on the child's estate; specialist advice should be obtained from a solicitor on this potentially useful tool. The effect of the deed of variation is to rewrite the will as if the deceased person had made the new and altered instructions in their will.

Executors

An executor is the person you appoint in your will to be responsible for handling your estate and making sure your wishes are carried out after you die. Think of a best man or chief bridesmaid at a wedding, only this time it's 10 times more important, so choose wisely. It is usual to appoint more than one executor and they should be over 18, so perhaps it could be your husband, wife or civil partner and a child, brother or sister. This could take some of the pressure off your husband, wife or civil partner in the initial period when emotions and loss are so significant.

Bear in mind that a complex estate can involve the executor in a significant amount of work and possibly stress. If the estate is complex and the will includes trusts, appointing a professional executor to act with lay executors is worth considering.

The main duties of the executor are:

1. Registering the death at the Register Office (find your relevant one at www.gov.uk) and locating the final will. You will need to take the medical

certificate signed by a doctor when you register the death. Once you register the death you will get a Certificate for Burial or Cremation (the 'green form') and a Certificate of Registration of Death. Think about how many copies of the death certificate you will need.

2. Arranging the funeral. The costs will usually be payable from the deceased's estate. Check on funeral wishes in any will or 'letter of wishes' or in any funeral plan (perhaps left with an undertaker) and with close family on the preparations. Notices may need to be placed in newspapers and social media informing people of funeral arrangements and any donation wishes (or the fact that donations should not be made). Emotions will be high and time is short, making this a difficult time, and so funeral specifications provided in the will can prove a blessing.

3. Valuing the estate. Gather in and ensure you have control of everything the deceased owned and also establish everything they owed. Obtain valuations from a professional valuer of expensive items and any residential property.

4. Apply for probate which gives the legal right to deal with someone's estate (for instance to sell their house), complete the relevant Inheritance Tax form and pay any tax due. The process varies between England and Wales, Scotland and Northern Ireland; the specifics can be found on www.gov.uk (go to 'probate').

Mike and Tom Bottomley of Ewart Price Solicitors share some suggestions and pointers on executors:

> *"Taking on the role on is a serious undertaking. It is one thing for a spouse to manage their deceased spouse's estate – they will have an intimate knowledge of their affairs and will likely be the sole/only beneficiary; it is quite another to appoint, say, a family friend to deal with a portfolio of assets and multiple beneficiaries. Even with the help of a solicitor it can be difficult and stressful to deal with assets, sell property, and keep a contingent of (potentially upset and impatient) beneficiaries informed and happy. People commonly leave gifts to their executors for taking on the role and more often than not, the executors are residuary beneficiaries anyway. This is up to the testator's discretion, but it makes sense to appoint someone as executor who has an interest in the estate as they will be motivated to get everything sorted. A professional executor will either charge by the hour or by a percentage of the estate."*

Lasting power of attorney

Dementia can develop slowly or suddenly, especially following a stroke or an accident, and the emotional turmoil will be substantial. There are one or two very simple procedures that can and should be done to ease the situation. The first is to set up a Lasting Power of Attorney (LPA); some solicitors consider this to be just as important as making a will. This has to be done before losing mental capacity, otherwise it is invalid. Before doing anything it would be wise to discuss the options with family or someone they trust to see what they think and whether they can help. To find out more about mental capacity and making decisions use www.gov.uk and go to 'make decisions for someone'.

An LPA gives someone you trust the legal authority to make decisions on your behalf and therefore you retain control through that person, known as the attorney. The attorney could be a husband, wife or civil partner, a son or daughter, a brother or sister, nephew or niece or just someone you trust. The person allowing the LPA to be drawn up is known as the donor. There are two types of LPA: one for *property and financial affairs* and another for *personal welfare*. It is safest to have both types. A health and welfare LPA allows others to make decisions about the donor's day-to-day care, where they live, who they should have contact with and, if desired, their choice for end-of-life care. The property and financial affairs LPA covers paying bills, collecting benefits, selling property and investing money. Without an LPA the only way a person can take charge of another person's finances is via the Court of Protection which is a lengthy, costly and stressful process.

Once you have made your LPA it is very advisable to register this immediately with the Office of the Public Guardian. This process takes at least two months, so if things deteriorate quickly an unregistered power is not valid.

The right time to draw up an LPA is while the individual is in full command of his or her faculties, so that potential situations that would require decision making can be properly discussed and the donor's wishes made clear. If you are considering setting up an LPA for yourself or an elderly relative it is important to consult both the relevant GP and the family solicitor as well as members of the family. When making an LPA make sure the attorneys can be relied upon to always and 100 per cent place your best interests at heart. Lasting Powers of Attorney were introduced in October 2007, replacing the old system of Enduring Powers of Attorney (EPA). An EPA created before October 2007 remains valid.

The personal welfare LPA could save endless amounts of angst amongst family and friends when dementia and then the end of life occurs. According to Compassion in Dying:

> *"Seventy per cent of us want little or no medical intervention at the end of life; 53 per cent believe family can make healthcare decisions on behalf of a loved one; and only 4 per cent of us have made our treatment wishes known in an Advance Decision."*

Being prepared will also allow more quality time with loved ones, particularly when those precious final months, weeks or days come. It will also relieve lots of strain and stress so consider incorporating the following in either your LPA or in a 'letter of wishes' appended to your will; your solicitor will be able to guide you on the best route:

- your end-of-life care plan;
- where you wish to be cared for;
- advance decision to refuse treatment (do not resuscitate (DNR) form);
- organ and tissue donation;
- planning your funeral.

The NHS website gives general advice on end-of-life planning at www.nhs.uk (go to 'end-of-life care') and there is also quality information available from Age UK: www.ageuk.org.uk.

Mike and Tom Bottomley of Ewart Price Solicitors share some suggestions and pointers on executors:

> *"If a person does not have a lasting Power of Attorney in place and they subsequently lose mental capacity, in order to manage their affairs, you will need to apply to the Court of Protection to obtain a deputyship: www.gov/uk/become-deputy. The application to become a deputy is expensive and time consuming, and far more hassle than simply registering a LPA. There are also additional requirements to act as a deputy than as an attorney, for example, you will need to submit an annual report to the Office of the Public Guardian to explain your decisions. Clearly, arranging a LPA while you still have capacity is far more preferable route - it is relatively inexpensive and the donor can have a say (by either limiting them or directing them) on the decisions their attorneys can/will make."*

Important wealth warning

This chapter is only a guide and it is neither legal nor taxation advice. Any potential tax advantages may be subject to change from the position as at Autumn 2020 and will depend upon your individual circumstances, so individual professional advice should be obtained.

Useful reading

The cost of care is an area subject to considerable pressure and potential change. Quality advice and updates can be found at www.citizensadvice.org.uk, www.ageuk.org.uk (go to 'paying for permanent residential care'), www.independentage.org (go to 'paying care home fees' to download their latest factsheet) and 'How to fund your long-term care - a beginners guide' (at www.moneyadviceservice.org.uk). Support is available for carers at both the national level and their local groups via www.carers.org.

Cruse Bereavement Care: www.cruse.org.uk or phone 0808 8081677;

Care for the Family and their specialist bereavement support:
www.careforthefamily.org.uk (go to 'bereavement support' or phone 02920 810800);

Samaritans: www.samaritans.org. With Samaritans remember their motto:
'Whatever you're going through, call us free any time, from any phone on 116 123.'

> **Reminder: Take any action points or follow up points to Chapter 12, Your Plan For A Better Retirement.**

Chapter Twelve

YOUR PLAN FOR A BETTER RETIREMENT

Things to actually get on with and start doing/planning now

	Page No.	Issue	Priority: High Medium or Low
1			
2			
3			
4			
5			
6			
7			
8			
9			
10			
11			
12			
13			
14			
15			

More information needed -things to follow up

	Page No.	Issue	Website or source of more help
1			
2			
3			
4			
5			
6			
7			
8			
9			
10			
11			
12			
13			
14			
15			
16			
17			
18			
19			
20			

Phil Haden
Independent Financial Adviser
Prosperity Wealth Ltd

Award winning 'Chartered Financial Planner'
Fellow of the Personal Finance Society
Advanced Pensions & Pension Freedom qualifications

t: 07486 462405

e: phil.haden@prosperitywealth.com

www.prosperitywealth.com

Printed in Great Britain
by Amazon